THE JOSEPH RC
CHARITABLE

A STUDY IN QUAKER PHILANTHROPY
AND ADULT EDUCATION
1904-1954

The Joseph Rowntree Charitable Trust:

A Study in Quaker Philanthropy and Adult Education 1904-1954

by

Mark Freeman

William Sessions Limited
York, England

ISBN 1 85072 310 9

Printed in 10 on 11 point Plantin Typeface
from Author's Disk
by Sessions of York
The Ebor Press
York, England

Contents

For Christine, Lucy and Dave

List of abbreviations

ABCA	Army Bureau of Current Affairs
BIAE	British Institute of Adult Education
CEdT	Community Education Trust
CEqT	Community Equipment Trust
CO(s)	conscientious objector(s)
COS	Charity Organisation Society
CSIR	Council for the Study of International Relations
ECA	Educational Centres Association
ESA	Educational Settlements Association
FAU	Friends Ambulance Unit
FRS	Friends Relief Service
FWCC	Friends World Committee for Consultation
IPC	International Peace Campaign
IVSP	International Voluntary Service for Peace
JRCT	Joseph Rowntree Charitable Trust
JRF	Joseph Rowntree Foundation
JRMT	Joseph Rowntree Memorial Trust
JRRT	Joseph Rowntree Reform Trust
JRSST	Joseph Rowntree Social Service Trust
JRVT	Joseph Rowntree Village Trust
LEA(s)	local education authority(ies)
LNU	League of Nations Union
LSE	London School of Economics
NASU	National Adult School Union
NCSS	National Council for Social Service
NFCA	National Federation of Community Associations
NMWM	No More War Movement
PPU	Peace Pledge Union
WEA	Workers' Educational Association
WVRC	War Victims' Relief Committee
YMCA	Young Men's Christian Association

Foreword
by Christopher Holdsworth

THIS BOOK IS the first scholarly examination of the first fifty years' work of the Joseph Rowntree Charitable Trust, one of three trusts established by Joseph Rowntree at a time when his flourishing business had brought him considerable resources. Mark Freeman writes with clarity and verve, as well as authority, since he has consulted a wide range of sources as well as the Trust's own archives. He successfully sets the developing story of the Trust against changes in wider society and those occurring in the small Society of Friends, to which the Founder and all his trustees belonged.

From the start, adult education, both among Quakers and more broadly, received a significant share of the Trust's resources. The trustees became increasingly focused upon the foundation and support of educational settlements, which in the 1920s and 1930s attracted between a third and a half of their grants. At the same time the trustees were involved in attempts to strengthen the fissiparous peace movement, as well as the religious work of British Quakers, while their total income often did not exceed £20,000 a year. Even so, the Trust was the major resource which enabled 32 educational settlements to come into existence across the country.

Mark Freeman reveals very frankly how marginal, in some senses, was the contribution of these settlements to the whole field of adult education, where local authorities, the Workers' Educational Association and university extension departments became far more significant. Yet the fact that by the end of the second world war local education authorities were themselves beginning to establish non-residential adult education centres demonstrates that some of the ideals behind those earlier settlements had been taken up, and developed.

The whole book should gain the attention of a wide readership, not just drawn from those concerned with adult education, or with the history of Quaker philanthropy, because it touches upon so many sides of life between 1904 and 1954. Mark Freeman doubts whether the Charitable Trust itself, or other grant-making bodies, could draw direct implications for their own work today from his account. Broadly speaking I share his doubt, yet, and here I write as one who served as a trustee of this Trust for forty years. I believe trustees of many trusts could read it with profit, since it raises so many questions about how trustees can easily lose touch with what is actually going on within institutions that they support, and may find it hard to allow those who use such institutions to take some share in their governance. Altogether, this is a book with a story which was worth discovering, and which has been well told.

Christopher Holdsworth
Exeter, November 2003

Preface and acknowledgements

IN 1904 THE York cocoa manufacturer and Quaker Joseph Rowntree set aside about half his personal wealth into three Trusts to be administered by members of his family in the interests of the community, each directed to specific objectives. The Joseph Rowntree Village Trust (JRVT),[1] intended to be permanent, was established to oversee the construction and administration of Rowntree's model housing project at New Earswick, just outside York; in 1959 this Trust obtained an Act of Parliament which allowed it to broaden the range of its activities, and changed its name to the Joseph Rowntree Memorial Trust.[2] Now called the Joseph Rowntree Foundation, it promotes research in the field of social policy, and continues to act as a housing association, managing the affairs of New Earswick. The Joseph Rowntree Social Service Trust (JRSST), which did not have charitable status, was designed to support overtly political projects, especially the purchase of newspapers, and was to last initially for a period of thirty-five years. It is now known as the Joseph Rowntree Reform Trust (JRRT), and finances a variety of political activity, across the party spectrum, focusing on the promotion of democratic citizenship, support for constitutional reform and the provision of research assistance for MPs.[3] The Joseph Rowntree Charitable Trust (JRCT), the smallest of the three in terms of assets and also with an initial lifespan of thirty-five years, was established, according to Rowntree's first biographer, 'mainly for research purposes [and] for the promotion of education';[4] and although this underestimates the range of projects it supported in its early years (and barely suggests the kinds of projects it funds today), it efficiently summarises the kinds of work Rowntree expected it to do. Both the JRSST and the JRCT were reconstituted at the end of their thirty-five-year remit, and, along with the Joseph Rowntree Foundation, are now approaching their centenaries. All three Trusts initially had the same board of trustees: Joseph Rowntree himself, his sons John Wilhelm, Benjamin Seebohm, Joseph Stephenson and Oscar Frederick Rowntree, and his nephew Arnold Rowntree. The Trusts have since grown apart in terms of membership, although their headquarters are all on the same site in York.[5]

This is the story of the JRCT, told in the context of wider currents of British philanthropy, changes in the Religious Society of Friends

(Quakers), of which the Rowntrees were members, and developments in adult education, with which, as will be seen, the JRCT was closely associated in the first fifty years of its existence. Essentially, it is the story of one manifestation of Quaker social concern. As one Friend has explained, 'Quakers use the word "concern" to indicate an over-riding compulsion to pursue a course of action inspired by compassion or inner ferment.'[6] During the first fifty years of the JRCT's existence, many opportunities arose for the expression of such concern, and the Trust was one of the most important grant-making bodies that provided financial support for the activities prompted by this concern. The story of all three Trusts in their early years is largely the history of the Rowntree family and a few of their collaborators; however, although several members of the family have been the subjects of biographies, none of these have devoted much space to the work of the Trusts.[7] Even Anne Vernon's biography of Joseph Rowntree does not discuss the Trusts in much detail, except for the establishment of New Earswick, which has been the single most tangible and lasting manifestation of the philanthropic work done in Rowntree's name.[8] Some Quaker historians have discussed the projects supported by the JRCT, and histories of adult education have usually accorded them a footnote, but little more. Additionally, historians of poverty have always found much to admire, and sometimes not a little to disparage, in Seebohm Rowntree's pioneering social investigations, many of which were also funded by the Trust.[9] This history will deal with as wide a range as possible of the areas in which the JRCT made grants in the first half-century of its existence; inevitably some areas will receive less comprehensive treatment than others, while some readers may feel that the concentration on the provision of adult education marginalises other areas in which the Trust supported work of at least as much value. In my defence I can only appeal to the authority of the Trust's account books, which show that educational grants formed by far the most substantial item of expenditure in this period, and to the centrality of education to the conception of Quaker philanthropy which the Trust embodied. Moreover, the history of social inquiry, the biographies of individual trustees, and the story of the Quaker peace testimony, have all been told more fully elsewhere.

The narrative has been set into a largely chronological framework, which has proved the most efficient way of detailing the changes in the conception and practice of philanthropy which modified the focus of the Trust's grant-making in this period. The one exception is the chapter on the support of initiatives in the field of peace in the interwar period, which is dealt with separately in the interests of clarity. The ending point of the story has been chosen for a number of reasons. Seebohm Rowntree, the last of the surviving original trustees, died in 1954, and his death symbolically marked the end of the first phase of the Trust's activity. The profile of the JRCT's grant-making altered substantially from the early 1950s, and although this history indicates some of the new directions the Trust took in later years, to attempt a realistic assessment of the very different kinds of philanthropic activity reflected in the later work of the Trust would bring an undesirable asymmetry to the narrative. Moreover, the scope of the JRCT's work, and the resources available to it – over £4 million was allocated to grantees in nine distinct areas in 1999 – have expanded so greatly since the 1950s that it would be difficult, if not impossible, to present the kind of unified organisational history that is offered here for the earlier period of the Trust's history. The volume of source material available for the second half of the twentieth century mirrors this expansion and diversification; it will support much further research, some of which has already been carried out, but presents significant obstacles to the writing of a single history. Finally, it is arguable that extending the history of the Trust to the present day, while enabling direct personal engagement with many of the individuals who have shaped its policies, would at the same time allow for less detachment than can be achieved when considering a period that ended nearly half a century ago. I have therefore confined myself to what is essentially the first half of the JRCT's history, and leave the serious interrogation of the second half to others.

The research on which this volume is based was carried out during the tenure of a research fellowship at the University of York, supported by the JRCT, to whose trustees and staff – especially Steven Burkeman, Stephen Pittam, Juliet Prager, Nick Perks, Tina Walker and Angela Forster – I am grateful both for the opportunity to pursue the work and for the access that has been provided to minute books and other archival material. Christopher Holdsworth read the first draft of the manuscript with great thoroughness, making a number of factual corrections and suggesting many revisions and further lines of inquiry. I must emphasise that neither the JRCT nor any individual trustee or member of staff has exercised any editorial control over the content of the book. I would also like to thank Elizabeth Jackson, Vaughan Birbeck and the staff of the Joseph Rowntree Foundation Library, where I have been able to consult a wide range of unpublished sources; and to the staff of Woodbrooke Quaker Study Centre, Friends House Library and the British Library. Among colleagues at the University of York, I am especially grateful to my collaborators Jonathan Davies, Lorna Gold and Lisa O'Malley, whose work on other aspects of the JRCT's history and current practice has been informative and helpful. Lorna Gold has allowed me to use material from her database of peace grantees, and from an unpublished analysis of the JRCT financial records which we carried out together; and Jonathan Davies has greatly assisted my interpretation of the educational settlement movement. I am also grateful to Neil Carter, who oversaw the research, and to

Jonathan Bradshaw for his encouragement. Thanks are also due to members of the Department of History, especially Bill Sheils, Jim Walvin and Allen Warren, all of whom have been immensely helpful in a variety of ways. I have been directed to useful material by, and enjoyed productive conversations with, Konrad Elsdon and Fiona Shaw. I am grateful to Phil Thomas and Stephen Warburton, Neil Brown, Richard Ennis, Fergus McGlynn, Matthew Roberts, Helen Smith, Isobel Todd and Louise Wannell; and also to Fiona Dalrymple and Gavin Deas, whose repeated hospitality enabled me to make frequent visits to Glasgow while the research was being carried out. Jennifer Watson has assisted in the final stages of the preparation of the manuscript. My continuing gratitude is due to colleagues at the University of Glasgow, notably but by no means exclusively to Anne Crowther, Mike French, Annmarie Hughes, Ray Stokes and Megan Smitley. Additionally, without the assistance of Mike Black, Louise Pollock and their colleagues at Arts Support, much of the manuscript could have been lost. I would also like to express my gratitude and appreciation to Georgia Toutziari for her friendship and encouragement, and similarly to Niall Barr, Irvine Johnston, Terry McBride, Lorna McKenzie, Natalie Milne, Adele and Alan Redhead and Jonathan Stewart. Finally, and as always, my parents, Alec and Catherine Freeman, have been an unfailing source of support.

Some portions of the book have appeared in revised form in the journals *Quaker Studies* and *History of Education*, and I thank the respective editors, Ben Pink Dandelion and Gary McCulloch, and the publishers, Continuum and Taylor and Francis, for their permission to reproduce them. I should also point out that during the bulk of the preparation of the manuscript, I was unable to consult two recent books: Thomas C. Kennedy's *British Quakerism 1860-1920: the transformation of a religious community*, Oxford 2001, a work of careful and thorough scholarship tracing the emergence of liberal Quakerism in the late Victorian and Edwardian period; and David Rubinstein's *Faithful to ourselves and the outside world: York Quakers during the twentieth century*, York 2001, which is referred to in places, but which contains much that would in other circumstances have been drawn on more fully. Finally, although I have been greatly assisted by all of the above, and by many who are not named here, any error of fact or interpretation is mine and mine alone.

Mark Freeman

Glasgow, August 2003

NOTES

1. On the JRVT see [Lewis E. Waddilove], *One man's vision: the story of the Joseph Rowntree Village Trust*, 1954.

2. Lewis E. Waddilove, *Private philanthropy and public welfare: the Joseph Rowntree Memorial Trust 1954-1979*, 1983.
3. For a brief history of the JRRT, see JRRT, *Trusting in change: a story of reform* (1st edn 1994), York 1998.
4. [Luther Worstenholme], 'Joseph Rowntree (1836-1925): a typescript memoir, and related papers', K7. (Each chapter of the memoir, in the library of the JRCT, The Garden House, York, is page-numbered separately. The second part of this quotation is a handwritten addition to the typescript.)
5. In 1994 one long-standing trustee could recall only one occasion on which all three Trusts collaborated on the same project (Grigor McClelland in *The Joseph Rowntree inheritance 1904-1994*, York 1994, 28-9).
6. Barrie Naylor, *Quakers in the Rhondda 1926-1986*, Chepstow 1986, 20.
7. Anne Vernon, *A Quaker business man: the life of Joseph Rowntree 1836-1925*, 1958; Elfrida Vipont, *Arnold Rowntree: a life*, 1955; Asa Briggs, *Social thought and social action: a study of the work of Seebohm Rowntree*, 1961; Stephen Allott, *John Wilhelm Rowntree 1868-1905 and the beginnings of modern Quakerism*, York 1994.
8. Vernon, *Quaker business man*, 147-50, 153-6.
9. The histories of Quakerism, adult education and social inquiry that have been drawn upon in the preparation of this study are all cited in full at the appropriate points in the text.

CHAPTER 1

Joseph Rowntree and the Charitable Trust: The Victorian background

JOSEPH ROWNTREE was something of an outsider. He spent almost all his life in a provincial town, York, and much of his philanthropic work was directed to specifically local objectives. Although politically active to a moderate degree, he never trod the national political stage, and his name was probably known to few outside Yorkshire except as a manufacturer of cocoa and confectionery. Although a member of the York Liberal Club, which presented him with a handsome tribute of the occasion of his golden wedding anniversary in 1917, he was never a strong party man.[1] He was an active member of a marginal religious sect, the Religious Society of Friends, or Quakers, who never numbered more than 60,000 in Britain and whose rather quaint behaviour, alienating mode of worship, archaic forms of speech and plain dress code marked them out in the first half of the nineteenth century as being different. Even within the Society of Friends, York Quakers were unusual. Rowntree moved within his own circles, not the least important of which was his large family, whose long-standing Quaker piety, liberal social outlook, business acumen and social concern were inherited by his children. Moreover, as an early biographer emphasised, Rowntree was not well known even to Quakers outside York.[2] Only rarely did he achieve prominence at Yearly Meeting, the national governing body of the Society of Friends, although he was a trustee of the Quaker periodical *The Friend*, and the bulk of the personal and financial benevolence in which he engaged had a distinctly provincial, if not local, focus. Nevertheless, the wider national and international changes wrought in Rowntree's long lifetime affected him, sometimes very deeply. As Anne Vernon, one of his biographers, has pointed out, he 'belonged to the generation which stared at the last stage-coaches in its childhood and the first aeroplanes in its old age'.[3] Born in the age of Whigs and Tories (Lord Melbourne was Prime Minister), he lived to see the first Labour government in 1924. He grew up in the 'Hungry Forties', read about the European revolutions and the Chartist demonstration of 1848, the

1

Crimean war and the rise of Gladstone and Disraeli; and in his dotage saw a world war and the heyday of Baldwin and MacDonald. Perhaps most significantly of all, he was born in a period when most of the British population lived in rural districts, and died when the overwhelming majority lived in towns, and he saw much of the social dislocation that went with this demographic transition.

Rowntree was born in York in 1836, the second son of a Quaker grocer into whose Pavement establishment he was apprenticed in the early 1850s. He received an early introduction to economic and social distress: in 1850 Joseph and his older brother John Stephenson Rowntree were taken by their father to Ireland, where they saw at first hand the sufferings of the victims of the potato famine, an experience that Joseph remembered for the rest of his life. Indeed, he could hardly avoid it, as York had its own Irish 'ghetto', the Walmgate area, where famine refugees were huddled together in overcrowded, insanitary and poverty-stricken conditions.[4] Apart from a brief sojourn in London in 1857, Rowntree lived in York all his life. In 1862, he married Julia Seebohm, a member of a noted German Quaker family, but this marriage was ended by her death in the following year; in 1867 he married Julia's cousin, Emma Antoinette Seebohm, the mother of all six of Joseph's children who lived to adulthood. In 1869 he joined his younger brother Henry Isaac Rowntree in a new cocoa works at Tanner's Moat, near Lendal Bridge. This new venture grew out of a long-standing firm, established by the Tukes, another family of York Quakers with whom the Rowntrees had close links, in the eighteenth century. The new firm grew slowly: Joseph was reluctant to advertise, which limited the range of markets for the Rowntree products, and it was only after the launch of 'Crystallised Gum Pastilles' in 1881 and 'Rowntree's Elect Cocoa' in 1887, accompanied by advertising campaigns, that real expansion began. In the year of Henry Isaac's death, 1883, the firm employed about 200 people; by 1894 the figure was almost 900; it doubled again between 1894 and 1899. In 1897, H. I. Rowntree and Company became a limited liability company, Rowntree and Company Ltd. In the 1890s it became necessary to move a new site, at Haxby Road, where expansion continued. The number of employees topped 2,000 in 1902, and 4,000 in 1906. As Rowntree explained in 1904, his great wealth only came to him 'late in life'.[5] It was as a result of the expansion of the Rowntree cocoa works that Joseph was able to establish the three Trusts that still bear his name, Trusts which embodied wider currents of Victorian and Edwardian philanthropy, Quaker social concern, and changing perceptions of poverty and social need in the nineteenth and early twentieth centuries. The object of this chapter is to contextualise Rowntree's attitude to philanthropy in terms of these wider developments.

Olive Checkland's history of philanthropy in Scotland divides Victorian philanthropy into three phases – each of which can also be applied to English developments[6] – and developments prior to and during the Edwardian period will be considered here as a distinct fourth phase. Although each of these phases was characterised by different dominant approaches to philanthropy, throughout each there runs a recurring theme: the idea that industrialisation and urbanisation fundamentally altered not only the economic and social, but also the charitable, relationships between men and women of different classes in Britain. The restoration of some elements of pre-industrial social and charitable relationships remained central to the theory and practice of British philanthropy from the early nineteenth century to the first world war, and beyond.

The first phase was a direct response to the industrialisation that crowded a population that had always been overwhelmingly rural and agricultural into towns and cities, which then experienced a rapid and unregulated growth. This unchecked outburst of urbanisation issued a fundamental challenge to English philanthropists. In the older towns, the well-established endowed charities and parochial charity systems were unable to cope with new patterns of residence and poverty; and in the newer urban units there were simply no philanthropic foundations on which to build.[7] More fundamentally, the transition to an urban society seemed to contemporaries to damage the organic communities and face-to-face social relationships associated with rural society. Industrial economic and social relations undermined the simple vectors between rich and poor through which pre-industrial charity could be bestowed. Thus one of the earliest philanthropic reactions to the twin cataclysms of industrialisation and urbanisation was the attempt to rebuild these social bridges by re-establishing the kind of neighbourly contact with the poor that had supposedly existed in the pre-industrial countryside.[8] Often prompted by religious zeal and concern for the souls of the urban heathen as much as for their short-term material well-being, such ventures involved personal visiting of working-class homes, the distribution of religious tracts, words of friendly and helpful practical and moral advice, and the provision of tangible relief in the form of food, clothing or money. Through 'district visiting' of this kind it was hoped that the virtues of thrift, diligence and self-sacrifice could be instilled into the English poor.

The promotion of these virtues essentially underpinned the Poor Law Amendment Act (1834), which clarified, in theory if not in practice, the demarcation between the statutory and voluntary sectors of welfare provision.[9] This Act, prompted by the belief that 'lavish poor relief led to insubordination and violence',[10] laid down the principles that 'outdoor relief', essentially doles of money or food, should not be given; and that 'indoor relief', that is the workhouse, should be provided on such 'ineligible' conditions that the poor would only apply for it if in the direst need.

It was hoped that, if statutory relief was given only under such conditions, private charity, which could be bestowed on a non-universal basis and hence could take account of personal character prior to almsgiving, would pick up a greater share of the growing cost of providing relief. These principles, established as much as a device for keeping the poor rates low as for any other purpose, and insofar as they were ever stringently applied except in the most punitive poor law unions, were gradually whittled away by the liberality of poor law boards of guardians over the next seventy years. In any case, they did nothing to stem the rising tide of indiscriminate voluntary charity. Indeed, the complexity of British charity was such that philanthropists often ended up competing amongst themselves; and the charitable world was beset with sectarian and denominational rivalries, not to mention simple personality clashes, which contributed to a large-scale misdirection of charitable benevolence.[11] It was not only mean-spiritedness that led many mid-Victorians to realise that the systems of poor relief and charitable welfare provision were in need of more efficient co-ordination.

This brings us to the second phase in the history of Victorian philanthropy, the period when large-scale attempts were made to organise and regulate charitable provision. The formation of the Charity Organisation Society (COS)[12] in 1869 made by far the most significant step in this direction. The COS was based on the premise that indiscriminate almsgiving had a pauperising effect on the recipient, and that the overlapping of charitable provision enabled and encouraged the poor to make repeated and frequently fraudulent claims on the philanthropic purse. The COS intended to restore the distinction between relief and charity through the establishment of a rigorous system of district offices for detailed investigation of the cases of individuals, who, if found 'deserving', would be directed to the appropriate charitable agency and, if 'undeserving', would be sent to the poor law guardians. The COS was not slow to condemn charity of which it disapproved on the grounds that it made no such distinction between 'deserving' and 'undeserving' and hence pauperised the recipient,[13] such as the efforts of the Salvation Army and Dr. Barnardo. The Society insisted that voluntarily provided and efficiently bestowed charity was the only means by which the poor could be led towards ultimate individual independence. Class separation and segregation 'demoralised' the poor and 'depersonalised' or 'deformed' the gift relationship that was the fundamental element of charity;[14] and hence the COS, like the district visitors of the early nineteenth century, aimed at raising the moral character of the poor through a restoration of the social relationships associated with the pre-industrial economy. Taking their inspiration from Edward Denison, who in the late 1860s went to live among the poor of London's East End in recognition of the obstacles to

4

personal charity posed by urban residential class segregation, and whose premature death gave him the status of a martyr in the cause of well-directed philanthropy,[15] the COS hoped that, in Gareth Stedman Jones's words, 'the capital city would be turned into a gigantic village, and its poor would be led back to manliness and independence under the firm but benevolent aegis of a new urban squirearchy'.[16]

The COS never fulfilled this aim, of course, and indeed its apparent meanness aroused intense opposition right from the outset.[17] Partly as a result of the limited appeal of COS doctrines, even its own practices deviated from them. The local district offices intended to organise rather than administer relief, nevertheless very quickly came to perform the latter function,[18] while the rigorous orthodoxy espoused by the metropolitan COS never wholly permeated the regions.[19] York, like most cities, had its branch of the COS, established in 1879, but its philosophy 'had only a very limited impact on the relief of poverty' in the city.[20] Yet York was in more need than most cities of a more regularised system of charity; indeed, the very prevalence of existing and often competing charities probably limited the effectiveness of the local COS.[21] The long tradition of philanthropy in York had left it, by the late nineteenth century, with an unsystematic, unorganised and anachronistic parochial charity structure, in no way geared to the requirements of a population that had been residentially dispersed by the demographic and industrial changes that had beset the city. (There was no complete register of York charities until 1911, and the system was not fully reorganised until 1956.)[22] York had more endowed charities than most cities, including the York County Hospital 1740), the York Dispensary (1788), The Retreat and Bootham Park Asylum (both for mental patients), the Yorkshire School for the Blind, York Emanuel (an institution for imbeciles and the blind), the Blue Coat (boys') and Grey Coat (girls') schools (both part-endowed), as well as such institutions as the York Benevolent Society (Wesleyan, 1793), the Soup Kitchen (1846) and the Discharged Prisoners' Aid Society (voluntary and endowed). There was plenty of opportunity for the local COS to criticise the unsystematic charitable provision in York, as it did, for example, when the high local unemployment of the mid-1900s was met by various schemes of work relief and indiscriminate charity, some of them supported by the Rowntree family.[23] As one York vicar claimed as late as 1909, 'every year we are manufacturing paupers in York by the rotten administration of the charities'.[24]

Although it can be asserted that the COS 'embod[ied] in institutional form the conventional assumptions which guided Victorian social action',[25] at least as far as welfare provision was concerned, it was also 'unfortunate for the advocates of philanthropy that just as they felt they were putting their house in order, assumptions about the causes of poverty were shifting and the government began to take a greater interest in social matters'.[26] The growing role of the state in welfare provision in the last third of the nineteenth and the first decade of the twentieth century changed the relationship between statutory and voluntary sectors, and issued a sometimes fundamental challenge to the precepts of the British philanthropic tradition. The appearance of groups such as the Fabian Society, formed in 1884, and other radical and socialist groupings, pressing for more active and interventionist government policies in a variety of areas, was just the most visible manifestation of a deeper change in the social thought of the British middle classes from the 1880s onwards; and this was the period in which Joseph Rowntree's children were becoming politically and socially aware. In her autobiography, Beatrice Webb remembered

> a new consciousness of sin among men of intellect and men of property; a consciousness at first philanthropic and practical – Oastler, Shaftesbury and Chadwick; then literary and artistic – Dickens, Carlyle, Ruskin and William Morris; and finally analytic, historical and explanatory – in his latter days John Stuart Mill; Karl Marx and his English interpreters; Alfred Russel Wallace and Henry George; Arnold Toynbee and the Fabians ... The consciousness of sin was a collective or class consciousness; a growing uneasiness, amounting to conviction, that the industrial organization, which had yielded rent, interest and profits on a stupendous scale, had failed to provide a decent livelihood and tolerable conditions for a majority of the inhabitants of Great Britain.[27]

Webb's array of exemplars of the 'consciousness of sin' projected back to the first half of the nineteenth century, but the apotheosis of the class guilt that she identified (and felt) was reached in the 1880s. Manifested in fierce debates in the newspapers, the periodical press, books and pamphlets on the 'meaning of the poverty of masses of men',[28] all of which took place against a background of social unrest and sometimes violent disorder,[29] the class consciousness that Webb described resolved itself through both new schemes of legislative reform and new vectors of philanthropy.

For Webb, one of the most important results of this new awareness of poverty was the impetus it gave to social inquiry. She worked on Charles Booth's investigation, instigated in 1887, into *Life and labour of the people in London*. This inquiry sought to measure the extent and the causes of poverty in the metropolis, and also included inquiries into the industries and the religions of London. Through detailed interviews with school attendance officers, who in the course of their work obtained information on all households with children of school age, Booth was able to construct 'poverty maps' of London, and arrive at a percentage of the population that lived 'more or less in want'. The figure, 30.7% of Londoners, shocked many of Booth's contemporaries, and appeared to many to imply that the magnitude of the problem was such that voluntary effort could not resolve it. Booth's findings appeared to suggest that structural factors might play as large a role as questions of individual character in explaining the amount and the persistence of poverty.[30] Booth's inquiry stimulated the Rowntrees into carrying out their own investigations. Joseph Rowntree had carried out a study of pauperism statistics and literacy rates, backed up by an inquiry into five hundred years of poor law history, which he presented at conferences in 1864 and 1865,[31] but his best known work was *The temperance problem and social reform*, written in collaboration with Arthur Sherwell and first published in 1899. This book examined alcohol consumption and licensing legislation in Britain and abroad. Perhaps its most startling finding was that the average working-class household in Britain spent six shillings a week, often as much as a third of its total income, on drink: this clearly implied that much working-class poverty could be blamed on alcohol consumption. Rowntree and Sherwell were reluctant to condemn drinking outright – they understood that it offered a temporary escape from poor housing and poor working conditions, which were general among even the more 'deserving' sections of the working classes[32] – but they hoped to effect changed habits through the provision of alternative forms of recreation, such as public parks, 'People's Palaces', temperance hotels and workplace social amenities.[33] Rowntree's own cocoa works are often cited as a model of the enlightened late Victorian factory: as well as educational projects, there were workers' committees to manage the hospital and library, and there were football, cricket, hockey, tennis, cycling, camping, rambling, boating, swimming, horticultural, allotment, angling, singing, lecture, drama, savings, medical and funeral benefit clubs.[34]

The inspiration of Charles Booth and his own father encouraged Seebohm Rowntree, Joseph Rowntree's second son, to instigate an inquiry of his own in York, the main purpose of which was to discover the extent and nature of poverty. He devised a 'poverty line', which stood at 21s. 8d. per week for a family of five; any household whose earnings were below this level (adjusted according to size of family) were deemed to be in 'primary poverty', in other words lacking the means to ensure the 'physical efficiency' of the inhabitants. Using information on household incomes divulged by York employers (of which his father, of course, was one of the most prominent), he found that 9.91% of the population of the city lived in primary poverty. Rowntree explained that he had deliberately set his poverty line at so low a level that nobody could seriously claim that it was too generous a standard, and that his figures for the proportion of the population in primary poverty were, if anything, underestimates. In addition, using impressionistic evidence – a visitor was sent to every working-class household to gather information and impressions – he decided that a further 17.93% of the population lived in 'secondary poverty', a condition in which the household income would be sufficient to maintain its inhabitants in a state of physical efficiency 'were it not that some portion of it is absorbed by other expenditure'.[35] A total of 27.84% of the population, then, was deemed to be in poverty of one kind or another. The main causes of secondary poverty, he thought, following his father, were drink and other vices including gambling (Rowntree also edited a book entitled *Betting and gambling: a national evil*), although he recognised that expenditure on non-essential items could be 'either useful or wasteful'.[36] But perhaps the most significant part of the poverty inquiry was the investigation of the causes of primary poverty, over half of which, according to Rowntree, could be blamed on the low wages of the chief wage-earner in the household: this suggested that structural causes accounted for at least a substantial proportion of poverty in Britain. Given the very different methods employed by Booth and Rowntree, the similarity between their figures for the proportion of the population in poverty – 30.7% in London and 27.84% in York – was largely coincidental, but it confirmed the suspicions of many that the problem of poverty could not be solved without a reappraisal of the role of the state in social reform. Rowntree's book, *Poverty: a study of town life*, first appeared in 1901, and like his father's went through a number of editions in the next few years; historians have repeatedly signalled it, along with Booth's survey, as an early landmark in the development of statutory welfare provision.[37]

The awareness of poverty challenged contemporary perceptions of the proper role of the state. Alfred Marshall, a leading Cambridge economist and charity organisation theorist and activist, told the Royal Commission on the Aged Poor in 1893 that 'while the problem of 1834 was the problem of pauperism, the problem of 1893 is the problem of poverty ... extreme poverty ought to be regarded, not indeed as a crime, but as a thing so detrimental to the State that it should not be endured'; this he called 'the fundamental position'.[38] The recognition of this change suggested to many that a more sympathetic approach was required in the treatment of destitution: indeed, the so-called 'Chamberlain Circular', issued five times by the president of the Local Government Board between 1886 and 1893, recommended that local authorities should create work during periods of high unemployment, although this was not given legislative force until 1905.[39] The impetus to social reform culminated in the 'new Liberalism' of the reforming government elected in the landslide of 1906. The social legislation passed in these years, most notably but by no means exclusively the Old Age Pensions Act (1908) and the National Insurance Act (1911), not to mention the establishment of trade boards and labour exchanges, the provision of free school meals and other

8

measures aimed at ensuring the welfare of children, was bitterly opposed by some spokesmen for the COS and similar bodies. Helen Bosanquet, for example, one of the most stringent of COS theorists, who along with the COS secretary Charles Loch had initiated a broadside against Seebohm Rowntree's structural explanations of poverty,[40] attacked free school meals as a measure that pauperised children and their families.[41] However, it would be wrong to suggest a simple antagonism between advocates and opponents of increased state involvement in social welfare. Even the leading members of the reforming Liberal government such as Winston Churchill stressed the primacy of the voluntary sector.[42] The more liberal wing of the COS was happy for state, municipal and voluntary welfare to coexist peaceably in the Edwardian period. Indeed, it can be argued that the spread of state-sponsored social welfare measures, some of which were administered by strengthened organs of local government in collaboration with voluntary organisations, actually gave voluntarists an opportunity to find a new role for themselves in shaping the collective futures of the communities in which they operated.[43]

To return for a moment to the 1880s, the 'consciousness of sin' also resolved itself through new vectors of philanthropy, many of which shared the underlying assumptions of the COS. The most tangible result was the establishment of university settlements.[44] The first and most noteworthy of these was Toynbee Hall in Whitechapel, established by Canon Samuel Barnett, vicar of St. Jude's Church. This involved the long-term residence of Oxford graduates in the East End, where it was hoped they would replace the resident gentry whose wholesale exodus from such poor districts was thought to bear much of the blame for the 'demoralised' condition of the urban poor. Here they would meet the working classes personally, educate them in practical and theoretical subjects, and discover 'new forms of religion more relevant to modern experience and thought'.[45] Although the settlements, by fusing the philosophical understanding of graduates with direct experience of work among the poor, acted as a finishing school for a generation of social reformers – R. H. Tawney, William Beveridge and Clement Attlee, to name just three, were residents at Toynbee Hall in the Edwardian period – the movement can also be viewed as an outgrowth and development of the social philosophy of the COS. Stedman Jones has argued that Toynbee Hall 'merely put into institutional form, ideas and practices which had largely been developed in the 1860s and 1870s';[46] while Standish Meacham has portrayed it as part of a long tradition of this kind of philanthropy that embraced such figures as Thomas Chalmers, Edward Denison and Octavia Hill.[47] Indeed, Canon Barnett was enthusiastic about the COS in its early years – although he later disagreed publicly with its principles and its leaders[48] – and like the COS he aimed explicitly at the restoration of 'individual connection'.[49] However, there was also a community focus to the settlement movement, and this marks it out from groups that aimed primarily to restore the individual reciprocity that had been the supposed hallmark of pre-industrial charitable relationships. Toynbee Hall was a centre of social inquiry as well as social work, and as Meacham explains, this element of settlement work transcended the individualism of much Victorian charity, aiming at 'the regeneration of individuals within a restored and revitalized community'.[50]

This emphasis on the community was crucial to the Edwardian conception of philanthropy, and represents perhaps the biggest change from the Victorian period; indeed, it justifies consideration as a fourth phase in the history of British philanthropy before 1914. Keith Laybourn and others have described in some detail the conception of the community that lay behind the new organising charities of the 1900s, especially the Guilds of Help and the Councils of Social Welfare, which represented more humane versions of the COS.[51] The older body was itself affected by these changes. As Jane Lewis explains in her history of the COS, voluntary charity in the Edwardian period was directed towards 'social efficiency and participation' rather than 'poverty *per se*'.[52] In modern parlance, we might say that the goal was 'social inclusion', and Joseph Rowntree and many of the other philanthropists of his age sought this aim through various economic, social and religious channels. The deflection of social concern from pauperism to poverty had direct implications for the community. Pauperism essentially entailed the separation of paupers from mainstream society: in York, for example, the Union workhouse, opened in 1849, was half a mile from Monkgate Bar to the north-east of the city.[53] The institutionalisation of the pauper cut him or her off from society; and the rigid distinction that the COS attempted to make between the spheres of charity and the poor law reinforced this separation. By contrast, poverty affected all members of the community, both directly and materially in the form of crime and other manifestations of social dislocation, and morally and culturally by imposing feelings of social duty onto the community's natural leaders. Hence more philanthropists came to define their responsibilities in terms of the community and the reciprocal social duties of its members. It might be argued that this represented a shift from the Judaeo-Christian concept of charity, with its emphasis on individual relationships and reciprocity, to a more classical one, based on a communal, or a civic, conception of gifting.[54] Thus many of the COS activists of the 1900s – still concentrating on urban communities – focused their attentions on the development of active citizenship through both philanthropic endeavour and the work of new institutions of municipal government.[55] Nevertheless, although it operated amidst modern institutions of urban governance, this philanthropic outlook was still fundamentally predicated on the superiority of pre-industrial social relationships. Thus Eglantyne Jebb, a member of the Cambridge COS and later a founder of the Save the Children Fund, remarked in 1906 that

> In old days, under the feudalistic regime, charity could undoubtedly do its work more simply. The mass of the poor were collected into villages under some roughly benevolent despot, whose lady too, often busied herself with the friendly oversight of village affairs. Under the different circumstances of the times the plan may have worked tolerably well, and the help may have been effective in a way it cannot be now, with our system of town life.[56]

A number of themes emerge from this discussion of the theory and practice of philanthropy in the Victorian and Edwardian periods which are of direct relevance to a consideration of Joseph Rowntree and the establishment of the JRCT. First, the development of systematic social investigation as an essential prelude to informed social work and reform (whether statutory or voluntary) influenced Rowntree to make this a feature of the planned expenditure of his Trust. Second, the establishment of Toynbee Hall and other university settlements had important ramifications for the Rowntrees. Unlike many provincial towns, York did not have a settlement: it lacked a university, and the early settlements were mostly established by academics and occupied by graduates. However, Rowntree was profoundly influenced by the settlement movement, as shown by the arrangement he made later in his life for the distribution of copies of a biography of Canon Barnett.[57] Third, the relationship between statutory and voluntary welfare provision was continually changing, and would continue to do so during the twentieth century, as many of the activities which were formerly the province of the voluntary sector were gradually, and sometimes suddenly, assumed as responsibilities of the state or local authorities. Finally, the theme of personal service that runs through the discussion of the four phases of British philanthropy, albeit expressed in different ways, was central to Rowntree's thought. Personal service both to the individual and to the community remained an essential calling of the philanthropist.

For Rowntree, and for most of his generation, personal service was allied to religious convictions and concerns; and we have not yet considered the religious impulses that lay behind late Victorian philanthropy. When Beatrice Webb was listing the various manifestations, philanthropic, literary, artistic, and philosophical, of the 'consciousness of sin', she also remarked on a 'theological' strand, citing Charles Kingsley, Frederick Denison Maurice, 'General' Booth of the Salvation Army and Cardinal Manning.[58] The development of practical Christian social involvement was carried on into the twentieth century by Anglicans such as Canon Barnett and by Nonconformists of whom Joseph Rowntree was one. Rowntree hoped that his own denomination, the Quakers, might through

11

the ethic of personal service link their spiritual work to the investigation of social conditions, and thereby help to bring about more profound social change than was possible through existing channels. No understanding of Rowntree's bequest, or of Victorian philanthropy in general, can be complete without some consideration of the rise of Quaker social concern, which reflected many of the broad trends of late Victorian social thought and also exhibited some distinctive features of its own.

The second half of the nineteenth century saw a transformation in the outlook of the Society of Friends, and a development of a social conscience that paralleled changes in other denominations and in society as a whole. The Quakers, at least at first, were slow to change. The Society's eighteenth-century legacy of 'quietism' – withdrawal from worldly affairs, silent worship and attachment to the doctrine of the Inward Light[59] – was reflected in the Quakers' quaintly archaic forms of address ('thee', 'thou' and 'thy', which feature heavily in Joseph and Arnold Rowntree's correspondence), their 'plain dress' code and their policy of disownment of any member who strayed from the tenets of the strict Book of Discipline. The most common reason for disownment was marrying outside the Society, a policy that caused much resentment and, on a more practical level, diminished the Society's already small membership. The 'quietism' that characterised early Victorian Quakerism manifested itself in an otherwordliness that scorned involvement in social questions and disdained politics. In any case, the Test and Corporation Acts, in force until 1828, prevented Quakers (and other Nonconformists) from holding public office, and the ancient universities and most professions were closed to them. This helped to explain their prominence in commerce and manufacturing, where their work ethic and connections with other Quakers put them at a distinct advantage.[60] Under the impact of evangelicalism, which came to dominate Yearly Meeting in the mid-nineteenth century, some alterations to Quaker practice were effected. Joseph Rowntree's brother John Stephenson Rowntree's provocative essay on *Quakerism: past and present*, published in 1859, called for the relaxation of Quaker discipline, for the enhancement of vocal ministry, and above all, as Thomas C. Kennedy has explained, for 'more knowledge of the wider world, deeper comprehension of the Bible as a guide to living in that world and stronger appreciation of the necessity for liberty of thought and action for both working through their own differences and providing a healing spirit for others'.[61] Some Friends were beginning to take a wider role in public life during this period.[62] The first Quaker MP, Joseph Pease, took his seat in 1833. As early as 1816 William Allen and Joseph Tregelles Price, both Quakers, had established the Peace Society, and Friends were involved in the anti-slavery campaigns of the early nineteenth century. By the 1840s and 1850s Quakers were involved in the temperance movement

– the Quaker Nathanial Card founded the UK Alliance, with which many other Friends were associated, in 1853 – in political campaigns – the Anti-Corn Law League attracted Quaker support – and in the campaigns against the Contagious Diseases Acts in the 1860s. The Society was changing internally as well: in 1859 the regulations against marriage outside the Society were relaxed, and in 1860 the plain dress code was made optional, under the influence of John Stephenson Rowntree's proposals for reform.

One result of these changes was to reverse the decline in membership of the Society; and nowhere was this more evident than in Joseph Rowntree's own city of York. York was at the centre of the 'awakening to a new life' among Friends.[63] Ever since George Fox, the founder of Quakerism, had been thrown down the steps of the Minster in 1651, York had been one of the largest centres of the Society in England, and was its unchallenged headquarters in the north. As Sheila Wright has shown, the York Meeting grew in the first half of the nineteenth century, while membership of the Society as a whole was in decline;[64] and this growth continued into the twentieth century: membership increased from around 200 in 1855 to 543 by 1915, while for Britain as a whole the increase was only about a quarter.[65] Quaker institutions, especially the schools at Bootham and The Mount, as well as employment opportunities in Quaker businesses, attracted many Friends to the city, and the high social status of the members of York Meeting gave them a local profile that was often denied to their co-denominationalists in other urban centres. Wright shows that an unusually high proportion of York Quakers in the nineteenth century were middle-class, and suggests that this contributed to their 'integration' into the economic and social life of the city. Long-standing friendships, marriage links between established Quaker families and the 'distinctive Quaker doctrine which had been engendered within York Meeting' under the influence of William and Esther Tuke in the late eighteenth century all contributed to the unique social environment of York Quakerism.[66] From 1828, when religious disqualifications from holding public office were removed, York Quakers began to involve themselves in local government, gaining a reputation for radicalism, although they remained disinclined to attach themselves to party labels. Many York Quakers also enjoyed a reputation for radicalism within the Society of Friends: as we have seen, it was John Stephenson Rowntree's essay that prompted the relaxation of Society discipline; and in the later nineteenth century a new generation of Rowntrees were at the centre of what Thomas C. Kennedy has termed the 'Quaker Renaissance' and the emergence of the 'new Quakerism'.[67]

The 'Quaker Renaissance' marked the triumph of liberal Quakerism over the evangelicalism that had gained a stronghold over the Society, or at any rate over 'official' Quakerism, in the nineteenth century. It was

13

symptomatic of more widespread changes in British Christianity, under the impact of the 'consciousness of sin' and one of its most influential voices, the Oxford Idealist philosopher T. H. Green. Young liberal Quakers, and above all Joseph Rowntree's eldest son John Wilhelm, embarked on a crusade to move Quakerism away from evangelicalism and towards a more contemporary faith, embodied in social action and based on the revival of the doctrine of the Inward Light which had been effaced by increasing reliance on scripture under the influence of leading evangelical Friends such as Joseph Bevan Braithwaite. Kennedy has identified four main strands of the 'Quaker Renaissance': the revival of the Inward Light doctrine; the maintenance of the free ministry, which had been effaced by the development of the pastoral system among American Friends and which appeared to be threatened by some of the activities of evangelical Quakers in Britain in the later nineteenth century; the rediscovery of the pursuit of Quaker history, under the direction of John Wilhelm Rowntree, who more than any other individual inspired this new interest in the history of Quakerism; and the revival of an active peace testimony among members of the Society of Friends.[68] A special conference, sanctioned by Yearly Meeting, held at Manchester in 1895 heard John Wilhelm Rowntree express his and his peers' 'overwhelming demand for a faith that was contemporary':[69] he claimed that the Society was failing to address the concerns of a younger generation which, having grown up in the social and intellectual ferment of the 1880s, desired above all other things a religion that would connect itself to the concerns of a rapidly changing British society. He argued that traditional Quaker quietism, which had been partly surpassed in previous decades, needed to be further subsumed beneath the urgent task of re-connecting Quakerism to the wider society of which its adherents remained a numerically insignificant minority. Under the impact of John Wilhelm's remarks, and of his influential *Present-Day Papers*, which appeared in the late 1890s, as well as books and pamphlets such as Edward Worsdell's *The gospel of divine help* (1886), young Friends began their drive to recapture and re-mould their Society.[70] At Quaker summer schools, held at Scarborough in 1897 and Birmingham in 1899, and at other locations in later years under the auspices of the Summer School Continuation Committee, young (and some not so young) reforming Quakers met in a spirit of fellowship to hear lectures about, and to discuss, the study of the Bible and the future of practical Quakerism.[71]

One of the most important expressions of this awakening of liberal Quakerism was a further development of Quaker social concern. Both nationally and in Rowntree's home city of York the calls to social action were being heeded. The new social involvement of the late Victorian generation of Friends often reflected long-standing Quaker interests: York

Quakers, for example, campaigned against the naval expansion programme in 1894 and, later, against the concentration camps established during the second Boer war. The Northern Friends Peace Board was founded in York in 1913, indicative of the revitalisation of the Quaker peace testimony. Similarly, the formation of the Friends Temperance Society and York protests against the extension of licensing hours echoed the traditional relationship of Quakers with the temperance movement. Yet, as Elizabeth Isichei has pointed out, in this period Quakers' concerns were shifting from the amelioration of distress – William Allen had established a 'soup society' to dish out food for the destitute Spitalfields silk weavers in the early part of the nineteenth century – to the 'social causes of distress': 'the channels through which the Quaker social conscience acted were changing, though the vigour and sensitivity of that conscience remained'.[72] Quakers sought a faith with direct relevance to solving the underlying causes of social problems. Politically, there was even a Socialist Quaker Society, established in 1898 (although it was not a mainstream body);[73] and many other Quakers adopted some of the outward characteristics of socialist and radical political groupings, a notable example being the 'Quaker Tramps', walks through the North Riding or Westmorland, to visit Quaker historical sites and to contemplate practical religion.[74] Less radical but no less important was the Friends Social Union, established in 1902, which under the leadership of Seebohm Rowntree attempted (with limited success) 'to grapple with the sort of social disintegration which reflected a deeper spiritual malaise in modern society'.[75] Under the influence of John Wilhelm Rowntree – who became almost a fully-fledged martyr to the cause of modern liberal Quakerism when he died suddenly in America in 1905 – Quakers in this period were seeking a new practical faith, and devising new mechanisms for the expression of it.

The most important involvement, however, was in the adult school movement. Developing from the Quaker 'First-Day Schools' (Sunday schools aimed at children aged 8-15), adult schools had been a Quaker concern for at least half a century. York's 'First-Day School' was founded in 1848. Joseph Rowntree taught there for forty years, beginning in the late 1850s, and was followed by his sons and his nephew Arnold Rowntree. Although the adult schools were non-denominational, a powerful Quaker influence was exerted, and Stephen Allott estimates that between a quarter and a third of new recruits to the Society of Friends in York between 1880 and 1918 were first introduced to Quakerism through the adult school movement.[76] The adult schools both grew out of and enhanced the developing social conscience of members of the Society of Friends, many of whom, including Joseph Rowntree, were themselves largely self-educated and desired to pass on the fruits of this self-education to others who had also been denied educational opportunities. But if these schools gave socially concerned Quakers the opportunity to educate the masses, it also taught them a lot about the way the poor lived, and gave them the sort of contact with the urban working classes that was only rarely, if ever, obtained in other ways. As such, the functions of the adult school movement were more than simply educational. Seebohm Rowntree dated his interest in the problem of working-class poverty to his years as an adult school teacher, remembering that he 'visited [his] scholars in their homes and thus got to know the conditions under which they lived'.[77] His brother John Wilhelm did the same.[78] The historian of English philanthropy David Owen has explained that, for George Cadbury, another Quaker confectioner and adult school teacher, adult school work was 'an education in the seamier side of working-class living'.[79] Rufus M. Jones, a Quaker historian and close friend of John Wilhelm Rowntree, explained why the adult school movement was the most significant of all the social and institutional manifestations of the Quaker social conscience:

> More than any other single thing which Friends have undertaken previous to the [first] world war, this work has taken the members of the Society out of themselves. It has made them unselfish and eager to live and to sacrifice for others. It has given them deep and intense human interests, sympathy and fellowship. The life and problems of a different class of persons from themselves have been brought home to their own experience, and their whole knowledge of the world has been transformed thereby, and not their knowledge only, but their entire human attitude as well ... Through this fellowship with the working men and their families Friends were brought face to face with problems of the social order which they would have known about only in an abstract way if it had not been for this direct contact ... as time went on and the living conditions and the environment of this class of labourers came to be fully revealed, interested Friends began to study the social and economic questions which were involved in the lives of these men whom they were teaching. It was a natural unfolding and maturing of social interest...[80]

In York, there were adult schools at thirteen separate centres by 1905, with a membership of 2,648 and an average attendance of 1,186;[81] and all told there were 288 such establishments in Britain by 1900.[82] Spawning interest in social investigation, they were the clearest expression of the interconnectedness of Quaker religious, economic and social concerns, and epitomised the overarching importance of personal service, which informed Joseph Rowntree's conception of social work and responsibility. Rowntree, like his sons, visited the homes of his adult scholars, some of whom testified to his personal influence on their lives;[83] and his interest in education was an integral part of the ethic of personal service to which he subscribed throughout his life. Education, he thought, should aim not just to train individuals for their role in the labour market, but also to 'develop the faculties upon the exercise of which a progressive civilised community must primarily depend'.[84] For Rowntree, York's long tradition of adult education served in some respects the connective functions of the metropolitan settlements; and, as later chapters will show, institutions which combined the aims of the settlements and the adult schools became the largest recipients of JRCT grants in the first thirty-five years of its existence.

Rowntree chose the institution of the charitable trust to fulfil his philanthropic aims. Another feature of the 1880s had been a mini-revival of this form of giving, which had a long history, having played an important role in Tudor and Stuart philanthropy, being regulated by the Statute of Charitable Trusts of 1601.[85] Originating as ecclesiastical foundations, trusts had come in time to embrace secular purposes, and English law has generally been 'relatively indulgent' towards them and their operations.[86] In 1895 the Charity Commissioners noted that thirteen new trusts of over £100,000 had been established during the previous twenty years; and on average in this period five hundred charitable trusts were being established every year.[87] In both Britain and America, the trust or foundation was a common creation of this period: the Carnegie (1911) and Rockefeller (1913) Trusts have become the best known.[88] However, the most important example to Rowntree was George Cadbury's Bournville Village Trust, established in 1903, and Rowntree corresponded with his fellow Quaker about the establishment of his own three Trusts. Cadbury's successful housing experiment at Bournville was followed by Rowntree's own venture at New Earswick, which the JRVT was established to administer; and Cadbury's political fund, spent mainly on the acquisition of newspapers, was also imitated in the establishment of the JRSST, which Rowntree explicitly wished to invest in the same area. The experience of the second Boer war (1899-1902), when the Rowntrees' pacifist stance was reviled in the jingoistic popular press (leading, among other things, to a violent attack on the Rowntree café at Scarborough), helped to impress on Rowntree the importance of encouraging Liberal control of the popular press, which he hoped to lead towards a more tolerant outlook and reflective disposition. The JRCT, with the least specific remit of the three trusts, was intended to fund projects with which the Rowntree family was closely associated, especially Seebohm's social investigations and John Wilhelm's Quaker and educational work. It came too late to pay for the *Poverty* inquiry, but it did support cheap reprints of the book; it post-dated the first Quaker summer schools with which John Wilhelm was associated, but it funded similar projects after his death.

By a deed signed on 13 December 1904, Joseph Rowntree transferred 800 ordinary shares and four deferred shares in Rowntree and Company to the trustees, the capital and dividends of which were to be spent 'for such charitable purposes and in such manner as the Trustees shall, in their uncontrolled discretion, think fit'.[89] The trustees were to meet at least four times a year, at a maximum interval of four months, at 'General Quarterly Meetings', and at other times where appropriate, with a quorum of three; and a simple majority of trustees was required for a motion to be passed. After thirty-five years the trustees were either to wind up the JRCT and transfer any remaining property to other charities (Rowntree specified the Village Trust as his preferred choice), or to establish a new Trust with broadly similar aims to the first. Although the trustees were to be given virtually unlimited powers to administer the Trust's property, the Trust Deed specified thirteen areas in which Rowntree envisaged grants being made. Although lengthy, these aims are worth reciting almost in full:

(a) The support, either by annual grants or capital sums, of the institution known as the 'Woodbrooke Permanent Settlement' ... or of any other establishment for the like purpose.

(b) The provision of religious teaching for the members of the Society of Friends, or for those associated with them in worship or Christian work.

(c) The improvement of the schools carried on by, or under the authority or direction of, the Society of Friends ... particularly by grants so made as to secure highly qualified men and women as teachers therein, and the provision of scholarships tenable at such schools or by scholars of such schools at any University or College in England or elsewhere.

(d) The foundation of scholarships to be held or enjoyed by members of the Society of Friends or those associated with them ... at any University, College, or school in England or elsewhere.

(e) The promotion of the study of the history of the Society of Friends or religious history generally.

(f) The promotion of temperance by investigation of the causes of intemperance and of remedies for the same or otherwise.

(g) The influencing of public opinion in favour of peace and the settlement of international disputes by arbitration or other pacific methods.

(h) The investigation of the causes of poverty and distress and of remedies for the same.

(i) The investigation of the causes of irregularity of employment amongst the working classes, and the provision of remedies for the same, including the provision of labour colonies and other works for the relief and training of persons out of employment.

(j) The provision of public parks and pleasure grounds.

(k) The acquisition of reports and information with regard to any of the matters in this clause mentioned, or with regard to the religious, moral, social, or educational condition of Great Britain and Ireland or other countries.

(l) The promotion of any of the objects in this clause mentioned, by the foundation of professorships, lectureships, or scholarships, or the giving of prizes, or other payments, for books, treatises, lectures, essays, or pamphlets.

(m) The publication and circulation of any such reports, information, books, treatises, lectures, essays, or pamphlets.[90]

The formal Trust Deed (along with the relevant deeds for the JRSST and JRVT) was accompanied by a memorandum circulated by Joseph Rowntree explaining some of the ways in which he intended the money available to his three Trusts to be distributed. This memorandum summarised Rowntree's conception of philanthropy, the fruits of half a century of social work and service. With regard to the JRCT, he suggested a number of specific and less specific areas in which his gift might be spent. For religious expenditure, he thought that grants should not be given towards buildings, preferring to see his gifts spent on '[r]eligious teaching to the Members of the Society of Friends of all ages, especially with a view to the fostering of a powerful Ministry', on 'strengthening the periodical or other literature of the Society', especially the history of Quakerism which John Wilhelm Rowntree had instigated, and on improved salaries for teachers in the York Quaker schools at Bootham and The Mount, as well as scholarships to those institutions.[91] Rowntree declared that the trustees 'should not, except in very special cases, make grants to existing associations, but should themselves direct and guide the appropriation of the funds' and that '[a]ny appropriations which tended to interfere with donations or subscriptions which others ought to give should be … very carefully avoided'.[92] In fact, the trustees always made grants to existing associations, and as Seebohm Rowntree explained at the end of the thirty-five year lifespan of the Trust, 'this expression of J. R.'s wish must not be interpreted literally … what he had in mind was that trustees should keep themselves fully informed as to the activities of any "existing associations" which they help'.[93] Indeed, in another section of the memorandum, Rowntree pointed out that, at least as far as religious work was concerned, 'there may be no better way of advancing the objects one has at heart than to strengthen the hands of those who are effectively doing the work that needs to be done'.[94] He envisaged that most of the projects supported, at least in the early years of the Trust, would involve members of his family personally, and that they would be able to maintain a 'watching brief' over the expenditure of sums they granted. These exhortations reflected Rowntree's continuing belief that the best form of charity was local and entailed close personal involvement, and that the community was the appropriate level at which to deliver it.

The JRCT was also to support projects concerned with 'the social question'; and in his advice under this heading Rowntree followed that delivered by George Cadbury in the establishment of his charitable trusts. Cadbury wished that his money be spent on the 'underlying causes' of social problems rather than the 'superficial evils' they manifested, and this was an important reason behind his involvement in newspapers.[95] As David Owen points out, '[s]uch expressions as "superficial evils" and "underlying causes" were commonplaces in the vocabulary of charity reformers, but to George Cadbury they conveyed something very different from what they meant to Charles Loch and the Charity Organisation Society'.[96] His utterances were made with a fuller understanding of the structural factors lying behind the problems of poverty, intemperance and improvidence; and Rowntree expressed much the same point of view in a much-quoted section of his memorandum:

> I feel that much of current philanthropic effort is directed to remedying the more superficial manifestations of weakness or evil, while little thought or effort is directed to search out their underlying causes. Obvious distress or evil generally evokes so much feeling that the necessary agencies for alleviating it are pretty adequately supported ... The Soup Kitchen in York never has difficulty in obtaining adequate financial aid, but an enquiry into the extent and causes of poverty would enlist little support.[97]

He cited his own temperance research as the sort of project to which philanthropy would be 'wisely directed', and clearly had in mind the social research in which Seebohm Rowntree was engaged; in particular, he wished to see more research into 'questions connected with the holding and taxation of land'.[98] It is easy to view this passage as suggesting that Joseph Rowntree disapproved of soup kitchens, much as the COS continued to do. This would be misleading, however: during the Edwardian winters of high unemployment York's soup kitchen was established and administered by a committee which included Arnold and Seebohm Rowntree, and was only seriously opposed by the Independent Labour Party, who argued rather unconvincingly that the kitchen would undercut wages.[99] Nevertheless, Rowntree would have concurred with the Labour representative who claimed that the persistence of unemployment in York was 'an eloquent tribute to the failure of ... local philanthropists to solve it'.[100] This section of Rowntree's memorandum emphasised his concern at the widespread misdirection of British charitable resources and the need for this to be at least partially redressed. As Brian Harrison has pointed out (quoting David Owen), '"to the mass of givers, the most appealing cases in order of preference were sailors, animals, and children" ... not necessarily the most deserving of relief either then or now. Money-raising for individual "causes" often led philanthropists to ignore the inter-relation of social ills, and promoted competition where co-operation was most desperately needed':[101] an assessment with which Joseph Rowntree would have wholeheartedly agreed.

Although much in this memorandum was 'splendidly far-sighted',[102] it is important not to lose sight of the fact that Joseph Rowntree was a man of his times, and in the present context it is particularly important to emphasise that he continued to subscribe to the prevalent assumption among Victorian philanthropists of the moral and cultural superiority of pre-industrial social relationships. His personal angst at the growth of his business beyond a size at which it was feasible to know all his employees individually is testament to this, and resulted (among other things) in his establishment of the *Cocoa Works Magazine* in 1902.[103] Involvement in adult school work and multifarious local projects, as well as the insistence on continuation classes and the provision of welfare officers at the factory, all illustrate Rowntree's concern about the impersonal nature of social relationships in the industrial town. Moreover, he felt that town and country had become sundered from each other. The creation of the model village of New Earswick fitted in with his belief that 'the residence of town workers in the country would help to bridge the gulf between town and country interests which for several generations had been slowly widening'.[104] Rowntree subscribed wholeheartedly to the Garden City ethos (Ebenezer Howard's influential *Garden cities of tomorrow* was published first in 1898 and again in 1902),[105] and his view was shared by his son Seebohm, who in his book *Land and labour: lessons from Belgium* (1910) looked to the Belgian model of residence in the country and work in the town as a means of reinvigorating the condition of the British worker.[106] Joseph himself rented a house in Westow, eleven miles from York, to which he occasionally retired to write, and Anne Vernon points out that, although he sometimes over-romanticised rural life, he was impressed by the 'corporate life' that Westow offered its inhabitants.[107] Thus when planning New Earswick, he tried to avoid the stultifying paternalism of William Lever's Port Sunlight,[108] but sought rather to establish 'civic interest' and 'civic responsibility' by giving tenants a substantial say in the management of the estate and its recreational amenities.[109] Nevertheless, the Rowntrees' only outright gift to New Earswick was the unusually named 'Folk Hall', at which religious services were held, but also country dancing and other rustic activities, embodying a partly conscious attempt to re-create a ruralised paternalistic atmosphere in the village.[110] Joseph's pastoralism – one relative remembered his 'almost Wordsworthian feeling for the countryside'[111] – made some of his projects seem rather quaintly anachronistic, but in this respect he drew fully on the guiding assumptions of Victorian and Edwardian philanthropy.

There was a more potentially serious side to this apparently harmless and eccentric pastoralism, however, striking at the heart of the sense of economic and social malaise that was arguably the central political concern of the Edwardian years. Ruralism had long been a part of the English literary tradition, but in this period its direct counterposition to the problems of urban life led many groups, from Tories to socialists, to project visions of national salvation onto the land. When theories of urban hereditary 'degeneration' began to circulate during the metropolitan crises of the 1880s, various half-baked proposals to revitalise the urban 'residuum' by moving them wholesale to rural locations and teaching them agricultural labouring skills were dreamed up; and the reports of widespread unfitness for military service of urban recruits during the second Boer war prompted a whole series of concerns about 'national efficiency' which led to the drawing of comparisons with other nations, especially the USA and most threateningly Germany, measured against whom Britain was undoubtedly in a period of comparative economic decline.[112] The Conservative government established an Interdepartmental Committee on Physical Deterioration in 1904 to examine the question, and although this inquiry revealed very little evidence of any such deterioration in urban physique and intelligence, it further fuelled the debates that continued to rage. The Rowntrees, although they never succumbed to the excesses of the 'national efficiency' enthusiasm (it was never coherent enough to be termed an ideology or organised enough to be termed a movement), subscribed with some vigour to its basic precepts. Rowntree and Sherwell, in *The temperance problem and social reform*, pointed to the implications of their findings for Britain's future industrial competitiveness:

> It is the more necessary to concentrate attention on this point by reason of changes that are rapidly shifting the centres of commercial activity and intensifying the forces of industrial competition ... Other nations have been moving up to our own standards of efficiency ... Within the last thirty years Germany, Belgium, and even Russia, have transformed themselves economically ... while we are also face to face with the unprecedented competition of the United States. The conditions of industrial competition are, therefore, wholly changed, and the question of efficiency – mental and physical – has become one of paramount importance.[113]

Seebohm Rowntree quoted these remarks in *Poverty*,[114] and by basing his primary poverty line on 'physical efficiency', he contributed to the ubiquity of the efficiency concept. He linked his researches specifically to the condition of recruits,[115] and accompanied the survey with an anthropometric and medical examination of schoolchildren in different areas of

York. These examinations of children showed, according to Rowntree, 'evidence of serious physical deterioration amongst the poorest section of the community'.[116]

It was partly Seebohm's awareness that conditions among agricultural workers in much of England were little or no better than those in the towns that prevented him from becoming a more enthusiastic supporter of the 'national efficiency' crusade. Nevertheless, as employers of labour, the importance of improving the efficiency and productivity of their workforce was not lost on the Rowntrees. Even workplace religious worship had its part to play in this. Both Fry's and Cadbury's introduced acts of compulsory daily worship at work, Joseph Fry remarking that these conferred the advantage of 'bringing the workpeople once a day under review. It is often a means of observing their conduct and checking any tendency to impropriety'.[117] It would be mean, however, to characterise the schemes to improve the welfare of Rowntree's workers as wholly motivated by such considerations; the Quaker social conscience, which the JRCT in its early years did much to satisfy, merits a less cynical interpretation. Although no historical analysis of the JRCT can be divorced from the wider economic and social currents of the period in which it was created, it must also take account of the longer-term developments within the Society of Friends and across the whole gamut of British philanthropy. The Rowntrees expressed these concerns in their role as enlightened employers, their long-standing associations with local social institutions, and their involvement in the 'Quaker Renaissance'. Above all, their interest in adult education – Quaker, non-denominational and even secular – fused their interest in social change with their belief in the necessity of personal service. The ideals that lay behind the adult education movement, linking religious, economic and social concerns, and subscribed to by Joseph Rowntree and his family in both their employment practices and their wider social involvements, were to guide the philanthropic enterprises in which they took part in the years to come.

NOTES

1. Worstenholme, 'Joseph Rowntree', G5-7.
2. Ibid. F12.
3. Vernon, *Quaker business man*, 9.
4. Frances Finnegan, *Poverty and prejudice: a study of Irish immigrants in York 1840-1875*, Cork 1982, esp. 35ff.
5. Joseph Rowntree, memorandum of 29 December 1904, 1, in JRCT, *Basic documents*, JRCT library. Hereafter Founder's memorandum.
6. Olive Checkland, *Philanthropy in Victorian Scotland: social welfare and the voluntary principle*, Edinburgh 1980, 3-4, 332.

7. See for example F. K. Prochaska, *The voluntary impulse: philanthropy in modern Britain*, 1988, 34; David Owen, *English philanthropy 1660-1960*, Oxford 1965, 444-8.

8. Anne Summers, 'A home from home – women's philanthropic work in the nineteenth century', in Sandra Burman (ed.), *Fit work for women*, 1979, 35-7; Prochaska, *Voluntary impulse*, 25-7, 34-58.

9. Prochaska, *Voluntary impulse*, 35.

10. Pauline Gregg, *A social and economic history of Britain 1760-1970* (1st edn 1950), 1971, 180.

11. Geoffrey Finlayson, *Citizen, state and social welfare in Britain 1830-1990*, Oxford 1994, 135-6 and passim; see also Brian Harrison, 'Philanthropy and the Victorians', *Victorian Studies* ix (1966), 367ff.

12. For general accounts of the history of the COS, see Helen Bosanquet, *Social work in London 1896-1912: a history of the Charity Organisation Society*, 1914; Charles Loch Mowat, *The Charity Organisation Society 1869-1913: its ideas and work*, 1961; Madeline Rooff, *A hundred years of family welfare: a study of the Family Welfare Association (formerly Charity Organisation Society) 1869-1969*, 1972; Jane Lewis, *The voluntary sector, the state and social work in Britain: the Charity Organisation Society/Family Welfare Association since 1869*, Aldershot 1995.

13. Owen, *English philanthropy*, 216-44, esp. 229.

14. Gareth Stedman Jones, *Outcast London: a study in the relationship between classes in Victorian society* (1st edn 1971), Harmondsworth 1984, ch. 13.

15. See *Letters and other writings of the late Edward Denison*, ed. Baldwyn Leighton, 1872.

16. Jones, *Outcast London*, 261.

17. See Robert Humphreys, *Sin, organized charity and the poor law in Victorian England*, Basingstoke 1995.

18. Owen, *English philanthropy*, 222-3.

19. Bosanquet, *Social work*, 392ff; Alan Kidd, *State, society and the poor in nineteenth-century England*, 1999, 99-100; Proschaska, *Voluntary impulse*, 25-6.

20. Anne Digby, 'The relief of poverty in Victorian York: attitudes and policies', in Charles Feinstein (ed.), *York 1831-1981: 150 years of scientific endeavour*, York 1981, 177.

21. Humphreys, *Sin*, 10: 'Ample evidence indicates that provincial COS revenues were not usually a match for many traditional charities. The COS explained that their *raison d'être* was not to disseminate alms but to investigate the justification of those who were asking for them. Such excuses about their financial weakness are unconvincing when it becomes known that provincial COSs were embarrassed by their inadequate public support making it impossible for them to succour some of those they had investigated and found deserving.'

22. Digby, 'Relief of poverty', 177; Owen, *English philanthropy*, 447-8.

23. A. J. Peacock, *York 1900 to 1914*, York 1992, 120-2, and passim.

24. Quoted in Digby, 'Relief of poverty', 167.

25. Owen, *English philanthropy*, 211.

26. Prochaska, *Voluntary impulse*, 70.

27. Beatrice Webb, *My apprenticeship* (1st edn 1926), Harmondsworth 1971, 191-3.
28. Ibid. 186.
29. The riots of 1886 (and the following year) are perhaps the best known outbreak of popular discontent in the 1880s. For an account see Jones, *Outcast London*, 290-6.
30. Charles Booth (ed.), *Life and labour of the people in London* (1st edn 2 vols 1889; 2nd edn 10 vols 1892-7), 17 vols 1902-3. There is a rich literature on Booth, of which the most recent and the most accessible examples are Rosemary O'Day and David Englander, *Mr Charles Booth's inquiry:* Life and labour of the people in London *reconsidered*, 1993; David Englander and Rosemary O'Day (eds), *Retrieved riches: social investigation in Britain 1840-1914*, Aldershot 1995.
31. Vernon, *Quaker business man*, 60-4.
32. Ibid. 137-8.
33. Ibid. 138; Worstenholme, 'Joseph Rowntree', H6-7.
34. Worstenholme, 'Joseph Rowntree', J7.
35. B. Seebohm Rowntree, *Poverty: a study of town life* (1st edn 1901), 1902, 8.
36. Ibid.
37. See for example Asa Briggs, 'The welfare state in historical perspective', in *The collected essays of Asa Briggs*, 3 vols Brighton 1985, ii. 201-5; Bentley B. Gilbert, *The evolution of national insurance in Great Britain: the origins of the welfare state*, 1966, 53-8, 82-91; Pat Thane, *The foundations of the welfare state* (1st edn 1982), 1996, 6-11, 14-19, 49-52; John Macnicol, *The politics of retirement in Britain 1878-1948*, Cambridge 1998, 76-84, 273-84.
38. *Official papers by Alfred Marshall*, ed. J. M. Keynes, 1926, 244-5.
39. Finlayson, *Citizen, state and social welfare*, 150-1.
40. Graham Bowpitt, 'Poverty and its early critics: the search for a value-free definition of the problem', in Jonathan Bradshaw and Roy Sainsbury (eds), *Getting the measure of poverty: the early legacy of Seebohm Rowntree*, Aldershot 2000, 23-38.
41. Owen, *English philanthropy*, 242.
42. Finlayson, *Citizen, state and social welfare*, 198-99 (but cf. 164).
43. See for example A. M. MacBriar, *An Edwardian mixed doubles: the Bosanquets versus the Webbs: a study in British social policy 1890-1929*, Oxford 1987, 182-95; Finlayson, *Citizen, state and social welfare*, 171-6; Lewis, *Voluntary sector*, 25-43, 69-79; Kidd, *State, society and the poor*, 95-107.
44. On settlements see Werner Picht, *Toynbee Hall and the English settlement movement*, 1914; J. A. R. Pimlott, *Toynbee Hall: fifty years of social progress*, 1935; Asa Briggs and Anne Macartney, *Toynbee Hall: the first hundred years*, 1984; Standish Meacham, *Toynbee Hall and social reform 1880-1914: the search for community*, New Haven, Conn., 1987; Jon Glasby (ed.), *'Back to the future': the history of the settlement movement and its relevance for organisations today*, Birmingham 2000.
45. Jose Harris, *Private lives, public spirit: Britain 1870-1914* (1st edn 1993), Harmondsworth 1994, 175.
46. Jones, *Outcast London*, 259.
47. Meacham, *Toynbee Hall*, 6-7.

48. See for example Mowat, *Charity Organisation Society*, 126-31; Finlayson, *Citizen, state and social welfare*, 140-1.
49. Meacham, *Toynbee Hall*, 37.
50. Ibid. 23.
51. See Keith Laybourn (ed.), *Social conditions, status and community 1860-c.1920*, Stroud 1997.
52. Lewis, *Voluntary sector*, 26.
53. Digby, 'Relief of poverty', 171-2.
54. Lewis E. Waddilove, *Foundations and trusts – innovators or survivals?*, 1979, 5.
55. See Mark Freeman, 'The provincial social survey in Edwardian Britain', *Historical Research* lxxv (2002), 73-89.
56. Quoted in ibid. 197-8.
57. Worstenholme, 'Joseph Rowntree', F10.
58. Webb, *My apprenticeship*, 192.
59. On 'quietism' see A. Neave Brayshaw, *The Quakers: their story and message*, 1921, ch. 15.
60. See James Walvin, *The Quakers: money and morals*, 1997, 209 and passim.
61. Thomas C. Kennedy, *British Quakerism 1860-1920: the transformation of a religious community*, Oxford 2001, 40-1.
62. The best general accounts are Elizabeth Isichei, *Victorian Quakers*, Oxford 1970, and Walvin, *The Quakers*. See also Rufus M. Jones, *The later periods of Quakerism*, 2 vols 1921, ii. ch. 24.
63. Jones, *Later periods*, ii. 942.
64. Sheila Wright, *Friends in York: the dynamics of Quaker revival 1780-1860*, Keele 1995.
65. Stephen Allott, *Friends in York: the Quaker story in the life of a Meeting*, York 1978, 78; Walvin, *The Quakers*, 137.
66. Wright, *Friends in York*, 134.
67. Kennedy, *British Quakerism*, esp. ch. 5.
68. Ibid.; Thomas C. Kennedy, 'Late Victorian/Edwardian Quakers and early Friends: clean connections or crossed wires?', lecture at Woodbrooke Quaker Study Centre, 1 May 2002.
69. Allott, *Friends in York*, 95.
70. See Kennedy, *British Quakerism*, 106-11, 155-71; Brayshaw, *The Quakers*, ch. 18.
71. Kennedy, *British Quakerism*, 171-7.
72. Isichei, *Victorian Quakers*, 256-7.
73. See Tony Adams, *A far-seeing vision: the Socialist Quaker Society 1898-1924*, Bedford n. d.
74. Allott, *Friends in York*, 95; Allott, *John Wilhelm Rowntree*, 110; J. Roland Whiting, *Ernest E. Taylor: valiant for truth*, 1958, ch. 4.
75. Kennedy, *British Quakerism*, 190.
76. Allott, *Friends in York*, 93.
77. Quoted in Briggs, *Seebohm Rowntree*, 13.
78. Allott, *John Wilhelm Rowntree*, 13-14.
79. Owen, *English philanthropy*, 436.
80. Jones, *Later periods*, ii. 956-8.

81. Allott, *Friends in York*, 92.
82. Walvin, *The Quakers*, 152.
83. Worstenholme, 'Joseph Rowntree', C4, D8-9.
84. Ibid. D4.
85. W. K. Jordan, *English philanthropy 1480-1660: a study of the changing pattern of English social aspirations*, 1959, 109-17.
86. Owen, *English philanthropy*, 5.
87. Finlayson, *Citizen, state and social welfare*, 133-4
88. On the role of the trust or foundation see Ben Whitaker, *The foundations: an anatomy of philanthropy and society*, 1974; Waddilove, *Foundations and trusts*; and for a critical interpretation from an American perspective Robert F. Arnove (ed.), *Philanthropy and cultural imperialism: the foundations at home and abroad*, Boston, Mass., 1980.
89. JRCT, Trust Deed, 1-2, copy in The Garden House, York.
90. Ibid. 2-3.
91. Founder's memorandum, 2-3.
92. Ibid. 1.
93. B. Seebohm Rowntree, 'Report on the work done by the JRCT 1905-1939 and suggestions ... regarding future policy', 1-2, JRF JRCT93/I/11 (d). Although these papers are housed by the JRF, they are the joint property of the JRF, JRCT and JRRT.
94. Founder's memorandum, 2-3.
95. Owen, *English philanthropy*, 434, 440-2.
96. Ibid. 434.
97. Founder's memorandum., 2.
98. Ibid. 2, 4.
99. R. I. Hills, *The inevitable march of Labour? Electoral politics in York 1900-1914*, York 1996, 13; Peacock, *York 1900 to 1914*, 57-8, 85.
100. Quoted in Hills, *Inevitable march*, 13, and Peacock, *York 1900 to 1914*, 85.
101. Harrison, 'Philanthropy and the Victorians', 367, quoting Owen, *English philanthropy*, 538.
102. Roger Wilson, *Money and power: reflections as a trustee*, 1972, 2 (pamphlet reprinted from *Friends' Quarterly*, July 1972).
103. Vernon, *Quaker business man*, 126-7.
104. Worstenholme, 'Joseph Rowntree', K3.
105. Waddilove, *One man's vision*, 2-3; Ebenezer Howard, *Garden cities of tomorrow* (1st edn 1898), 1902. (The first edition was entitled *To-morrow: a peaceful path to real reform*.)
106. B. Seebohm Rowntree, *Land and labour: lessons from Belgium*, 1910, 288-94.
107. Vernon, *Quaker business man*, 145-7.
108. Gillian Wagner, *The chocolate conscience*, 1987, 71.
109. Waddilove, *One man's vision*, 8-10, ch. 8.
110. Ibid., photograph facing p. 83: a group of Swedish folk dancers on the lawn outside the Folk Hall.
111. Jean Rowntree, 'The Founder's commission: some reflections and guesses', 19 March 1973, 16, in JRCT, *Basic documents*.
112. See for example Jones, *Outcast London*, esp. chs 6, 16; G. R. Searle, *The quest for national efficiency: a study in British politics and political thought 1899-1914*

(1st edn 1971),1990, (pp. 64-5 on Seebohm Rowntree); Eileen Janes Yeo, *The contest for social science: relations and representations of gender and class*, 1996, 223-9.

113. Joseph Rowntree and Arthur Sherwell, *The temperance problem and social reform*, 1899, 48.
114. Rowntree, *Poverty*, 220-1.
115. Ibid. 216-21.
116. Ibid. 214.
117. Wagner, *Chocolate conscience*, 50-1.

CHAPTER 2

The Rowntrees and their Trust: early grants and the challenge of war, 1904-1918

WHEN JOSEPH Rowntree established the JRCT and its sister Trusts, there were a number of circumstances that he could not foresee. He could not foresee the outbreak of war in 1914 and the challenges this would issue both to the nation and to the Society of Friends; he could not foresee the importance that adult education and educational settlements would come to have both to the Society of Friends and to his own family; he could not foresee the death of his son John Wilhelm Rowntree within months of the establishment of the Trust; and perhaps most importantly he could not have foreseen that he would live until the age of 89, dying in 1925, when 21 years of the intended 35-year lifespan of the JRCT had passed. In other words, he did not expect when establishing the Trust that he would have so much personal direction over its resources for so long. His initial memorandum, circulated to the trustees of his three Trusts in December 1904, although still important to the trustees and still cited in the JRCT's triennial reports late in the twentieth century,[1] had in some respects become obsolete during his lifetime, and was modified by later memoranda. This chapter examines the early grant-making activities of the JRCT, under the direct influence of the 1904 memorandum and its author, and goes on to consider how the first world war modified the Rowntrees' views of their Trust in the context of Quakerism and philanthropy. In these early years the JRCT (together with the JRVT and JRSST) was very much the Rowntrees' Trust, pursuing the philanthropic interests of members of the family, usually through channels with which they were personally associated.

The original trustees, charged with administering the distribution of the funds allotted to all three trusts, were Joseph Rowntree himself, his sons John Wilhelm, Benjamin Seebohm, Joseph Stephenson and Oscar Frederick, and his nephew Arnold Stephenson Rowntree. Oscar and

Joseph Stephenson (known as Stephen) both joined the board of Rowntree and Company in 1905. Oscar, born in 1879, was active in the Edwardian Liberal party, as secretary and treasurer of Bootham Ward Liberal Association and Liberal Club, and was elected to York City Council for Castlegate Ward in 1905. The least active of the original trustees, and not an active member of the board of the cocoa works either – he was 'first and foremost a pig farmer'[2] – he resigned his trusteeship of the Charitable Trust in 1919.[3] Stephen, born in 1875 and educated at Bootham School and King's College, Cambridge, took more interest in the JRVT, of which he was later chairman, than the JRCT. Like the other Rowntrees, he was interested in education, and took the main responsibility for this area in New Earswick.[4] A 'man of retiring nature',[5] he was nevertheless mayor of Harrogate from 1911 to 1913. He remained a trustee of the Charitable Trust until his death in 1951, and was interested in Quaker worship, on which he published a number of works.[6] He was an active member of the Society of Friends' Peace Committee and Northern Friends Peace Board, and treasurer of Yorkshire Quarterly Meeting from 1922 to 1945. With the possible exception of John Wilhelm, he was more concerned with the internal structures and practices of the Society of Friends than were the other trustees, and this was to be seen later when he regularly pleaded for a more distinctively Quaker dimension to the increasingly non-denominational and even secular educational endeavours that the JRCT funded.[7]

John Wilhelm, Joseph's eldest son, born in 1868 and the only trustee mentioned by name in the Founder's memorandum, died after just one meeting of the trustees, but his inspiration lay behind much of the work that they funded in the early years.[8] As we have seen, John Wilhelm was one of the leaders of the young Friends who did much to change the outlook of the Society in the 1890s. Like the other members of his family, he was a practical educationalist: he began teaching at the York Adult School in the 1880s, and he and his friend Edward Worsdell opened the branch school in Acomb in 1893.[9] After the Manchester conference in 1895, at which John Wilhelm (supported in the discussion by Worsdell) had given one of the most stirring addresses, urging wider and more imaginative social involvement, especially in the field of education, by Friends, he edited *Present-Day Papers*, a short-lived Quaker journal in which he advocated the development of summer schools, and pleaded for the establishment of a 'Quaker settlement'.[10] Together with his father, his uncle John Stephenson Rowntree (himself a young Quaker radical in the midnineteenth century) and George Cadbury, he was involved in the establishment of the 'settlement' or college at Woodbrooke in Birmingham, the opening of which, in 1903, he just lived to see. (Woodbrooke is examined in more detail below). Because of his poor health – he was physically weak, visually impaired and partially deaf – John Wilhelm was unable to play as large a personal part in many of these endeavours as he would have wished, but on moving to Scalby, near Scarborough, in the interests of his health in 1899, he and his wife established a guest house, known as Friedenstahl, for the use of Quakers and adult scholars, which opened in 1905. In that year John Wilhelm died, but many of his friends carried on this kind of work. He was a close friend of the American Quaker scholar Rufus M. Jones,[11] of the English Quaker Edward Grubb, and of many other leading Friends of his time. He had pioneered the idea of the 'Quaker Tramps', given practical form after his death by his cousins Arnold and Arthur Rowntree (the latter was headmaster of Bootham School), and suggested lines along which the educational and pastoral work of the Society might progress; and many of the early JRCT grants were given to his personal friends to further these aims.

Joseph's second son Seebohm, three years younger than John Wilhelm, shared his older brother's interest in adult education, but differed from him in many other respects. Although a Quaker himself, he was less directly involved in the internal business of the Society of Friends, preferring to find an outlet for his energies in social investigation and the promotion of workplace welfare initiatives at Rowntree and Company and elsewhere. Although a supporter of the Liberal party, and later a friend and close associate of David Lloyd George, he was never a strong party man, content to avoid the spotlight of politics and concentrate on the careful analysis of social problems. He studied chemistry at Owen's College, Manchester (later Manchester University), and Asa Briggs, in a biography published soon after Seebohm's death, has pointed to the importance of this scientific background to the future directions his life took.[12] Seebohm entered the cocoa works in 1889, where he was interested in the development of new products, reflecting his scientific knowledge and interest; and in 1901, as we have seen, he published the results of a social survey of York carried out two years earlier, in which he described how nearly a third of the city's population lived in poverty, and that almost a tenth lived in 'primary poverty', in other words lacking a sufficient income to enable them to purchase enough shelter, food and household sundries to maintain their physical efficiency.[13] Joseph Rowntree envisaged an important role for the JRCT in funding work of this kind, and Seebohm was the largest individual recipient of grants in the first ten years of the Trust's existence, which he spent in carrying out similar kinds of social inquiry. From 1904 to 1906 he served as the Trust's unpaid secretary, and remained a trustee until his death in 1954. For much of this time he lived at the Homestead in York, now the headquarters of the Joseph Rowntree Foundation.

Although born only one year later than Seebohm, his cousin Arnold Rowntree was a very different character, and became perhaps the most influential trustee, and certainly the trustee with the highest public pro-file.[14] Nevertheless, like Joseph and Seebohm, he was first and foremost a York man. The son of Joseph's brother John Stephenson Rowntree, Arnold was educated at Bootham and indentured to the grocer's shop in the Pavement where Joseph Rowntree had served his own apprenticeship four decades earlier. Arnold joined the cocoa works in 1892, where he quickly came to specialise in advertising and marketing, the kind of activ-ity which suited his outgoing personality. Like his cousin Oscar, he was involved in the York Liberal Association, serving as secretary from 1901 to 1904, president from 1904 to 1909, and as MP for York from 1910 until 1918. He was also chairman of the North of England Newspaper Company, and a founding member of the governing council of Woodbrooke college (of which he wrote a history, published in 1923).[15] Having married Mary K. (May) Harvey, sister of another Quaker MP, T. Edmund Harvey, in 1906, Arnold lived at Chalfonts, near Mount Villas in York, for most of the rest of his life. Education, and especially adult education, was a lifelong interest of Arnold's. His father had been involved in the establishment of The Mount girls' school; and Arnold taught from an early age in the Leeman Road Adult School. From 1903 to 1945 he was honorary secretary of the York Schools Committee (dealing with The Mount and Bootham), from 1906 president of the Yorkshire Adult School Union, and from 1905 honorary secretary of the National Adult School Union (NASU). His personal secretary Frederick J. Gillman was the author of a history of adult education in York, and wrote a series of hymns for adult school use.[16] Even after his election to parliament in 1910, Arnold continued his education work, and after losing his seat in 1918 he gave most of the rest of the life to adult education: much of this work was funded in whole or in part by the JRCT. Arnold's physical bulk earned him the nickname 'Chocolate Jumbo', and he was a well known public figure in York for most of his life.

The first trustees, then, all came from the same family and worked within a series of traditions that derived from their home city, their Liberalism, their business interests and their Quakerism. As Arnold Rowntree's biographer remarked, he was 'a Yorkshireman, descended from many generations of Yorkshiremen; a Quaker, descended from many generations of Quakers; a humanitarian, descended from many genera-tions of humanitarians'.[17] These distinctive traditions were reflected in the early work of the Trust, which awarded grants on a distinctly local basis, and in most cases to promote the work of the Society of Friends. It was also a cocoa works trust: its original assets consisted wholly of shares in Rowntree and Company, all the trustees were directors (Oscar and Stephen only by virtue of being trustees), and meetings were usually held at the company's Haxby Road premises. Moreover, the crossover of trustees between the JRVT and JRCT meant that all were involved in the practical improvement of working-class life within the city of York. Joseph Rowntree was reluctant to allow non-Rowntrees to become trustees: thus although John Wilhelm died in 1905, he was not replaced on the board of trustees until 1913. (Even Rowntree and Company was at first unwilling to diversify its directorate: when it was incorporated in 1897, of the six directors only J. B. Morrell, a long-standing family friend, was not a Rowntree.)[18]

Unsurprisingly, then, many of the early grants made by the Trust went to support members of the family and their friends. Seebohm Rowntree's social investigation work was supported handsomely, Arnold brought many applications for grants to the attention of the trustees, and regular transfers of assets between the Village, Charitable and Social Service Trusts suggest a strategy for grant-making whereby the family decided where their money should go and then worked out the most efficient and legally acceptable way of dispersing it.[19] Grants were often given informally: for example, when the trustees formally approved a small book grant to Edward Worsdell in July 1907, it was noted that this had been 'already approved by all the Trustees at an informal meeting' in May.[20] When an external application for funding was received, the trustees were generally reluctant to grant money, conscious of their duty to maintain a 'watching brief' over the expenditure of their grants. More formally, it might also be unclear whether the project fulfilled the terms of the Trust Deed: thus when the Rev. H. S. Grinling applied somewhat vaguely for money to help with his social work in Woolwich (a long way from York), discussion was deferred until Seebohm was able to gather more information.[21] The trustees were always willing to spend money on their own relatives. Maurice Lotherington Rowntree, son of Joseph's cousin Joshua Rowntree, received a grant to visit the United States, partly in the interests of the Society of Friends and partly for his own personal development;[22] and the Trust took a great interest in his welfare and future prospects. Seebohm Rowntree gave him employment on one of his social studies, and hoped he might be trained to carry out settlement work,[23] and when it was pointed out at a meeting that Maurice was thinking of visiting the Holy Land, '[s]ome discussion took place as to a travelling companion for him'.[24] Another regular recipient of grants, Wilfrid Crosland, a student at Woodbrooke and later sub-warden of the settlement at St. Mary's in York, was a cousin of Arnold Rowntree.

The first non-Rowntree trustee of the JRCT, E. Richard Cross (1864-1916),[25] who served as a trustee from 1913 until his death, and acted as the paid secretary of the Trust from 1906, was the Rowntree family solicitor and a signatory to the original Trust Deed, with long-standing connections to the family. Brought up as a Wesleyan Methodist, Cross began

33

attending Quaker Meetings in the early 1890s, took part in the Manchester conference of 1895, and finally joined the Society in 1898. He grew up in Scarborough, where he was articled to Joshua Rowntree, and only moved to York in 1913, when his Rowntree commitments necessitated it. He was an active member of the Scarborough Liberal Association, chairman of directors of the Liberal *Nation* periodical from 1907 until his death, and in 1912-13 worked with Seebohm Rowntree on the Liberal party's Land Enquiry Committee. During the war he was appointed to the Central Control Board (Liquor Traffic) by Lloyd George; and he died suddenly from drowning in the Lake District in August 1916. Cross was always sceptical of the Quaker belief in the unlawfulness of war under all circumstances; but he opposed the second Boer war, being present at the violent break-up of the peace meeting at the Rowntree café in Scarborough in 1900. He did not take the same view of the first world war, but nevertheless kept up his peace work, acting in collaboration with Lord Bryce and the Council for the Study of International Relations (of which more later).

The next two non-Rowntree trustees were Ernest E. Taylor and William Charles Braithwaite, both appointed at the same meeting in 1915 (although Taylor had begun attending JRCT meetings regularly in 1912).[26] Braithwaite,[27] in terms of the Trust, was the less active of the two, but he was an important figure in the history of both Quakerism and adult education. Born in London in 1862, the son of the noted Quaker minister and influential evangelical Joseph Bevan Braithwaite,[28] William, though legally trained, spent most of his working life as a banker in Banbury, where he was active in the magistracy, the Education Committee from its inception in 1902, the management of the Friends' co-educational boarding school at Sibford, and the local adult school. He was one of the speakers at the Manchester conference in 1895 which had done so much to pave the way for the increased social involvement of young Friends. Most important perhaps, in 1900 Braithwaite succeeded the adult education pioneer William White as chairman of the National Council of Adult School Unions (which became the NASU); and in this capacity he was also involved in adult school exchange visits to Germany in the years before the first world war. As a friend of John Wilhelm Rowntree, Braithwaite was enthused by the idea of the history of Quakerism, proposed by John Wilhelm and largely funded by the JRCT, and he wrote two of the seven volumes, *The beginnings of Quakerism* (1912) and *The second period of Quakerism* (1919). Braithwaite's remoteness from York and his other commitments made him an only occasionally active Rowntree trustee; but his connections in the adult education movement – he was also chairman of the Woodbrooke Committee from its formation in 1903 – made him a useful point of contact for the other trustees.

34

Probably the most important of the non-Rowntree trustees in this period was Ernest E. Taylor.[29] Born in Malton in 1869, Taylor spent most of the period 1891-1905 living and working in Kendal, as a partner in the Northern Newspaper Syndicate. Through this professional interest and his Quaker connections, he knew Arnold Rowntree, who brought him back to Yorkshire in 1905 to become secretary of the North of England Newspaper Company, which owned the *Northern Echo* and the *Yorkshire Gazette* as well as Taylor's home-town *Malton Gazette*. Taylor was also one of the first directors of the British Periodicals Limited, which included the *Nation* and the Quaker journals *The Friend* and the *Friends Quarterly Examiner*, and he later wrote various works on Quaker history;[30] but his main contribution both to the Society of Friends and the JRCT was in the field of adult education and extension work. He helped to run the 'Quaker Tramps', started in the aftermath of John Wilhelm Rowntree's death, and in the same year became honorary secretary of the Yorkshire 1905 Committee, of which Arnold Rowntree was the president and John Stephenson Rowntree the treasurer. This committee was formed with the aim of improving the vocal ministry in Meetings in the north of England, as well supporting existing Quaker endeavours in the field of adult education and the distribution of pamphlets. Kennedy has characterised it as 'a sort of "ginger group" dedicated to pursuing the objectives which John Wilhelm Rowntree had articulated'.[31] Its work was summarised in a report of 1913 as including 'Visitation arrangements, Lecture Courses, Study Circles, Sunday Evening Addresses, Children's School Work, and Settlements';[32] and it effectively became an overseeing body for the still somewhat chaotic Quaker adult education provision in Yorkshire. In fact, its role was sometimes proactive and innovative, as in the case of the establishment of educational settlements (which will be explored in more detail below). Taylor remained a trustee until 1951, serving as secretary after the death of Richard Cross until 1936.[33]

The workers and initiatives of the Yorkshire 1905 Committee received substantial JRCT support in this early period of the Trust's history. Even where the Committee was not directly involved, its vision of the Quaker religious and social mission lay behind most of the grant-making priorities of the trustees. Thus by far the largest number of grants were given to Quaker groups and individuals, under sections (a) to (e) of the Trust Deed, and especially towards the salaries of individuals working for the Society or in some way under its auspices. The most prominent of these was Edward Grubb (1854-1939),[34] who had been working as secretary of the Howard Association, and on resigning this post was employed full-time in Quaker service by the JRCT. A product of Bootham School, Grubb was one of the most important Quaker teachers of the period: a friend of John Wilhelm Rowntree, he became joint secretary of the Woodbrooke committee (with John H. Barlow) on the formation of the settlement in 1903; and in 1907 he was appointed the first secretary of the Woodbrooke Extension Committee. The range of Grubb's work was impressive. During the first six months of 1907, he reported to the Trust that he had given 25 lectures, helped to organise summer schools in Maidstone and Cambridge, worked as secretary to the London Meeting of Recorded Ministers and to the Ministry Committee of his own Monthly Meeting, acted as chairman of his own Quarterly Meeting Committee on Poverty and Social Science, and written the American Epistle at Yearly Meeting.[35] In the first half of the following year he was even more active, organising summer schools at Guildford, Kendal and Glasgow, giving addresses in Leeds, Bradford and Ipswich, lecturing weekly at both York and Luton, spending almost every Sunday attending Meetings away from home, and acting as secretary of the Yearly Meeting Ministry Committee; and on top of this he was preparing to write two books and to endeavour to boost the circulation of *The Friend*.[36] Even when in his sixties, during the first world war, Grubb continued his frenzied activities, lecturing, visiting Meetings, and writing: his *What is Quakerism?*, first published in 1917, was an accessible introduction to the principles and some of the practices of the Society of Friends, and went through a number of editions in subsequent decades.[37]

Another itinerant Quaker lecturer supported by the Trust in its early years was Herbert Waller, appointed as librarian at Woodbrooke in 1906, who rivalled Grubb in his assiduous visitation of Quaker groups across Britain, and especially in Yorkshire. In 1911, for example, Waller gave courses of lectures at Huddersfield, Leeds and Malton, and made week-end visits to a number of Yorkshire Meetings, was involved in the organisation of two 'settlements' (in this case, the word refers to short-term residential courses) and other Quaker social gatherings, as well as being a member of the London Home Mission and Extension Committee.[38] The Trust also contributed to the salary of Foster Brady, appointed field secretary of the Yorkshire 1905 Committee in 1908, about whom detailed reports were received from Ernest Taylor.[39] In 1910 Brady was involved in large Quaker 'Settlements' at Settle and Rawdon, visited adult schools and Meetings in Yorkshire most weekends, gave various lectures, and was commended for his 'personal influence ... over younger members [of the Society] especially'.[40] He was also involved in Taylor's adult education work at Leeds, and in the following year continued to visit meetings, went for walks with young Quakers on Saturday afternoons, and lectured and 'met with groups of earnest minded people' at Skipton and Barnsley.[41] George Willey, another itinerant lecturer, based initially at Woodbrooke, was employed by the JRCT on an annual basis from 1912, to work in Yorkshire, where he was involved in adult schools, public preaching and extension work. Grants to these men were supplemented by smaller contributions to scholarships at Woodbrooke, Bootham and The Mount, and donations to the Woodbrooke library. Such grants were central to Rowntree's aims in establishing the Trust, and long remained a source of pride among the trustees: Roger Cowan Wilson, a trustee from 1948 to 1977, claimed as late as 1973 that the most important thing the Trust had done was 'the liberation of certain Friends [such as Grubb, Waller and Brady] for the service of the Society'.[42]

The important point about these grants is that most were made for Quaker work within Yorkshire or nearby, or at Woodbrooke, and mostly to recipients who were personally known to the Rowntrees or to men like Ernest Taylor who were heavily involved in Quaker educational work. They were local grants to men over whom the trustees could exercise considerable supervision, and the grants could be withdrawn if the recipients were not acting to their satisfaction. The Founder's memorandum had made the point that the income of the JRCT 'must not be too widely scattered' if it were to achieve positive results, and this exhortation seems to have been taken to heart in the concentration of grants on Yorkshire and Quaker objects.[43] Grubb and his colleagues worked within the structures of the Society of Friends, disseminating their work through lectures to Meetings or adult schools, through periodicals such as *The Friend* and through institutions such as the Swarthmore lecture. This lecture, established by the JRCT in association with the Woodbrooke Extension Committee in 1907, was delivered the evening before Yearly Meeting: the first was given by Rufus Jones in 1908.[44] The lecture was designed, as Arnold Rowntree explained to the trustees in 1907, to be one 'in which the religious problems of the present day might be treated from a progressive point of view';[45] and early lectures were given by such men as W. C. Braithwaite, Edward Grubb and Joshua Rowntree.[46] The Trust also supported the *History of Quakerism*, envisaged by John Wilhelm Rowntree and undertaken by Braithwaite and Jones, covering both sides of the Atlantic and itself growing from the changes that took place within the Society in the 1890s and after.[47] Again, as Braithwaite was a friend of the Rowntrees and later a trustee, a close eye could be kept on this work, the proceeds of which the Trust had a claim to, and which became known as the 'Rowntree histories'.

Woodbrooke in Birmingham was the institution around which this variety of work undertaken by and among members of the Society of Friends coalesced and from where much of it was directed.[48] The first item of expenditure by the JRCT authorised in the Trust Deed was the support of Woodbrooke, and it received grants every year. The idea of a 'Quaker settlement' was propounded by John Wilhelm Rowntree in the aftermath of the Manchester conference, in order to promote Bible study among Friends and non-Friends in a supportive, studious and reflective environment. John Wilhelm envisaged a 'Bible school' along the lines of 'a Way-side Inn, a place where the dusty traveller, stepping aside for a moment from the thronged highway, shall find refreshment and repose';[49] and the 'social wing' he wished to see annexed to the school reflected the influence of the social settlements such as Toynbee Hall.[50] The idea was given practical form through the generosity of the Cadbury family, who supplied the premises in Birmingham and who contributed much to the settlement's early development.[51] The JRCT, reluctant to spend money on buildings, subscribed from a sense of duty to various appeal funds issued by Woodbrooke,[52] but preferred to concentrate on providing books for the library and scholarships for individual Friends to spend a term or a year (or sometimes longer) studying at the settlement. Indeed, on one occasion the trustees voted a sum of up to £1,000 to pay for the construction of a house for a lecturer at Woodbrooke, but this grant was later rescinded in view of the passage in Rowntree's 1904 memorandum expressing his 'regret if it were necessary to make grants on account of buildings'.[53] Woodbrooke aroused some opposition from within the Society of Friends, some members arguing that the Cadburys and the Rowntrees were preparing 'a theological college and a paid ministry',[54] although John Wilhelm had attempted to allay these fears in his 'plea for a Quaker settlement' published in *Present-Day Papers*.[55] Although one of the few bodies outside Yorkshire funded by the JRCT in this period, Woodbrooke nevertheless had many close connections with the family: Joshua Rowntree was its first warden, and Arnold Rowntree and other family members served on the governing body. The settlement – which should properly be called a college, and was more frequently referred to as a college from the early 1920s[56] – grew from the long-standing Quaker involvement in educational work, and it was later envisaged as a training-ground for wardens of educational settlements and other workers in the field. The JRCT regularly discussed the progress of Woodbrooke at length, and it was an integral part of the broader Quaker educational schemes into which they were firmly locked.

The distinctively Quaker conception of education for and through fellowship and service that emerged from adult school work, and was reflected in the development of the curriculum and social life of Woodbrooke, is essential to any understanding of the kind of schemes which the JRCT was trying in this period to promote. Woodbrooke's stated aim was 'to provide an opportunity for those who desire, by study and fellowship with others of kindred spirit, to equip themselves for the service of God. No narrow interpretation is set upon such service, which may be directly spiritual or simply social; in the vocal ministry, Adult or Sunday School work, or in civic and other spheres.'[57] The settlement enjoyed close links with local colleges and halls of residence, but also attracted many overseas scholars and many non-Friends: it was not unusual for over half those in residence to be non-Quakers, and by 1922 foreigners represented over a third of all those who had been admitted to Woodbrooke since its foundation.[58] Within this broad collegiate atmosphere, a distinctive Woodbrooke tradition was invented, owing much to the wardenships of William and Margaret Littleboy (1904-7) and Isaac and Mary Braithwaite (1907-14), and involving the creation of an 'Old Woodbrookers Association' and similar ventures.[59]

Woodbrooke stood at the hub of the network of educational settlements that grew up in the decade following its foundation. Like Woodbrooke, these settlements were envisaged as training centres for adult school teachers and students, and like Woodbrooke the Rowntrees were attracted to funding them. As we have seen, Joseph Rowntree was interested in Toynbee Hall, at one point arranging for the distribution of copies of Henrietta Barnett's biography of her husband,[60] but it was recognised that such settlements were expensive, and that, appropriately for the Quakers, 'something along simpler lines should be attempted'.[61] The resultant non-residential educational settlements, in Thomas Kelly's words, 'held their primary purpose to be education, not social missionary work', and 'represented a re-statement in the twentieth century of the belief that had led fifty years before to the foundation of the working men's colleges, namely that adult education, to be successful, must have both a home and a spirit'.[62] Arnold Rowntree had been taking tentative steps in this direction for some time. In 1906 he had organised a course of lectures in York, growing from a visit of adult school members to Woodbrooke; and the establishment of the Woodbrooke Extension Committee in the following year provided a body of lecturers and organisers who might be employed in such ventures.[63] In 1909 Arnold was able to tell the JRCT that a joint committee of Leeds Monthly Meeting and the Yorkshire 1905 Committee had been formed to oversee the establishment of a Friends' settlement in Leeds, and that Gerald K. Hibbert (a Baptist minister who was keen to join the Quakers) had agreed to be the warden and Maurice Rowntree the sub-warden. No doubt partly in recognition of the exhortation in the Founder's memorandum that Trust money should not if possible be spent on buildings, Arnold paid the rent of the premises himself, and asked the Trust to pay the salaries of Hibbert and Maurice Rowntree, which it agreed to do.[64] The settlement became known as Swarthmore educational settlement, and was perhaps the logical extension of a tradition of adult education in the city among Quakers and non-Quakers alike. Recently Ernest Taylor, under the auspices of the Yorkshire 1905 Committee, had been arranging 'Tea Table Talks', held in Friends' homes, to try to bring 'peripheral' young Quakers more directly into the fold and to recruit them for adult education work;[65] and the Leeds branch of the Workers' Educational Association was formed in 1907.[66] By 1910 Swarthmore was affiliated to the WEA and recognised by Leeds City Council.[67] Swarthmore and its ethos fitted in neatly with the broader conception of education (for children and adults) among Yorkshire Quakers, basing its appeal on the personal direction of the teachers and the friendly and co-operative atmosphere it sought to promote. Thus the JRCT was glad to note Maurice Rowntree's 'very strong personal influence over individuals',[68] and Ernest Taylor's biographer remembered Swarthmore's communal ethos, and that 'some classes of a more informal kind, and personal talks with members, were carried on in the cosy atmosphere of a private sitting room'.[69]

The settlement at St. Mary's in York, established in the same year as Swarthmore, did not grow directly from Quaker initiatives, although many of the part-time lecturers, such as George Willey, worked at both settlements. A. J. Peacock has suggested that the York venture 'came out of the same social climate that produced aggressive trades unionism, suffragism, a new lease of life for liberalism and, in York itself, Seebohm Rowntree's revelations about the extent of poverty'.[70] Again, Arnold Rowntree subscribed personally to the expenses,[71] and the JRCT supported the salaries of the warden Richard Westrope and the sub-warden Wilfrid Crosland. The first curriculum consisted of a series of classes on Biblical matters, a series on Christianity and the 'social problem' and a more popular series on literature, economic and social history and other general topics; but Peacock maintains that the settlement in York was mainly 'designed to produce class teachers, skilled in scriptural knowledge', although this aim clearly failed.[72] In fact there was much co-operation in the pre-first world war years in York and elsewhere between the educational settlements, university extension courses, adult schools, and the WEA: Basil Yeaxlee, himself a close collaborator of Arnold Rowntree and Ernest Taylor, saw the settlements as 'community centres of adult education' whose importance lay in 'devising a method of true community education which secures a complete range of provision from the most informal groups to the most advanced type of class'.[73] The collaborative impulse that lay behind this conception of the settlement stood at the heart of Quaker social service, and inspired the JRCT to take a leading role in the development of settlements. Joseph Rowntree told a meeting of the trustees in 1912 that '[t]his Trust and others would have to start the movement first', envisaging a more proactive role for the Trust in collaboration with bodies like the Yorkshire 1905 Committee;[74] and during the next few years a large proportion of the Trust's financial support went on the development and staffing of educational settlements, a proportion that would be increased in the years after the first world war.

In 1914 another educational settlement was established: the Beechcroft settlement at Birkenhead, also under Quaker influence, and perhaps even more typical of the Quaker educational ethos than Swarthmore and St. Mary's. Its founder, Horace Fleming, believed it to have been the first truly educational settlement, recognising the claims of the institutions in Leeds and York, but arguing that the breadth of Beechcroft's curriculum from its inception made it a more genuine 'community centre of adult education'.[75] Like its predecessors, Beechcroft grew out of the local adult school movement, but it was also influenced by the WEA and other educational bodies. Originally in Fleming's own home, it was intended from the start to create the atmosphere of 'fellowship' that lay at the heart of the educational settlement ethos. It was also influenced by the model of the Danish Folk High Schools, the practices of which were admired by a variety of adult educationalists in this period. However, as A. J. Allaway explained, although Beechcroft 'owed something' to the Danish example, as well as to Swarthmore and St. Mary's,

> it differed from all of them, and a great part of the difference was due to its founder and its earliest membership. Unlike Arnold Rowntree, who had wealth, and Samuel Barnett of Toynbee Hall, who had a university background and influential connections, Horace Fleming was a small-scale business-man with little more than average schooling. And the earliest members were men and women of his own kind – small traders and weekly wage-earners, keenly interested in political, social and religious questions, and having a great faith in education as a means for equipping themselves with the power to make the world a better place in which to live. The differences provided the conditions under which the ordinary members could undertake the shaping of the settlement's destinies. Beechcroft never stood in need of personal rule; it could be a democracy from the beginning.[76]

Although, as we will see in later chapters, this optimism about the democratic governance of Beechcroft and other settlements was misplaced, the settlement at Birkenhead became an important pioneering educational institution which, mainly through the zeal of Horace Fleming, would exercise an important influence on the educational settlement movement as it developed after the first world war. During the war, the JRCT donated small sums of money (£75 in February 1916) to Beechcroft, an indication of the prioritisation of educational initiatives, even where the Rowntree family was not directly involved, in the years after 1914.[77] As early as 1914, the total amount spent on grants for educational work by the JRCT was £5,248.[78]

By far the largest recipient of money in the earliest years of the JRCT, however, was Seebohm Rowntree, whose grants in some years amounted to over fifty percent of the total amount given. In 1907, for example, when

41

the total given to Quaker projects was £794 15s. 6d., Seebohm received £2,000; and in 1908 the respective amounts were £1,450 16s. 11d. and £1,500.[79] Seebohm repeatedly overspent the amount he had been allocated and went back to the trustees to ask them to make up the difference.[80] Seebohm was effectively working as a full-time social investigator for much of this period, and although his best known and probably most influential work, *Poverty*, pre-dated the formation of the JRCT, in the Edwardian years he carried out, usually in collaboration with others, a number of important pieces of social research. Joseph Rowntree's recognition in his 1904 memorandum of the importance of the land question as a fundamental underlying cause of many of the social problems that Seebohm had identified was confirmed in the later Edwardian years by the explosion of interest in the land question and rural social conditions.[81] The discovery that the rural population was living in conditions in many respects no better than town-dwellers necessitated a reassessment of the priorities of the 'Back to the Land' movement: Harold Mann and Maud F. Davies, applying Rowntree's poverty survey methods to rural theatres of inquiry, showed in 1905 and 1909 respectively that poverty was at least as widespread in villages as in towns.[82] The revelations of the unenviability of the condition and outlook of the rural population compromised the siting of the rural as the solution for various social problems associated with urban life: Joseph Rowntree's admiration for village life did not accord with the 'realities' as presented by these researchers. Therefore, as the Liberal government looked to other countries for templates on which to model its social reform legislation,[83] Rowntree looked abroad to draw lessons for the future of the English countryside. His *Land and labour: lessons from Belgium* (1910), largely if not wholly funded by the JRCT, was a large-scale inquiry into Belgian social conditions and an attempt to draw conclusions relating to his own country. This was followed up by a book co-written with May Kendall, *How the labourer lives: a study of the rural labour problem*, published in 1913, which examined the domestic budgets of 42 English agricultural households and commented on 'The Labourer's Outlook'. While this inquiry was being carried out (mainly, it would appear, by Kendall), Rowntree was also involved in the Land Enquiry Committee, a body established by Lloyd George in 1912. Over a two-year period, Rowntree regularly spent four days a week in London working on this inquiry.[84] He also joined enthusiastically in the propagandist side of the Committee's work: his contributions to Lloyd George's 'land campaign' included a series of lectures and a pamphlet, *The labourer and the land* (1914). The Land Enquiry Committee was funded in part by the JRSST, which made grants totalling over £7,000 in 1912-13 and also supported J. St. George Heath's work as secretary to the Committee.[85] In the midst of this activity, Seebohm Rowntree did not forget his interest in problems of urban life: his *Unemployment: a social*

42

study (1911), written in collaboration with his private secretary Bruno Lasker, was a survey of the extent and character of unemployment in York, based on detailed case-study information. This research was also largely funded by the JRCT.

In these researches Rowntree extended the range and ambition of his work beyond the relatively narrow enumeration of the extent and causes of poverty that had characterised his first social survey. Although *Poverty* had included some information about a variety of subjects – including housing, local government, charity, public houses and working men's clubs, friendly societies, trade unions, co-operation, temperance, the competence of housewives as domestic managers, education, poor relief, district visiting and religion – none of these were integral to his analysis. Possibly under the influence of a number of Edwardian social surveys which did integrate subjects like this into their social diagnoses,[86] Rowntree gave a more central place in these later surveys to a greater variety of social factors, especially urban and rural leisure and the opportunities for the purchase of land. The importance of education was also emphasised. In *Poverty* he had pointed to the narrowness of outlook and the limited education enjoyed by the classes who lived just above the primary poverty line,[87] and in *Unemployment* he and Lasker extended this line of thought to argue that giving the unemployed man greater responsibility, and to an extent directing his exercise of it, was the way to restore individual self-respect and social usefulness. In *Unemployment*, therefore, the education, organisation and direction of youth was given a central place. In the Edwardian period children and youths were placed at the heart of discourses of national efficiency, and various investigators showed that one of the main factors in the creation of an unemployed, and arguably unemployable, class was the unsystematised and ill-directed employment of both the work and the leisure time of the young: short-term casual employment engendered bad habits that stayed with the individual for a lifetime. Thus Rowntree and Lasker proposed school care committees (along the lines of those already established by the London County Council) to help children from disadvantaged homes;[88] and their belief that 'juvenile unemployment has a vital connection with adult unemployment, and ... the latter problem can never be solved if the former is neglected'[89] confirmed them in the conviction that 'self-sacrificing voluntary work' and 'the comradeship and help of men and women of strong moral fibre ... given ... intensively to three or four persons related to them by bonds of sympathy and mutual understanding' was essential to the prevention of inefficiency and moral deterioration among the young.[90] The concern for national efficiency, then, was expressed in terms of the personally directed philanthropy that remained the central aim of men like Seebohm Rowntree and his father. Seebohm's faith in the power of educative measures, rooted in his own long experience of adult education work, suggested a proactive rather than a penal approach to labour market reform: notwithstanding section (i) of the JRCT Trust Deed, Rowntree rejected, by and large, the use of labour colonies for the long-term unemployed.[91] The JRCT seems to have agreed with this, rejecting, in 1911, an application for a grant of unspecified size from W. A. Albright to put towards the establishment of a Farm Colony for Unemployables.[92]

At the same time, there was an evident need for more efficient organisation of the labour market, and Rowntree fully supported the development of the labour exchange as a means of disseminating labour market information. William Beveridge had argued the case for labour exchanges in his book on *Unemployment* in 1909, and some of his proposals were incorporated into Winston Churchill's Labour Exchanges Act (also 1909). Such measures reflected the preoccupation with organisation that characterised the legislative culture of the 'new Liberalism': a recognition that state intervention could impose order on inefficient and unregulated areas of economic life. Seebohm Rowntree shared in this recognition. However, like Rowntree, the new Liberalism, while admitting the possibility and asserting the necessity of certain collectivist measures of social welfare and labour market reform, retained its association with individualism. For Leonard Hobhouse, one of the leading new Liberal theorists, what he called 'Liberal Socialism' was characterised by two impulses: first, democratic collectivism, seeking 'to secure a fuller measure of justice, and a better organisation of mutual aid', and, second, creative individualism, aiming to 'make its account with the human individual ... [and] give the average man free play in the personal life for which he really cares'.[93] These twin tenets clearly informed Seebohm Rowntree's social thought in this period, and were of particular importance at a time when the relationship between statutory and voluntary social welfare provision was undergoing significant modification. Thus his social inquiries of the period, as funded by the JRCT, although frequently used to justify schemes of state-sponsored social reform, embodied very strongly the Quaker belief in personal service, and as such they resonated with the other kinds of work that the Trust funded during its first ten years. No less importantly, they reflect the Quaker sense of the interlinkage of religious and social concern, a sense that profoundly influenced the liberal wing of the Society of Friends during and after the 'Quaker Renaissance'. Nowhere was this link more clear than in Seebohm Rowntree's leadership of the Friends Social Union, which sought to involve Quakers in research into a number of fields, 'including housing, poverty, unemployed and unemployable labour, constructive philanthropy, labour colonies, and "How to Form a Social Services Committee"'.[94] The failure of the Union – dominated by more conservative Quakers with only Edward Grubb and the non-Friend

Radical MP Percy Alden to represent the younger and more liberal generation – to produce more than 'a paucity of meaningful social consequences'[95] only emphasises the importance of Rowntree's own research work in expressing the link between social concern and social action among Friends. The JRCT can be credited with cementing this link in the early years of the twentieth century.

Although Seebohm Rowntree was always intended as a recipient of JRCT monies, the social dimension of Quakerism was also reflected in some of the more imaginative grants made by the JRCT in its first decade. At Woodbrooke, for example, the Trust supported the appointment of a lecturer in economics, J. St. George Heath, who, as indicated above, left to work with Seebohm Rowntree on the Land Enquiry Committee, and later became warden of Toynbee Hall. John Wilhelm Rowntree had suggested that courses on 'the economic aspects of the stewardship of wealth' might be held at a 'Quaker settlement' as a supplement to courses of Bible study and Quaker and Church history;[96] and prior to Heath's appointment lectures on social topics had been given by George Shann and Tom Bryan, both working-class Labour men and graduates of the University of Glasgow who had fallen under the influence of Henry Jones, Professor of Moral Philosophy and a leading philosopher of social reform.[97] Bryan collaborated with George Cadbury Junior to write a textbook on the land question and land reform;[98] and he became the first warden of the nearby Fircroft College, a working men's college in Birmingham founded in 1909, which had a broader curriculum than Woodbrooke, including economics, political philosophy, literature and history, and was shorn of most of Woodbrooke's religious associations.[99] Both Bryan and Shann concentrated on classical ideas of citizenship, and it was as a teacher of practical citizenship (with a Quaker focus) that Heath was appointed. The JRCT recognised in 1906 the 'importance of developing the social side of the work of Woodbrooke',[100] and agreed to pay a salary of £250 if a suitable candidate could be found. Within a year of his appointment, Heath had helped to establish a diploma in social study, offered in conjuction with Birmingham University, part of which was taken at Woodbrooke. Although Heath left in 1911, the course continued and became one of the most important features of Woodbrooke's work. Branching out into this kind of study was representative of a tendency in the Edwardian period for social work and social study to become professionalised, moving away from the amateur ethos that had prevailed among nineteenth-century philanthropists. Courses at the University of Liverpool, the London School of Economics (established in 1895) and elsewhere were mirrored in the Birmingham/Woodbrooke initiative; and even the Charity Organisation Society set up a School of Sociology in 1903, which was merged into the LSE as the Department of Social Administration in 1912.[101] At

Woodbrooke, Heath was succeeded in 1911 by James Cunnison, later lecturer in economics at Fircroft and at the University of Glasgow, who was also supported by the JRCT; and Elizabeth Newcomb, 'tutor-organiser in social work' alongside Heath, and also supported by the JRCT, was replaced by Janet H. Kelman in 1914.[102]

These developments at Woodbrooke, as indicated, reflected the professionalisation of much of the work that would previously have been done by largely untrained amateur social workers. Social survey work, which the amateur Seebohm Rowntree had done much to promote, was also becoming professionalised, often within a university context: Maud Davies's rural survey was supervised by Sidney and Beatrice Webb at the LSE, and Arthur Bowley's survey of poverty in different parts of England, published in 1915, was also based there, funded by the wealthy Ratan Tata Foundation.[103] However, the JRCT continued to support, to an appropriately modest extent, social survey work carried out by groups with whom the Rowntrees did not have close links: for example, the trustees considered funding an abortive project to carry out a survey of Bolton (this may have been a survey later carried out by Arthur Bowley under the auspices of the LSE),[104] and they gave £50 to Professor Michael Sadler of Manchester University for a survey of 'moral training in schools'.[105] More significantly, they also supported the Outer London Inquiry Committee,[106] a body representative of the transition towards the professionally conceived and executed social investigation. Established to carry out an investigation into poverty, casual labour, unemployment, rent and local government in West Ham,[107] and including among its members such luminaries as William Beveridge, Beatrice Webb and Canon Barnett, the cash-strapped body received £100 from the JRCT, as well as a personal donation of ten guineas from Seebohm Rowntree (and £100 from Charles Booth). It received only a total of about £1,200; and when it overspent and had to beg for help to pay off its losses, it appealed to the trustees again, who agreed to underwrite them if necessary: eventually a further £50 was given.[108] The Outer London Inquiry was a good illustration of the truth of the passage in Rowntree's 1904 memorandum suggesting that although a soup kitchen would always attract donations, a social inquiry would not.[109] Whereas the Committee was able to raise only £1,200, this figure was dwarfed by the total of £25,000 raised by short-term unemployment relief funds in West Ham during the winter of 1904-5 alone.[110] Thus George Arkell, a veteran of Booth's inquiry and the secretary of the Committee, complained that most '[p]eople are ready to give to fashionable relief funds but not to scientific research'.[111]

Social surveys of this kind often suggested areas of state or municipal intervention into labour markets, wage fixing, or the provision of leisure or educational initiatives; and the landslide victory of the Liberal party in the general election of 1906 initiated a period during which the incursion of the state into many areas of the nation's economic and social life necessitated a reappraisal of many of the traditional Victorian assumptions about the respective roles of legislation and charity. Perhaps the most significant feature of the period was a growing awareness among men and women of all political complexions of underlying structural causes of social problems that were not wholly or even partly susceptible to the solutions that would have been attempted in earlier years. Thus the introduction by the Liberal governments of non-contributory old-age pensions, national unemployment and health insurance, free school meals, labour exchanges and trade boards (to fix wages in certain low-wage industries) created a series of new governmental structures and new administrative institutions to deploy the resources of a more benevolent state. However, as we have seen, the Liberal governments could not – and did not wish to – sweep away the voluntarist tradition, and as the individualism of the Victorian Liberal heyday gave way to the more insecure collectivism of the Edwardian Liberal swansong, the reinvention of the English civic community proceeded apace within the context of municipal governance and locally inspired and delivered philanthropy.

The JRCT and its activities in the 1900s and early 1910s should be viewed in this wider context of changes in English philanthropy, and although their Quakerism significantly affected the trustees' grant-making priorities, they fitted easily into the tradition of localism and the revitalisation of citizenship that many of these wider developments implied. Thus in its work in Yorkshire, especially its support for the Yorkshire 1905 Committee, the Trust demonstrated its concern for the development of ideals of citizenship among the local population and the promotion of Quaker social leadership. Similarly, the work of the JRVT in New Earswick, along with the workplace reforms at Rowntree and Company, embodied a conception of citizenship that emphasised working-class participation in the management of industrial and social initiatives. Joseph Rowntree's establishment of the Cocoa Works Debating Society, the works library and the *Cocoa Works Magazine* were all part of a strategy designed to furnish his factory 'with those amenities which might make it easier for men and women "to develop all that is best and most worthy in themselves"'.[112] In this kind of development, there could never be a significant role for the state, as only personal service and direction could help the less fortunate achieve this kind of personal advancement.

The Rowntrees recognised this in the various schemes they sponsored and the perceptions of the role of the state and the voluntary sector that they endorsed. An ongoing reappraisal within the ranks of Quakerism of the importance of social service was epitomised by Joseph's cousin Joshua Rowntree's[113] Swarthmore lecture in 1913, in which he noted that the 'desire to ameliorate the outlook and the conditions of the great mass of the toilers under the strain of modern civilization is surely one of the most encouraging signs of our times',[114] and recognised that the growing involvement of the state and municipalities in social matters (and the greater involvement of Quakers in national and local politics) could be a beneficial force for change. Nevertheless, the limitations of these developments were clear:

> It may be said that the world has got beyond the stage of voluntaryism [sic] in social service. It must now be handed over to the legislature, and enforced by the State. No doubt steam rollers are invaluable for certain purposes, but where you are dealing with the higher needs of the mysterious compounds of body, soul, and spirit, – the growth of character in the most sensitive organisms of creation, – their usefulness may easily be overestimated. Life only proceeds from life ... By all means let the ground upon which humanity builds and lives and rears its young be made as sanitary and secure as possible; but let the gardens of the soul and the fruits of the spirit rejoice in a liberty and guidance above and beyond the control of civil engineers, and the shaping even of the best town Councils.[115]

As an illustration of this, Rowntree turned to the perennial Quaker favourite, education, arguing that much remained to be done in this sphere, and that many of the developments in educational reform over the past four decades had stripped education of much of its personal value both to the child and the adult. The Rowntrees, in their writings and at the cocoa works, attempted to build on the Quaker conception of the Inward Light in every man and woman, and to provide through their philanthropic donations every opportunity for this Inward Light to find expression in the self-development of the individual.

Nevertheless, behind much of this activity, both at the cocoa works and more broadly in the field of adult education and social inquiry, there lay a lingering paternalism that cannot simply be explained away as a relic of Joseph Rowntree's Victorian background. Even Rowntree's admiring biographer Anne Vernon admitted that he had found it difficult to shed the '[b]enevolent autocracy' associated with the paternalistic employer, and that he frequently 'gave his employees such things as he thought it good for them to have'.[116] In New Earswick, although the structure of village governance was ostensibly democratic, based on household suffrage, the JRVT could veto any decision arrived at 'democratically' by the residents.[117] Even the establishment of organs designed to promote and refine Quakerism, doctrinally perhaps the most democratic of all Christian denominations, was based on a perceived need for guidance and leadership, and arguably a residual suspicion of democracy and of complete freedom of thought. This was not only Joseph's view. His son John

Wilhelm, proposing the establishment of a 'Quaker settlement', argued that in the development of higher religious thought it was 'dangerous to rely on untutored freedom. If liberty is to be with power, it must be cherished by those who know the discipline of mental and spiritual training. Fervent zeal must be tempered by knowledge, and warmth of heart must be supplemented by intellect that is under the dominance of truth.'[118] Inquiring minds must be led to the truth through a combination of their own earnest and inward desires and the spiritual guidance of men and women trained for the task. The frequent complaints by members of the JRCT and others that adult school teachers lacked sufficient knowledge and understanding of the Bible to teach their scholars efficiently suggest the perception of a need for (middle-class) educated leadership of the open discussion that was supposed to prevail in the schools. As Arnold Rowntree pointed out, 'many who come into the schools, have little interest in the Bible and are suspicious of organised Christianity', and needed to guided by trained teachers.[119] It is unsurprising, perhaps, that the York branch of the WEA came to distrust the St. Mary's settlement, which grew out of adult school endeavour, as 'philanthropic and condescending on the surface, bourgeois and reactionary in reality'.[120]

The high hopes the Rowntrees and many of their collaborators held for the development of their adult education initiatives, while not dashed, were undoubtedly tempered by the outbreak of war in 1914. The first world war had especially profound implications for the Society of Friends, as a body committed to the peaceful resolution of conflict and to the rejection of outward violence.[121] There was no single Quaker response to the war; the divisions among members of the Society that the tensions of war engendered were often very bitter and in many cases the wounds never healed. Moreover, Quakers were not the only pacifists in Britain or elsewhere in the world, and much of the Quaker response to conflict is best examined as part of a wider resistance to an unprecedented 'total war'. Nevertheless, by 1914 many Quakers already had experience of overseas relief work in the context of war or militarism – for example, they had supported the resistance to conscription in Australia and New Zealand in 1910-11,[122] and some Friends had been involved with relief work during the Balkan conflict that preceded the world war[123] – and many threw themselves into such work in the early months of war. The best known Quaker response was the establishment of the Friends Ambulance Unit (FAU), organised and commanded by Philip Noel-Baker, Olympic athlete and later Labour MP and cabinet minister, which undertook a variety of war work, including the support of refugees, the provision of medical care and clothing, and general social service including farm work, forestry and education.[124] It was a controversial body, never enjoying the official support of Yearly Meeting – it was disowned by the 'official' Friends

Service Council in 1916 – and was opposed by 'absolutists' who viewed even this kind of work as morally untenable because of its indirect links to the 'war effort'.[125] Nevertheless, the Rowntrees supported the FAU, which staffed the hospital housed from 1915 in Rowntree and Company's refectory and recreational facilities, as well as a similar establishment at a house in Birmingham donated by the Cadbury family. Arnold Rowntree and Sir George Newman, a Quaker and chief medical officer at the Board of Education, both gave their support, while William Braithwaite served as the FAU's treasurer throughout the war. However, although the JRCT supported the FAU to the extent of six or seven hundred pounds a year during the second world war, they contributed nothing to its funds during the 1914-18 conflict.

A second outlet for Quaker energies during the war was the War Victims Relief Committee (WVRC), chaired by Sir George Newman and enjoying the official support of Yearly Meeting. Before the war, the WVRC had been involved in administering relief during the Balkan conflict, and after 1914 it worked in Holland, Belgium and France.[126] The work ranged from dispensing medical aid to both civilians and soldiers, through rebuilding a large district in Verdun and establishing a maternity hospital at Châlons-sur-Marne, to teaching handicrafts to inmates of refugee camps.[127] Quakers were also involved in many non-denominational anti-war groups, including the Union of Democratic Control, the Women's International Relief Committee, and the Fellowship of Reconciliation, and later Eglantyne Jebb's Save the Children Fund (established in 1919)[128] and the League of Nations Union (see chapter 6). Carl Heath, secretary of the National Peace Council, joined the Society of Friends in 1916, and although the Peace Council collapsed during the war, Heath's work, especially his vision of 'Quaker Embassies' in the capital cities of the world to promote peaceful conflict resolution, had a powerful influence on the post-war development of Quaker and non-Quaker peace work. After the war Heath became secretary of the Friends Council for International Service, established in 1919.[129] There was also substantial Quaker involvement in campaigning groups with a more domestic focus, especially Fenner Brockway's No-Conscription Fellowship. This was mainly an Independent Labour Party body, but a third of the committee were Quakers, and the ubiquitous Edward Grubb was the treasurer.[130]

The Quakers in York suffered from the closure of the Meeting House, which was turned into a reception centre for refugees, and later into a hospital for the duration of the hostilities. This lack of premises meant an inevitable decline in attendance – and in any case some Quakers enlisted and others did non-military war work away from the city – and it seems to have been difficult to keep the Meeting going at all.[131] The consciences of many local Quakers came under severe strain. Lawrence Rowntree (only son of John Wilhelm), for example, joined the FAU early in the war, but later enlisted as a private, was wounded at the Somme and was killed in 1917.[132] Maurice Rowntree, sub-warden of the Swarthmore settlement in Leeds, was denied exemption, and eventually imprisoned, and on his 'removal' from Swarthmore the JRCT agreed to use the money set aside for his salary to pay replacements.[133] Others were more fortunate. Edward Grubb, in his sixties, was too old for military service, while George Willey, continuing in the Trust's employment, was given conditional exemption by the York military service tribunal and was able to continue teaching at St. Mary's and Swarthmore.[134] A member of the No-Conscription Fellowship and the Peace Society, Willey helped organise anti-war protest meetings in the city, and in 1917 was involved in peace work in working men's clubs and study circles:[135] his ability, noted by Ernest Taylor following peace meetings in 1914, to deal effectively with hecklers must have been very useful.[136] He was heckled at an anti-conscription meeting in 1916,[137] for example, by one of the many citizens of York who turned against the Quakers and the Rowntrees.

The Rowntrees suffered greatly at the hands of the local press, especially Arnold Rowntree, who was one of the most vociferous opponents of the war in the House of Commons, allying himself with the Asquithian Liberal rump after the formation of the Lloyd George coalition government in 1916. Rowntree opposed conscription and supported conscientious objectors, including his cousin Maurice.[138] He had offered to resign his seat at the outbreak of hostilities, and again during the passage of the Military Service Act, and vigorously and unsuccessfully opposed the electoral disqualifications imposed on conscientious objectors in an amendment to the Representation of the People Act of 1918 (the Act which conceded full men's and partial women's suffrage). During his eight years as an MP, he maintained his interest in the various educational projects with which he and Ernest Taylor had been associated, and his support for the educational settlements at York, Leeds and Birkenhead was reflected in the continuing attention given to these projects during the war by the JRCT.[139] The settlements themselves, to the outrage of some of their opponents, played their part in the peace movement. For example, when Arnold's wife May Rowntree gave a lecture at St. Mary's on 'the story behind the war', she was, unsurprisingly, 'clobbered' in the Yorkshire press.[140] An unusually large proportion of Rowntree and Company's employees were conscientious objectors, and the Rowntrees did not help the situation by applying for exemption for many of them themselves: the most notorious case came when Seebohm applied for exemption for his coachman and two nurserymen at the Homestead.[141] Unsurprisingly, Arnold Rowntree was heavily defeated in the 'hang the Kaiser' general election of 1918.

Arnold Rowntree and Richard Cross were prominent supporters of the Council for the Study of International Relations (CSIR), a body which the JRCT supported during the war. The Council, according to the note inserted at the beginning of each of its pamphlets, existed 'to encourage and assist the study of international relations from all points of view', but this broad-mindedness did not stop it from being widely identified as an anti-war body, which to all extents and purposes it was. Supported until 1915 by the Joseph Rowntree Social Service Trust,[142] the CSIR published pamphlets and bibliographies intended to assist careful study of the problem of war and the history of international relations,[143] and because its work was wholly educational, and based around traditional Quaker forms of education, the JRCT was keen to support it as much as possible.[144] Indeed, the Council grew out of the adult school movement: Arnold Rowntree was prompted to initiate the scheme following an interview with Lord Bryce reported in the adult school periodical *One and All* just before the war, in which the latter had advocated a 'cheap text-book on foreign policy'.[145] The CSIR held conferences, lecture courses at the LSE, University College London, and at Glasgow, Aberystwyth, Bangor and Newcastle, and a course in association with the YMCA. It was involved in some 150 such courses in 1916, as well as summer schools and study circles, of which there were about 500, with an average membership of about eighteen. The CSIR's president was Lord Bryce, its general secretary Arthur Greenwood of the University of Leeds, later a Labour cabinet minister, its honorary secretary Percy Alden; and Henry Clay was secretary of its board of studies, which consisted of eight eminent historians including G. P. Gooch. Greenwood and Clay, along with Norman Angell, author of *The great illusion* (1909) and perhaps the best known pacifist of the period, attended a meeting of the JRCT in September 1916, the result of which was that Arnold Rowntree and William Braithwaite joined the board of studies and that JRCT support for the CSIR was confirmed.[146]

In York the CSIR was associated with the local branch of the Union of Democratic Control, a national organisation prominently supported by Ramsay MacDonald, and in York enjoying the backing of Arnold Rowntree. As A. J. Peacock has explained, the CSIR's York branch was also supported by groups as varied as the Fabian Society, the YMCA, the Railway Institute, the adult school, the New Earswick Village Guild, the York Liberal Club, the Church of England Men's Society, the Co-operative Women's Guild and the York Trades Council.[147] It was actively supported by Wilfrid Crosland, sub-warden of the St. Mary's settlement, who organised study circles and lectures.[148] The prominent involvement of local Quakers, including Arnold Rowntree himself and the solicitor K. E. T. Wilkinson, contributed to the CSIR's credentials for receipt of

JRCT support, and a total of £3,000 was granted during the three years in which calls on Trust funding were made.[149] Nevertheless, despite the optimism engendered among the membership of the CSIR – it developed an ambitious programme of connecting its work to co-operative societies, Education Committees, secondary schools and organisations such as the Women's Co-operative Guilds, and appeared to be booming during 1917, when the Carnegie Endowment for International Peace also made a substantial donation – the departure of Henry Clay and Arthur Greenwood and the realisation that the task of post-war reconstruction was coming to assume more immediate importance than peace work led to a rapid decline.[150] By June 1917 much of the work it wanted to do was already being done by the League of Nations Society;[151] and by October it had been wound up, its continuing literary work having been taken over by the Athenaeum Literature Department.[152]

Early in the war the JRCT also gave £275 to Meeting for Sufferings (the standing executive committee of Yearly Meeting) to help with the costs of the Quaker 'Message on the War', and later gave small grants for the circulation of books on peace and reconstruction to 'carefully selected leaders of opinion;[153] and Norman Angell remembered later that the Rowntree family had approached him, through Richard Cross, with whom he worked on the CSIR's publications, and offered him an income to continue his work for peace.[154] Whether this was under the auspices of the JRCT is unclear: the JRSST had paid Angell a modest salary and secretarial expenses prior to the war, and continued to support his work after the onset of hostilities.[155] Although a non-Friend himself, Angell was a popular figure among British Quakers: the Yorkshire 1905 Committee and the Peace Committee were involved in the production and distribution of some 10,000 copies of a pamphlet summary of *The great illusion*.[156] Angell was one of those who occasionally accompanied Joseph Rowntree on his regular Saturday afternoon walks in Scarborough, and was part of that group of pacifists of whom Arnold Rowntree and his brother-in-law T. Edmund Harvey were probably the most prominent parliamentary representatives. In general, however, the war did not move the JRCT very far from its Yorkshire, Quaker and family concerns. As a direct influence on grant-making, with the single exception of the large grants made to the CSIR, the war impinged little. George Willey, Edward Grubb, Herbert Waller, Foster Brady, the *History of Quakerism*, *The Friend*, the Swarthmore lecture, the educational settlements and the adult schools all continued to receive JRCT money during the war, although the work of these individuals and groups was often directly related to the Quaker response to the conflict. Thus when Edward Grubb reported to the trustees in November 1917, he explained that he had been able to give fewer lectures than normal because of the war, but had done lots of writing and had given talks to 'friends of COs'.[157] Likewise, although the educational settlements still received substantial backing – a total of £1,836 between July 1915 and June 1916, including £430 to Swarthmore and £300 to St. Mary's[158] – their work was necessarily altered and in some respects compromised by the war. Similarly, Woodbrooke found it difficult to attract students, serving instead as a base for refugees and a centre for conscientious objectors, many of whom went there to await arrest;[159] and although it was able to pick up the occasional student who was unable to study at Ruskin, Westminster College (Cambridge) or Carey Hall (a women's Baptist college near Woodbrooke), all of which were closed for at least a part of the war,[160] the average annual number of students declined from about 45 before the outbreak of hostilities to 23 at the end.[161] Some training was also provided for FAU and WVRC volunteers. Although reluctant to bear too high a proportion of the costs associated with Woodbrooke's declining enrolments, the JRCT was occasionally required to bail the settlement out at times of crisis in both peace and war.[162]

The trustees were able to give less time to their favoured projects during the war years: Arnold Rowntree's parliamentary workload reduced the direct involvement he was able to have in his educational schemes; and Seebohm's wartime activities took him away from his social investigation work. Although he began the war by initiating (under the guidance of his father) a new series of welfare reforms in the York cocoa works, by September 1915 Lloyd George had appointed him to a committee at the Ministry of Munitions, chaired by his fellow Quaker Sir George Newman, charged with reporting on the health of munitions workers. Early in the following year he was appointed as the director of the new Welfare Department at the Ministry, in which capacity he applied many of the innovative business practices pioneered at Rowntree and Company and other 'progressive' firms to the employment of munitions workers.[163] Like Rowntree and Company, the munitions factories employed a great deal of female and child labour, groups whose welfare needs had usually been identified and responded to earlier than those of their male counterparts. Nevertheless, the near absence of welfare officers and other trained staff capable of making the improvements Rowntree wanted hampered the progress he was able to make; and he was not helped by the opposition, or at least suspicion, that his schemes aroused among many fellow industrialists.[164] Rowntree was later appointed to membership of the Reconstruction Committee and worked for the newly constituted Ministry of Reconstruction, charged with a wider brief which included housing, in which he took a special interest. However, it is for his workplace welfare initiatives that Rowntree is probably best remembered (especially in York, where he returned after the war). Rowntree put as the basis of what he saw as the necessary welfare reforms the payment of a living wage, arguing that 'we must look forward to a very much higher standard of wages in this country', based on higher productivity, and starting at a minimum of about 35s. a week at pre-war prices, nearly double the cash value of his primary poverty line devised in 1899.[165]

On top of this improved money wage, Rowntree envisaged a whole series of reforms designed to improve productivity and the morale of the workforce. The impulses that went towards making up these schemes of improvement were an intriguing mixture of, on the one hand, a desire for greater workplace efficiency, founded on the premises of the 'national efficiency' discourses that had emerged in the Edwardian years, and on the other, a long-standing Quaker humanitarianism which saw in the awakening of the 'higher side' of the individual nature the path both to divine inspiration and to useful citizenship. Thus work before breakfast was 'notoriously uneconomic' and should be ended;[166] greater security against unemployment was a necessary prerequisite for increased output;[167] and even after measures of this sort had been taken, the 'problem of how to deal with the inefficient or "unemployable" class' would remain.[168] However, greater efficiency went hand in hand with justice in the community: in a just community, Rowntree argued, 'each personality should be regarded as something of ultimate value', and 'men and women ... are not tools but ends in themselves'.[169] As an example of the too prevalent economic and social distance between employers and their workforces, he cited the frequent and demeaning use of the word 'hands' to describe employees.[170] Rowntree did not distrust trade unionism as much as his father did,[171] but he saw industrial conflict in the same unfavourable light as military conflict, and it was part of the mission of Quakerism to diminish conflict of all kinds. In sketching out a framework for the future of industrial relations, Rowntree, whose own cocoa works were viewed as a model of the enlightened factory which promoted industrial efficiency while safeguarding the welfare of the workforce through a range of voluntary initiatives, was proposing a new settlement between employers, workers and the state: a settlement which would itself have profound implications for the future of the philanthropic enterprises with which he was associated, and in particular the JRCT. The more that was provided by the state, the greater the challenge to philanthropists to find useful channels for their service and effective destinations for their benevolence.

NOTES

1. See for example JRCT, *Triennial report 1997-1999*, 54, JRCT library.
2. Robert Fitzgerald, *Rowntree and the marketing revolution 1862-1969*, Cambridge 1995, 280.
3. JRCT minute book, no. 1, pp. 237-8. The minute books are in the offices of the JRCT, The Garden House, York. For minute book no. 1, page references are given; for subsequent minute books the minute numbers are used.
4. Waddilove, *One man's vision*, 106-7, 130-1.
5. *The Friend*, 3 August 1951, 700-1.
6. See for example J. S. Rowntree, *The sincere desire: a study in prayer*, 1907.
7. See for example JRCT minute book, no. 1, pp. 110, 112-13, 126.
8. For an account of John Wilhelm's life see Allott, *John Wilhelm Rowntree*.
9. Frederick John Gillman, *The story of the York adult schools from the commencement to the year 1907*, York 1907, ch. 6. See also John Wilhelm Rowntree and Henry Bryan Binns, *A history of the adult school movement*, 1903.
10. Many of the more important articles he wrote for this periodical were reprinted posthumously in John Wilhelm Rowntree, *Essays and addresses*, ed. Joshua Rowntree (1st edn 1905), 1906.
11. For accounts of Jones's life, see David Hinshaw, *Rufus Jones: master Quaker*, New York 1951; Elizabeth Gray Vining, *Friend of life: the biography of Rufus M. Jones*, Philadelphia and New York 1958.
12. Briggs, *Seebohm Rowntree*, 9-10.
13. Rowntree, *Poverty*; see above, pp. 7-8.
14. See Vipont, *Arnold Rowntree*.
15. Arnold S. Rowntree, *Woodbrooke: its history and aims*, Birmingham 1923.
16. Gillman, *Story of the York adult schools*.
17. Vipont, *Arnold Rowntree*, 11.
18. Fitzgerald, *Rowntree and the marketing revolution*, 280.
19. JRSST general minute book, no. 1, pp. 134, 181, 196, 202, 209-10 for grants and loans made to the JRVT, and pp. 72, 106, 125, 142, 181, 186, 230-2 for grants to the JRCT; JRCT minute book, no. 1, p. 124. One of these grants amounted to £10,000.
20. JRCT Minute book, no. 1, p. 29.
21. Ibid., p. 30.
22. Ibid., pp. 133-4 (inset).
23. Ibid., pp. 49-50.
24. Ibid., p. 46.
25. Most of this account of Cross is based on Marion Wilkinson (ed.), *E. Richard Cross: a biographical sketch, with literary papers and religious and political addresses*, 1917; but see also Briggs, *Seebohm Rowntree*, 65, 92, 100-1, for the range of Cross's links with the Rowntrees. For a potted biography see Kennedy, *British Quakerism*, 324 n. 41.
26. JRCT minute book, no. 1, pp. 152, 162, 167. Taylor's first recorded appearance was on 22 September 1911; he also attended on 3 May 1912, and was at most meetings from 23 December 1912 onwards (pp. 88, 95, 104).
27. Much of this account is based on Anna L. B. Thomas and Elizabeth B. Emmott, *William Charles Braithwaite: memoir and papers*, 1931. The authors were Braithwaite's sisters.

28. See *J. Bevan Braithwaite: a Friend of the nineteenth century, by his children*, 1909.
29. See Whiting, *Ernest E, Taylor*.
30. See for example Ernest E. Taylor, *The valiant sixty*, Swindon 1947.
31. Kennedy, *British Quakerism*, 289.
32. 'The Yorkshire 1905 Committee, May 1913', inset in JRCT minute Book, no. 1, pp. 119-20.
33. For Taylor's appointment see JRCT minute book, no. 1, p. 177.
34. See James Dudley, *The life of Edward Grubb 1854-1939: a spiritual pilgrimage*, 1946.
35. JRCT minute book, no. 1, p. 31.
36. Ibid., pp. 51-2.
37. Edward Grubb, *What is Quakerism? An exposition of the leading principles and practices of the Society of Friends, as based on the experiences of 'the Inward Light'*, 1917.
38. Report on Herbert I. Waller, inset in JRCT minute book, no. 1, pp. 85-6.
39. See for example JRCT minute book, no. 1, pp. 37-8, 45-6, 129-30.
40. Report on Foster E. Brady, 28 November 1910, inset in JRCT minute book, no. 1, pp. 69-70.
41. Report on Foster E. Brady, September 1910, inset in JRCT Minute book, no. 1, pp. 85-6.
42. Roger C. Wilson, 'The Founder's commission', 21, in JRCT, *Basic documents*.
43. Founder's memorandum, 2.
44. Rufus M. Jones, *Quakerism: a religion of life*, 1908.
45. JRCT minute book, no. 1, p. 34.
46. William C. Braithwaite, *Spiritual guidance in the experience of the Society of Friends*, 1909; Edward Grubb, *The historic and the inward Christ*, 1914; Joshua Rowntree, *Social service: its place in the Society of Friends*, 1913.
47. Volumes included W. C. Braithwaite, *The beginnings of Quakerism*, 1912; W. C. Braithwaite, *The second period of Quakerism*, 1919; Jones, *Later periods*.
48. For accounts of the formation and early history of Woodbrooke see Kennedy, *British Quakerism*, 177-96; Rowntree, *Woodbrooke*; Robert Davis (ed.), *Woodbrooke 1903-1953: a brief history of a Quaker experiment in religious education*, 1953.
49. Rowntree, *Essays and addresses*, 144.
50. Ibid. 146.
51. See A. G. Gardiner, *The life of George Cadbury*, 1923, ch. 10.
52. JRCT minute book, no. 1, pp. 36, 155-6, 191.
53. Ibid., pp. 54, 56; Founder's memorandum, 2.
54. Rowntree, *Woodbrooke*, 23.
55. Rowntree, *Essays and addresses*, 135-50.
56. William E. Wilson, 'Post-war conditions in Woodbrooke', in Davis, *Woodbrooke*, 64-5.
57. Quoted in Rowntree, *Woodbrooke*, 29.
58. Ibid., 39, 44, 46.
59. Ibid., 31-4.
60. Worstenholme, 'Joseph Rowntree', F10.

61. G. Currie Martin, *The adult school movement: its origin and development*, 1924, 351. Martin's research for this volume and other research into adult education and its history was supported by the JRCT.
62. Thomas Kelly, *A history of adult education in Great Britain*, Liverpool 1962, 261, 265. See below, p. 69.
63. Martin, *Adult school movement*, 346; A. J. Peacock, 'Adult education in York 1800-1947', in A. J. Peacock (ed.), *Essays in York history*, York 1997, 283-4.
64. JRCT minute book, no. 1, pp. 59-60.
65. Whiting, *Ernest E. Taylor*, 52-3.
66. See J. F. C. Harrison, *Workers' education in Leeds: a history of the Leeds branch of the Workers' Educational Association 1907-1957*, Leeds 1957.
67. 'Report from the executive committee of Swarthmore to the council meeting held on 25 February 1910', inset in JRCT minute book, no. 1, pp. 69-70.
68. JRCT minute book, no. 1, pp. 97-8.
69. Whiting, *Ernest E. Taylor*, 78.
70. Peacock, 'Adult education in York', 266.
71. JRCT minute book, no. 1, p. 83.
72. Peacock, 'Adult education in York', 284.
73. Basil A. Yeaxlee, *Lifelong education: a sketch of the range and significance of the adult education movement*, 1929, 84-5.
74. JRCT minute book, no. 1, p. 109.
75. Horace Fleming, *Beechcroft: the story of the Birkenhead settlement 1914-1924: an experiment in adult education*, 1938, 14.
76. A. J. Allaway, *The educational centres movement: a comprehensive survey*, 1961, 11.
77. JRCT minute book, no. 1, p. 170.
78. Ibid., p. 145.
79. JRCT financial records, The Garden House, York.
80. See for example JRCT minute book, no. 1, pp. 58, 69, 71-2, 76, 85-6.
81. See Mark Freeman, *Social investigation and rural England 1870-1914*, Woodbridge 2003, ch. 6.
82. Ibid., ch. 4.
83. See for example E. P. Hennock, *British social reform and German precedents: the case of social insurance 1880-1914*, Oxford 1987.
84. Briggs, *Seebohm Rowntree*, 65-6.
85. JRSST general minute book, no. 1, pp. 176-7, 194-5, 201, 212.
86. See Freeman, 'Provincial social survey'.
87. Rowntree, *Poverty*, 74.
88. B. Seebohm Rowntree and Bruno Lasker, *Unemployment: a social study*, 1911, 18.
89. Ibid. 16.
90. Ibid. 196.
91. Ibid. 510 (but cf. 199); John Brown, 'Charles Booth and labour colonies 1889-1905', *Economic History Review* 2nd ser. xxi (1968), 353.
92. JRCT minute book, no. 1, p. 87.
93. L. T. Hobhouse, *Liberalism*, 1911, 172-3.

94. Kennedy, *British Quakerism*, 281.
95. Ibid.
96. Rowntree, *Essays and addresses*, 145 n.
97. H. G. Wood, 'Wardens and staff', in Davis, *Woodbrooke*, 38-9; H. G. Wood and Arthur Ball, *Tom Bryan, first warden of Fircroft: a memoir*, 1922, 35-42.
98. George Cadbury Junior and Tom Bryan, *The land and the landless*, 1908.
99. Wood, 'Wardens and staff', 40-1; Martin, *Adult school movement*, 347-50. As Martin and others have pointed out, Fircroft was inspired by Bryan's visits to the Folk High Schools in Denmark; although Bible scholarship did form a part of the curriculum and Fircroft reached out through its students and former students to the adult school movement, the atmosphere was more secular than at Woodbrooke.
100. JRCT minute book, no. 1, p. 21.
101. See Jose Harris, 'The Webbs, the Charity Organisation Society and the Ratan Tata Foundation: social policy from the perspective of 1912', in Martin Bulmer, Jane Lewis and David Piachaud (eds), *The goals of social policy*, 1989, 27-63.
102. Wood, 'Wardens and staff', 39-40
103. A. L. Bowley and A. R. Burnett-Hurst, *Livelihood and poverty: a study in the economic conditions of working-class households in Northampton, Warrington, Stanley and Reading*, 1915.
104. JRCT minute book, no. 1, pp. 123-4, 132.
105. Ibid., p. 28.
106. Most of the account below is based on Mark Freeman, 'The Outer London Inquiry Committee 1905-1908: a study in Edwardian social investigation', unpublished paper, Economic History Society annual conference, 2000.
107. Published as Edward G. Howarth and Mona Wilson, *West Ham: a study in social and industrial problems*, 1907.
108. JRCT minute book, no 1, pp. 18-19, 39, 80.
109. Founder's memorandum, 2.
110. Freeman, 'Outer London Inquiry Committee'.
111. Ibid.
112. Vernon, *Quaker business man*, 102-3 (quote unattributed).
113. Joshua Rowntree (1844-1915) was a member of the Scarborough branch of the family, involved in the organisation of the Manchester conference of 1895, and for six years Liberal MP for York. He was well known for his visits to concentration camps in South Africa during the second Boer war, and was the first warden of the Woodbrooke settlement. For an account of his life see S. Elizabeth Robson, *Joshua Rowntree*, 1916, and for his work in South Africa see Hope Hay Hewison, *Hedge of wild almonds: South Africa, the 'Pro-Boers' and the Quaker conscience 1890-1910*, 1989, esp. 163-5, 190-200.
114. Rowntree, *Social service*, 10.
115. Ibid. 107-8.
116. Vernon, *Quaker business man*, 93, 94.
117. Waddilove, *One man's vision*, 8-9, ch. 8; see Jonathan S. Davies and Mark Freeman, 'A case of political philanthropy: the Rowntree family and the campaign for democratic reform', *Quaker Studies* (forthcoming).

118. Rowntree, *Essays and addresses*, 138-9.
119. Rowntree, *Woodbrooke*, 37; quoted in Martin, *Adult school movement*, 346.
120. Peacock, 'Adult education in York', 287.
121. Kennedy, *British Quakerism*, contains an excellent account of the challenges posed by the first world war to the Society of Friends.
122. See Peter Brock, *The Quaker peace testimony 1660 to 1914*, York 1990, 276-89; John Ormerod Greenwood, *Quaker encounters, volume I: Friends and relief*, York 1975, 166-7.
123. Greenwood, *Friends and relief*, chs 8, 12.
124. For the 'official' account of the FAU during the First World War see Meaburn Tatham and James E. Miles (eds), *The Friends' Ambulance Unit 1914-1919: a record*, 1920; and for an alternative account, Greenwood, *Friends and relief*, ch. 11.
125. On these disagreements see Kennedy, *British Quakerism*, ch. 9.
126. Brock, *Quaker peace testimony*, 294-5; Greenwood, *Friends and Relief*, ch. 5.
127. For a description of this work see Greenwood, *Friends and relief*, 197ff.
128. For an account of Jebb and the Save the Children Fund, see Edward Fuller, *She championed children: the story of Eglantyne Jebb* (1st edn 1953), 1956.
129. See C. H. Mike Yarrow, *Quaker experiences in international conciliation*, New Haven, Conn., 1978, 23-31. For a brief account of Carl Heath's life see Frederick J. Tritton, *Carl Heath: apostle of peace*, n.d.
130. See Greenwood, *Friends and relief*, 180; Thomas C. Kennedy, *The hound of conscience: the story of the No-Conscription Fellowship 1914-1919*, Fayetteville, Arkansas, 1981.
131. Allott, *Friends in York*, 101-2; David Rubinstein, *York Friends and the Great War*, York 1999, 6-7.
132. A. J. Peacock, *York in the Great War 1914-1918*, York 1993, 329-30.
133. JRCT minute book, no. 1, pp. 184-5.
134. Peacock, *York in the Great War*, 394, 519.
135. JRCT minute book, no. 1, p. 183.
136. Inset in JRCT minute book, no. 1, pp. 145-6.
137. Peacock, *York in the Great War*, 379.
138. Ibid. 478-88; Vipont, *Arnold Rowntree*, ch. 6; Rubinstein, *York Friends and the Great War*, 16-17.
139. For Arnold Rowntree's relationship with these settlements, see Vipont, *Arnold Rowntree*, 58-62.
140. Rubinstein, *York Friends and the Great War*, 15-16; Peacock, *York in the Great War*, 328-9.
141. Peacock, *York in the Great War*, 415.
142. See JRSST general minute book, no. 1, pp. 218, 224-5. The JRSST agreed to pay the salary of a director of studies for the CSIR if a suitable candidate for the position could be found.
143. See for example H. C. [i.e. Henry Clay], *Notes on the countries at war*, n.d., which recommended (p. 12) Rowntree, *Land and labour*, as a good guide to Belgian conditions.
144. JRCT minute book, no. 1, pp. 171-2, 174-5, 186-8, 193-4, 197-8.
145. Martin, *Adult school movement*, 191 (and see 343).
146. JRCT minute book, no. 1, pp. 174-5.

147. Peacock, *York in the Great War*, 327-8.
148. Peacock, 'Adult education in York', 293.
149. £500 was given in 1915, £2,000 in 1916 and £500 in 1917 (JRCT financial records). There was some disagreement between Arnold and Seebohm Rowntree about whether the work of CSIR was worthwhile: JRCT minute book, no. 1, pp. 186-8, 193-4.
150. JRCT minute book, no. 1, pp. 186-8.
151. Ibid., pp. 193-4.
152. Ibid., pp. 197-8.
153. Ibid., pp. 149, 200.
154. Norman Angell, *After all: the autobiography of Norman Angell*, 1951, 198-9, 286.
155. JRSST general minute book, no. 1, pp. 171-2, 195-6, 215, 230, 245, 258, 284.
156. Kennedy, *British Quakerism*, 303.
157. JRCT minute book, no. 1, pp. 202-4.
158. Ibid., pp. 184-5.
159. H. G. Wood, 'The first world war', in Davis, *Woodbrooke*, 44-5.
160. Ibid., 45; JRCT Minute book, no. 1, pp. 150, 197.
161. Wood, 'First world war', 43.
162. See for example JRCT minute book, no. 1, p. 191. Woodbrooke needed £1,300 of losses paid off, towards which the JRCT donated £100.
163. Briggs, *Seebohm Rowntree*, ch. 5.
164. Ibid. 122-3, 125-6.
165. Ibid. 130.
166. B. Seebohm Rowntree, 'Prospects and tasks of social reconstruction', *Contemporary Review* cxv (1919), 8.
167. B. Seebohm Rowntree, 'Labour unrest', *Contemporary Review* cxii (1917), 373-4.
168. Ibid., 374 n.
169. B. Seebohm Rowntree, 'Labour unrest and the need for a national ideal', *Contemporary Review* cxvi (1919), 496, 498.
170. Rowntree, 'Labour unrest', 374.
171. Briggs, *Seebohm Rowntree*, 71, 146-8 and passim. However, note that in his 1904 memorandum Joseph Rowntree implicitly expressed approval of Joseph Arch's National Agricultural Labourers' Union, established in 1872 (Founder's memorandum, 3).

CHAPTER 3

'From Philanthropy to Education': the end of the war to the death of the Founder, 1918-1925

THE IMPACT of the first world war on the principles of Quaker social service was demonstrated in the Swarthmore lecture for 1918, when Lucy Fryer Morland assessed the Quaker commitment to social service in the light of the experience of war.[1] Her lecture assessed the collectivist impulse that was developing among Friends, quickened by the catalyst of the needs of war, and reflected in the increasing attraction among Quakers to Labour and socialist politics. Morland argued that 'self-determination' and 'co-operation' could and must co-exist. The former, defined as 'the freedom for each individual to work out his own destiny, to develop to his full manhood', entailed a return to the principle of the Inward Light, or the Divine Seed; while 'co-operation' involved 'the voluntary merging of some personal and private liberty into that of the organised group, in order to achieve a wider freedom'.[2] The argument that collectivism undermined 'self-determination', Morland thought, was fallacious: unrestricted economic and social competition was what really stifled the cultivation of the Divine Seed, and the state itself provided the 'public spirit of the individual' with an opportunity to serve, in the same way as philanthropy had done in earlier times.[3] Like Seebohm Rowntree, Morland was more sympathetic to the claims of trade unionism than were many members of the older generations of Friends, and she saw the unions' demands as entailing not simply a living wage but a more fundamental stake in society and opportunities to shape their own lives beyond the workplace, especially in regard to leisure provision.[4] Moreover, as the labour movement became increasingly associated with the provision of adult education, Quakers needed to reassess their position even in this field of social endeavour. One member of Morland's audience recorded how '[g]radually we realised that here from the desk of Yearly Meeting was being expounded the view that the implications of the Quaker faith led to that which in effect is

Socialism as the true theory of life'.[5] At the same Yearly Meeting, the Society of Friends adopted a statement on the 'Foundations of a True Social Order'.[6] Tony Adams ascribes the acceptance of this statement to pressure from the Socialist Quaker Society: although the wording was 'purged of socialist terminology', the adoption signified that the 'aims of mutual service were found acceptable' to the Society as a whole.[7] Although the activities of the 'War and the Social Order Committee' (established by Yearly Meeting in 1916), which drafted the statement – and on which members of the Socialist Quaker Society were disproportionately represented – met with suspicion from many moderate Friends, Thomas C. Kennedy has pointed out that the statement's provisions 'reflect just how far to the left the wartime Society of Friends had moved with regard to social policy'.[8] The Committee's victory at Yearly Meeting represented perhaps the most impressive manifestation of the Quaker social conscience since the Manchester conference in 1895, and bore the additional stamp of the official approval of the governing body of the Society.

Only a minority of Quakers were socialists, however; and for Joseph Rowntree the lessons of the growth of state intervention before and during the war held different implications for the future of Quaker service. More sceptical than Morland about the value of Quaker service in an official or statutory context, he argued in an article in *The Friend* in August 1918, three months before the end of the war, for the continuance and revitalisation of Friends' service in the voluntary sector. Like his cousin Joshua Rowntree five years earlier, he argued that the expansion of the state necessitated an even greater expansion of voluntary social service:

> The substantial increase of taxation, the growing claims made by the State upon each citizen, the manifold services now undertaken by the community on behalf of the individual, and the spread of collectivism would seem at first sight to be factors which reduce, even if they do not remove, the responsibility of the individual in respect of private benevolence in the public welfare. The springs of voluntary effort and personal sacrifice seem to be in danger of drying up; the more the community does for those in need, the less apparently is the occasion for organised charity. And yet, paradoxical as it may seem, the result is otherwise. The more the State does for the individual the greater and not the less becomes his responsibility; an increase of privilege from the whole to the part creates an increase of debt from the part to the whole; the further communal enterprise develops the more insistent is the need for voluntary spirit and for voluntary service.[9]

He went on to urge Friends to establish charitable trusts similar to his own, echoing his own concern for addressing 'underlying causes' rather than 'superficial manifestations' of social problems in exhorting them to 'be concerned with the creation and working of schemes of permanent and positive value, leaving to current subscription the more transient, temporary and occasional needs'.[10] His call appears to have been heeded: in the early 1920s there was 'a flurry of trust making' among Quakers, and especially among the Cadbury family, including the Barrow and Geraldine Cadbury Trust, the Barrow Cadbury Trust (which, like the JRSST, gave grants for non-charitable purposes), the G. W. Cadbury Trust and the William Adlington Cadbury Trust.[11]

In the midst of this flurry of new trusts, the JRCT was placed in the forefront of the movement to enhance and expand the work of the educational settlements and their associated bodies, institutions which appeared to offer the kind of 'communal enterprise' that Joseph Rowntree wanted to encourage. Signalling this focus of attention, in the first two years after the war, both Joseph and Arnold Rowntree made substantial donations of shares to the JRCT, each accompanying his gift with a memorandum suggesting the ways in which the money should be spent. Both referred implicitly to the experience of war, and linked their view of education with the cause of international peace. Joseph suggested that more scholarships at Bootham and The Mount be provided, that teachers' salaries be supplemented, and that settlements be supported. These settlements, he urged, were 'so manifestly what the country is needing now', and he hoped that they would 'link on naturally to the work of the Workers' Educational Association and to Associations for strengthening the International spirit'.[12] Arnold's gift, donated in 1920, was intended to support his work at the educational guest house at Cober Hill, which had replaced John Wilhelm's early experiment at Friedenstahl, as well as to encourage the trustees to continue to support adult education.[13] Together these two large donations and the memoranda that accompanied them were to do much to shape the course of the JRCT's grant-making during the inter-war period. As Arnold Rowntree explained, '[r]ecent experience has convinced me that the creation of a new spirit is needed before we can really solve our International and Industrial problems and in this connection I am increasingly impressed with the necessity, if the right atmosphere is to be obtained, of at times bringing people together for the discussion of these problems in an environment of quietness and beauty.'[14] Joseph and Arnold still saw the role of the JRCT in essentially local terms: over half of Joseph's memorandum dealt with the York Quaker schools, Bootham and The Mount, and their value to the Society of Friends, and Arnold's memorandum, as well as outlining the benefits of nearby Cober Hill, also drew trustees' attention to the 'the question of providing adequate help for maternity and child welfare work in York', in which his wife was much interested.[15] The trustees, conscious of their duty, as outlined in the 1904 memorandum, to keep a close watch on what was being done with their money, were also reminded by Joseph

Rowntree in *The Friend* that 'the administrative control of the resources of the Trust should be placed in the hands of like-minded trustees, and laid out and expended by them rather than allocated by them to other associations or bodies'.[16] Concentration on the expanding educational settlement movement did not at this point entail an abandonment of this principle: in 1918 there were only three such institutions, and only one outside Yorkshire. However, given the subsequent rapid expansion of the movement into new areas, the control which the trustees could exercise over its development would soon be compromised.

During this period only two new trustees were appointed, Arthur Bevington Gillett of Oxford and Francis L. P. Sturge of Woodbrooke, both in 1922, nominally in place of Oscar Rowntree, who resigned in 1919, and William Braithwaite, who died in 1922. Both were related to the Rowntrees by marriage. Gillett (1875-1954), who was to serve as a trustee until his death, was the third son of George Gillett and Hannah Elizabeth Gillett, younger sister of Joseph Rowntree. George Gillett had worked with Josephine Butler in her campaigns against the state regulation of prostitution, and Arthur inherited at least some of his campaigning zeal, being described by one of his many admirers, in an arguably oxymoronic phrase, as a 'belligerent Quaker'.[17] Educated at King's College, Cambridge, he became a partner in the family bank, Gillett and Company, in 1904, and was a member of Oxford City Council and treasurer of the council of the (then all-female) Somerville College, reflecting the long-standing Quaker interest in the education of women. In 1919 Gillett and Company merged with Barclay's Bank, of which Gillett served as a director from 1921 to 1949. Like his uncle Joseph Rowntree, he was a lover of long walks, and taught basic literacy in his local adult school. In 1909 he married Margaret Clark of Street in Somerset, who had worked with Emily Hobhouse among Boer women during the South African war, and through these connections he developed a friendship with Jan Smuts, the Boer general and moderate nationalist who was later to become prime minister of South Africa. (Gillett's eldest son was named Jan, presumably after Smuts.) Although a Quaker of strong pacifist sympathies, Gillett had attempted to enlist in 1914, but was 'thwarted by age and physical condition'.[18] He supported the war from start to finish, but took an unconventional and occasionally provocative view of conflict. As a friend remembered, '[s]oon after the first world war he took me to tea with a well-known Oxford Professor. Discussion turning a little hotly on the so-called German atrocities, the Professor exclaimed indignantly – "Do you then expect me to forgive the Germans?" "No," said Arthur, "I expect you to ask them to forgive *you*."'[19] Although Gillett's residence in Oxford made it difficult for him to take as active a role in the proceedings of the JRCT as the other trustees, he was nonetheless a valuable member of the

Trust, not least because of his family's connections with adult education in South Wales, of which more later.

Francis (Frank) Sturge (1871-1948) and his wife Edith M. Sturge (Arnold Rowntree's sister) were wardens of Woodbrooke, having taken over from Herbert and Dorothea Wood in 1918 (Wood replaced the influential Rendel Harris as director of studies), and Frank played as full a part as was possible for a resident of Birmingham in the work of the York-based JRCT. Warden until 1930, and a Charitable Trustee until 1948, Sturge took particular reponsibility on the board of trustees for the administration of the annual and one-off Woodbrooke grants. His appointment strengthened the relationship of the JRCT with the educational institutions which they funded; and the trustees devoted an even greater proportion of their resources and time to adult education after the war than they had done before 1914. They also insisted on as broad a definition of education as possible. Thus in 1921, a rough breakdown of the total expenditure of Joseph Rowntree's three trusts established that 40% went on housing (almost all administered by the JRVT), 13% on 'social reforms' (including Seebohm Rowntree's social inquiries), 2% on administration and 45% on 'Education (including book[s] & the Press)'.[20] The press, of course, was still the province of the JRSST, but the three trusts were still essentially part of the same Rowntree philanthropic whole, in which education, including political education, was a central feature.

Education, always central to Quakerism's social mission, was in some respects even more important to the Society after the war. Given the declining numbers of adult school members,[21] and the waning of Quaker influence within the schools – which according to some accounts was discernible as early as the 1890s[22] – the educational settlements, which had grown out of the adult school movement when at its peak, were now viewed as the most suitable way forward for Quaker educational endeavour. This was in part a reaction to the fact that the basic teaching of the 'three Rs', filling in the gaps left by an inadequate system of elementary education, was not now the urgent necessity it had been among the generations who passed through the pre-1870 school system; but it was also partly the result of a belief among Friends and many others that the systematised teaching now given in local authority-managed schools tended to denude children's education of its spiritual side and thus compromise the development of individual personality. This unwelcome development was the educational side of a more general mechanisation of human life, the result of a drive towards universality of state welfare provision, in the course of which religion (especially the distinctively personal religion epitomised by Quakerism) had been forgotten or at best marginalised. Thus in the Swarthmore lecture for 1923 Helen M. Sturge explained the dangers of over-reliance on the state and municipalities for the provision of material needs to the detriment of the spiritual side of life:

> Society is awakening to the fact that it has a corporate duty to the community as such, which can often only be accomplished through corporate action. We are indeed only beginning to realise the implications of this wide view of our duty as citizens and members of a State. But it does not cover all the ground. It may be that the earnest hope of many hearts will be fulfilled, and that material conditions will be so improved as to bring to all a good degree of comfort, with education and a fair measure of freedom. But nothing can abolish the accidents of life – sickness, suffering, sorrow and death. Nor will sin be eliminated even in the best of external conditions – nor all those subtle forms of torture that arise from joining temperaments and varieties of mental constitution. Would there be, in the absence of religion, any satisfying message for people in the grip of these things? It looks as though we might ... fail our friends just when their need is greatest and do everything for them but the highest thing of all.[23]

Quakerism was an essentially individualist religion trying to come to terms with its place in a society organised along increasingly collectivist lines, and personal philanthropic service was viewed as an antidote to impersonal statist social reform. Thus Joseph Rowntree insisted that '[d]irect personal control and active personal guidance and inspiration are of the first importance both in initiating and maintaining any scheme which is to be a living organism and not a mechanical contrivance'.[24]

Importantly in the context of Rowntree's philanthropic objectives, education of all kinds was a cornerstone of the national reconstruction programme. During the war the Ministry of Reconstruction had recognised the importance of adult education in its appointment of the Adult Education Committee, which delivered its final report in 1919. This Committee was headed by the Master of Balliol, A. L. Smith, and included trade unionists such as Ernest Bevin (who had himself attended an adult school in his teenage years),[25] the founder of the Workers' Educational Association Albert Mansbridge, university extension lecturers such as R. H. Tawney, and the social reformer, philosopher and educationalist Sir Henry Jones. (As noted earlier, Jones was an important influence on Tom Bryan and George Shann, who inspired the Fircroft experiment.) Basil Yeaxlee, who was to become secretary of the Educational Settlements Association in 1920, and Arthur Greenwood, who had been general secretary of the Council for the Study of International Relations, were also members. The Education Act of 1918 had drawn the local education authorities more closely into the realm of adult education, and the Adult Education Committee recognised the importance of the interlinkage of various responsible bodies in adult educational work. The report showed that 'there is a great opportunity before the State, the Universities, Local Authorities, and voluntary bodies, that there is ample scope for the activities of all these agencies, and that the development of adult education, if it is to fulfil its possibilities, depends upon the utilisation of the resources of the State, the Universities, and the Local Authorities, and on the free and vigorous service of voluntary organisation[s]'.[26] From 1924, officially designated 'Responsible Bodies', of which the WEA was the most prominent, were entitled to state financial support: another example of a partnership in provision between the state and voluntary sectors.

One of these 'Responsible Bodies' would be the Educational Settlements Association (ESA), founded in 1920 as a successor organisation to the short-lived Northern Settlements Association (1919). In the years after the war, following to a greater or lesser extent the models of York, Leeds and Birkenhead, new educational settlements were established at Bristol (the Folk House), Plymouth (Swarthmore Hall), Rugby, Letchworth, Gateshead (the Bensham Grove settlement) and Wilmslow (the Beacon Guild), to name just a few. Not all these were Quaker foundations, although members of the Society of Friends played a role in the majority of them, and all were informed by aspects of the Quaker educational ethos. By May 1921 there were fourteen settlements affiliated to the ESA, and by 1935 this figure would increase to 32.[27] The formation of the ESA gave greater coherence to the otherwise rather disorganised emergence of educational settlements; and the JRCT decided that, rather than supporting individual settlements, the bulk of its adult education funding should be delivered in the form of block grants to the ESA, which would in turn offer financial support to the individual settlements. The rapid spread of the educational settlement model meant that it was impossible for the trustees to keep a close eye on the developments and needs of each settlement, and it was one of the cornerstones of Joseph Rowntree's benevolence that its recipients should be in close contact with the organisations that provided their financial support. Settlements were so widely dispersed that it was only through a central and specialised agency that their needs could be efficiently met. The JRCT was represented on the ESA's governing body by the ESA's president Arnold Rowntree, and at times by other trustees, and was to remain closely associated with the educational settlement movement throughout the interwar years and beyond, being easily the largest contributor to the funds of the ESA for most of the period. In the early 1920s over half the JRCT's annual expenditure was laid out under the heading 'adult education and settlements' – peaking at £11,753 (of a total Trust expenditure of £18,728) in 1922 – and as such it is difficult to disentangle the Trust from the wider educational settlement movement in this period of its history. There follows, therefore, a more detailed consideration of this distinctive and in some respects unique expression of the Quaker approach to the education of adults.[28]

The earliest educational settlements, as explained in chapter 2, grew from the adult school movement, as did many of the post-war settlements, and the ethos of the adult schools was transmitted as far as possible to the new institutions. The pre-war pioneers were keen to emphasise the links between the new settlements and the adult schools: Arnold Rowntree, speaking at the official opening of the St. Mary's settlement, pointed out that its establishment did not mean 'any break in connection with the past history of the Adult School Movement', but was rather 'only the necessary growth and extension of the activities of that movement'.[29] The extension was necessary because it was felt that the original remit of the adult schools, which met only on a Sunday, for a short period, had been superseded by the spread of near-universal elementary education. There was less need for the 'three Rs', and more desire among the working-class consumers of adult education for subjects such as economics, literature and history, subjects which could not be covered in any depth in the half hour available before the weekly Bible lesson. Moreover, as became clear during and after the Great War, a rapidly secularising society exhibited less desire for Bible study; and Joseph Rowntree was especially hopeful that the settlements might come to do the work of churches and chapels, where attendance was decreasing in shaping 'the spiritual fellowships of the future'.[30] He was particularly interested in discovering '[a]ny evidence that the Settlements were meeting the deeper needs of men and women who had ceased to attend places of worship'.[31] Rowntree saw in the establishment of new settlements under the auspices of existing Quaker educational bodies a means of re-establishing the central place of Quakerism in adult education. As Edward Grubb pointed out in 1917, adult schools had long served a social function of sorts – '[e]very real Adult School gathers other activities round it than the Sunday morning or afternoon lesson: Savings Funds, Libraries, Temperance Societies, Sick Clubs, and the like'[32] – but the establishment of settlements represented a more ambitious attempt to endow adult education with what one historian has called 'both a home and a spirit'.[33]

The result of this transfer of the attention and energies of both teachers and students from the adult schools to the settlements was, somewhat inevitably, detrimental to the success of the older institutions. Together with the growth of university extension work, the WEA and other providers, the new developments spelt the end of the adult school movement as a major player in the field. As Arnold Hall, the adult schools' historian, has noted,

> It was now [by 1920] clear ... that for the great majority of Adult Schools – many of them scattered over the country in rural as well as urban areas – the way forward could not be on the same scale or style of educational provision as would be available at the Settlements ...

large numbers of Adult School members enrolled as students at the Settlements, besides belonging to their own School ... As time went on, therefore, there would doubtless be those – members or potential members – who found their educational needs more fully met at the Settlements, where professional teachers were in operation, supplied by the W.E.A. or the Universities or from elsewhere. This would draw off a considerable number from the Schools. It is equally certain that the Adult Schools lost a fair number of leaders or potential leaders to the Settlements. From this point of view the older Movement was being superseded by the new one.[34]

Indeed, as George Currie Martin – an adult school lecturer and the author of a JRCT-supported history of the adult school movement published in 1924 – pointed out, Woodbrooke, envisaged partly as a resource for adult school teachers, was becoming increasingly viewed as a training centre for settlement work.[35] By this time the membership of adult schools stood at considerably less than half its peak level – it reached 113,789 in 1910, and fell to 91,751 in 1914 and 50,761 by 1922-3[36] – while the number of students catered for by the ESA was continuing to increase. Seebohm Rowntree believed the schools had been superseded by other institutions, and not only the settlements, which fulfilled the same need: he told the JRCT in 1918 that '[t]he Adult School is only a means to certain ends, and it is possible that the work which has been done by the Schools in past years may have to be carried out in different ways and through different agencies in the future'.[37]

Despite being viewed by their founders as outgrowths of the adult school movement, the bodies with which the educational settlements were most naturally compared were the older social settlements, and between the two types of institution there were clear and marked distinctions, reflected in the fact that there was no joint meeting of the councils of the ESA and the British Association of Residential Settlements until 1939, and only two settlements (the Mary Ward Settlement and Toynbee Hall) were affiliated to both.[38] The distinction is complicated by the sometimes very striking differences between the educational settlements themselves, which although combined into the ESA from 1920, differed greatly in aims, governance and effectiveness. Moreover, the social settlements, to varying degrees, themselves served an educational function.[39] The Ministry of Reconstruction's Adult Education Committee, reporting in 1919, described education provision at Toynbee Hall, the Passmore Edwards Settlement, Oxford House, the Canning Town Women's Settlement, the Bermondsey Settlement, Mansfield House, the Browning Settlement, Birmingham Women's Settlement, the Bristol University Settlement, the Victoria Settlement in Liverpool and the Sheffield Neighbour Guild Settlement.[40] At Toynbee Hall, for example, university extension and tutorial courses were held, as well as a programme of WEA classes, and the curriculum for 1913-14 ranged from industrial history through home nursing and Esperanto to nineteenth-century English literature, not to mention flourishing drama, art and natural history societies.[41] At the Browning Settlement in Walworth, university extension work had proved less popular, but a wide range of non-vocational courses were taught in connection with the adult schools and the 'Pleasant Sunday Afternoon' movement; while the Bermondsey Settlement had an attached Educational Institute at which 600 students were enrolled during the 1912-13 academic year.[42]

Nevertheless, none of these settlements had as their *raison-d'être* the provision of adult education, which was only one part – and a subsidiary part – of the settlements' activities. As A. J. Allaway explained,

> Settlements, such as Toynbee Hall ... had educational programmes that were as comprehensive as could be imagined ... But these settlements were, of course, far more than educational centres: they engaged in social welfare work on a grand scale. The name 'settlement', by which Toynbee Hall and other similar ventures were known, was intended to convey the idea that they were places which, among other things, housed settlers: men who had come, even if only temporarily, to live in poor districts in order to remedy 'the habitual condition of this mass of humanity...'[43]

Toynbee Hall, for example, was an important recruiting ground for researchers to work on Charles Booth's survey of *Life and labour of the people in London*;[44] and in 1903 residents were represented on the London County Council, the London School Board and Stepney Borough Council, some were active in the Charity Organisation Society, the Mansion House Unemployed Scheme and the Prisoners' Aid Society, and some were carrying out 'Economic Inquiries'.[45] As well as involvement in boys' clubs and social activities for men and women, residents carried out social investigations published under the settlement's auspices.[46] Moreover, the educational work of these settlements was viewed within a broader context of social reform. As Basil Yeaxlee, secretary of the ESA, explained, whereas the bodies with which he was associated concentrated on educational work, the social settlements were 'constituted on the more general principle of social science'.[47] (For this reason, the educational settlement was not as restricted in location as the social settlement: almost by definition, the social settlement needed to be in a more or less deprived area, where some kind of social inquiry and social service could be carried on by the residents, whereas the educational settlement needed only to be within reasonable walking distance of those whose needs it was intended to meet.)

71

Residence, in the early years of the movement, was seen as essential for the practical realisation of this broader conception of what the social settlement could and should do. Whereas Toynbee Hall accommodated 20 men in 1914, and even the the smaller settlements four or five,[48] the educational settlements (sometimes after brief but unsuccessful attempts at providing short-term residential courses) usually housed only the warden and sub-warden.[49] This distinction was important: when the German observer Werner Picht compiled his list of British settlements in 1914, he did not include the non-residential ones.[50] Residence made possible the work of what Horace Fleming called 'social investigation and social amelioration';[51] it was intended also to facilitate the cross-class 'connection' that Samuel Barnett wanted to promote;[52] but it also had arguably negative implications for the diffusion of mutual social knowledge. As Standish Meacham has pointed out, the early social settlements were 'established on the basis of hierarchy',[53] and the Oxbridge-inspired physical shape and surroundings and more intangible 'atmosphere' of Toynbee Hall 'encouraged a kind of theater [sic] that could ... only serve to impede connection'.[54] R. H. Tawney, an early pioneer in the Workers' Educational Association, found that the WEA gave him the kind of intensive personal contact with the working classes that he had failed to obtain at Toynbee Hall.[55] The undergraduates at the settlement swapped their college 'scouts' for Cockney servants, and, although living in a working-class district, did not necessarily interact with their working-class fellows on terms of particular cordiality, let alone equality. This in turn had implications for settlement governance: the social settlements were largely patrician in spirit and undemocratic in structure, whereas the educational settlements, unencumbered by residence and its associated social implications, were in theory freer to develop along at least outwardly 'democratic' lines. From the adult schools they inherited the concept of 'membership', which was much less class-specific than 'residence', and although in practice the involvement of students in shaping settlement policy was limited, and although the definition of 'membership' was unclear,[56] the educational settlements were in a better position to foster a sense of settlement identity among the population of their local area than were the residential institutions.

From a practical point of view, the establishment of a residential presence depended on the availability of resources to construct or procure large enough premises to house settlers, and by the availability either of funds to pay them or of men and women of independent means who were able to devote their whole time to residence at a settlement. The early settlements enjoyed the patronage of their parent colleges, and undergraduates of independent means were able to stay for an average period of over two years during the first thirty years of Toynbee Hall's existence.[57] A salary of £250 was set aside for the warden, but before the outbreak of the first world war it had never been taken. It was recognised by the pioneers of educational settlements that they were unlikely to enjoy these advantages: thus Arnold Rowntree told his fellow trustees that he hoped the new venture at Leeds would enable well-meaning people to gain 'some of the advantages of institutional life without actually entering into residence at a Settlement'.[58] Swarthmore did attempt to organise some residential courses in its first years, but the residential accommodation was quickly converted into classrooms: even this short-lived residential element, involving mostly working men staying for a short period only, hardly fulfilled the functions of a true residential settlement.[59] George Currie Martin recalled that the residential settlement was 'very expensive in building and equipment, and demanded University people as residents, so ... [it was] felt that something along simpler lines should be attempted'.[60] Indeed, Joseph Rowntree warned that there should be an element of 'self-sacrifice' in the educational settlements, believing that 'whilst Settlements should be homelike they should not emphasise comfort';[61] and this simplicity of surroundings, partly necessary and partly encouraged, may have had a less alienating effect on the local population.

Nevertheless, 'connection' was important to the pioneers of the educational settlements, just as it was to the Quaker adult school teachers, who saw home visitation of scholars as a central aspect of their work.[62] This social aspect of the adult school was paralleled in the conception of the settlement as a homely environment, where freedom of expression went hand-in-hand with spiritual guidance in a supportive and unintimidating environment. Just as the residents of Toynbee Hall were engaged in the 'search for community', Horace Fleming believed that the educational settlement played a role in re-establishing community relationships:

> The Settlement, in drawing together larger numbers of the sundered units of humanity and reconciling them into a community, is providing in our modern complex society facilities for growth similar to those created by the family in simpler forms of social organisation. The same qualities of sympathy, tolerance, understanding and comradeship are induced, and in group activities values are discovered which include the welfare of others. These community groups, in providing a stand against the disintegrating forces of modern life, are comparable to the family group in primitive times.[63]

The aim, then, was to provide a collegial, even a familial environment, where the work of education in its truest and most general sense could be carried on. In some cases, as at Beechcroft in its earliest years, the settlement was literally in somebody's home; this was the epitome of the connective spirit of education that bodies like the Yorkshire 1905 Committee sought to promote. Thus a conference of Quaker extension secretaries held at Colwyn Bay in 1912 discussed the idea of the 'House Settlement', and it was explained that

> The idea would be for some Friend and his wife or sister to take a house conveniently situated, and keep one or two rooms at liberty for evening callers, taking care, however, that these rooms remain home-like. The host or hostess would entertain simply those who came, perhaps sometimes introducing a friend who wanted to tell a fresh experience, or discuss a living problem, or ask a vital question. Gradually there might grow up continuous teaching work, but not so much as to overshadow the ministry of the host and hostess in their own home. The quality of the personal service rendered would be the first thing.[64]

The key word, used repeatedly by all educational settlement propagandists, was 'fellowship'. As J. F. C Harrison has remarked, 'fellowship' was a word frequently used in adult school circles, and translated to the settlements, but 'it is difficult to determine exactly what this meant to a majority of the students';[65] nevertheless, the idea permeated the whole movement and was central to the conception of education that lay behind it. For example, Basil Yeaxlee saw the value of the settlements as lying in their 'bringing into fruitful fellowship men and women of the most diverse views, interests and circumstances', and in seeking 'to foster an education which is indeed spirit and life', all under the overarching idea of 'freedom and fellowship'.[66] The intangible 'spirit' of adult education which was supposedly fostered in these 'homes' evoked metaphors that stressed the familial characteristics of the settlements and the idea that in the common room and in friendly intercourse the religious and social sensitivities of the individual could be moulded and channelled in the direction of social and religious service. Indeed, the common room was central to the idea of the settlement – the ESA's journal was entitled *The Common Room* – envisaged as the nucleus of a social centre that enabled fellowship to be grafted onto education. Although in practice the common room tended to be unattractively decorated, poorly heated, too small and not frequented by more than a small minority of members,[67] there were some exceptions, notably the café at the Folk House, Bristol, voluntarily staffed by members and serving as a comparatively pleasant centre for social intercourse.[68]

Growing as they did from Quaker social concern, the educational settlements were conceived as contributing to the fostering of what one Quaker historian has called 'those omnipresent magic words, "Fellowship" and "Service"'.[69] Although most of the settlements discarded many of the trappings of their denominational heritage very quickly, many in the interwar period still viewed them as central planks in the educational structure of the Society of Friends. Horace Fleming, having spent a year a Woodbrooke, supported by the JRCT, researching the history and condition of adult education and other Quaker work, saw the settlements as occupying an essential bridging position between the adult schools and the Quaker Meeting. Fleming identified three stages of adult education: the first stage was the adult school, 'where the individual self is thawed out from the ice block of instincts, prejudices and habits of the mass'; the second the settlements, 'where the self flows through self-effort into identity, gains a soul and desires to express it'; and the third and final stage the Meeting, 'where the individual self [feels] the need for expansion into the worship of the highest'.[70] Each of these stages entailed a different, and developing, expression of fellowship, while the institutional permanence of each of the three bodies (in contrast to the temporary influence of the missionary worker or the itinerant teacher) contributed to the wider 'leavening of the local community life'.[71] This link to the community – as well as the internal structures of the Society of Friends – emphasises the importance of the ideal of settlement, if not of residence, in a specific locality. John Wilhelm Rowntree had envisaged his 'Quaker settlement' as having a 'social wing', which would serve as 'an outlet for practical Christianity',[72] and although this was intended to be subordinate to the Biblical scholarship for which his settlement was to be established, it emphasised the importance of active citizenship to the Quaker community. Woodbrooke never really developed this 'social wing', although from 1908 onwards students had the opportunity of taking the diploma in social study inaugurated by J. St. George Heath, and Fleming recommended in 1928 that an educational settlement be established in Birmingham which would better serve Rowntree's purpose.[73] (The city already had the Birmingham Women's Settlement, founded in 1899.)

The educational settlement, then, was viewed as a civic centre, where citizenship and training for social leadership could be actively pursued. Fleming declared in 1929 that '[f]or a knowledge of human, industrial, and civic problems, there is no finer school than a Settlement',[74] and hoped that yet more Quakers might be drawn into the movement. He remembered that in Birkenhead 'though the Settlement dates only from the outbreak of war, the dynamic effect of the student community has resulted in the revolutionising of the housing conditions, and the changing of the composition of the civic Council'.[75] Here, settlement students and workers, many of whom had a long-standing interest in housing issues, were closely involved in the establishment of a Housing Inquiry Committee in 1922, which undertook careful investigation of slum housing and a variety of propagandist work.[76] Other educational settlements followed the lead of Toynbee Hall and worked on social surveys: residents at Bensham Grove, for example, assisted with Dr. Henry Mess's survey of *Industrial Tyneside*, and the warden Lettice Jowett was a member of the

Survey Committee.[77] Others had branches of the League of Nations Union or the Left Book Club, and, in the case of the settlements at Plymouth and Bristol, were closely associated with the Youth Hostels Association.[78] In engaging in activities like this the educational settlements were following the lead of the social settlements; and in some respects they tended, during the interwar years, to adopt more of the characteristics of their Victorian predecessors, developing the 'social wing' that John Wilhelm Rowntree envisaged. Some viewed this as a dangerous tendency. Although social service under settlement auspices fostered 'fellowship', for some wardens there were limits to the convergence of 'education' and 'fellowship'. This was clear even at the level of teaching methods. John A. Hughes, warden of St. Mary's from 1921, contrasted small-group teaching, which was 'the real educational work' of the settlement, with large popular lectures, which were 'more valuable from the Fellowship point of view'.[79] Similarly, and less ambiguously, the influential 'Guildhouse Report' of 1924 – prepared by a committee of the British Institute of Adult Education chaired by Harold Laski – emphasised the importance of keeping education at the centre of the settlements' activities, warning that '[t]he College must not be lost in the club, nor the class in the common-room'.[80] These concerns pre-empted those that would be expressed in the 1930s, when the educational settlements would feel the pressure of competition from alternative institutions which offered a somewhat different version of 'fellowship'.

The association in the popular mind of the educational settlements with the Canon Barnett type of institution was also detrimental to the impact of the new movement. The idea of the social settlement seemed essentially outmoded by 1918: it was more appropriate to a late-Victorian society in which the encroachments of the state and municipalities into social work were essentially limited, and the residence of educated men and women in poor working-class districts was seen as a useful vector of social service and a necessary prelude to greater understanding and more effective amelioration of the conditions under which a large proportion of the population lived. The assumption by statutory and municipal authorities of many of the basic social functions served by the early settlements had, according the one observer in the 1930s, 'reduced the need for residential workers, and the usefulness of the untrained volunteer ha[d] decreased as the scope of official action ha[d] expanded'.[81] Indeed, it could be argued that 'the "settlement" concept itself ha[d] lost much of its meaning'.[82] Yet the freeing up of the energies of the voluntary sector represented by the deeper incursions of the state into the economic and social life of the nation, together with the extension of democracy (the parliamentary franchise had been conceded to men aged 21 and over and women aged 30 and over in 1918), gave new scope for a more imaginative development of the settlement model as an organ of voluntarism.

Fleming viewed the shift from social to educational settlements as representative of a transition 'from Philanthropy to Education';[83] while the ESA declared that the educational settlement, in contrast to its Victorian predecessors, should be 'essentially democratic'.[84] Education for citizenship became an important theme of the movement in these years. Fleming hoped to see the educational settlements become training centres for local municipal leaders: he told an international conference of settlements held at Toynbee Hall in 1922 that 'Local Government will always halt by the way until all are equipped to take up the burden of citizenship', while another delegate believed that the more specialised kind of settlement would be 'the surest foundation of a new order'.[85] The settlement should be a centre for citizenship, where training for social work could take place, and local people could be encouraged to examine the lives of their own communities and suggest remedies for the social problems they encountered, and often experienced themselves. Arthur Greenwood (who had attended meetings of the JRCT during the war as a representative of the Council for the Study of International Relations), speaking in 1922, saw the educational settlement as a vehicle of working-class self-expression, in a way that the social settlement could never have been:

> There is much objection to the carrying on of research by settlers assisted by working people. What is needed is subjective research on the part of the workers assisted by the settlers. I want to see the workers articulate. That involves a great educational question. The workers have a heritage common to all, and a special experience since the Industrial Revolution which ought to be utilised, because the people who know most can say least. Settlements should gather groups of workers together for team work of this kind.[86]

Training for active citizenship was also seen as an important role for the Quaker schools, of which Bootham and The Mount in York were of particular interest to the Rowntree family, who sought where possible to develop links between the schools and the settlements. For John Wilhelm Rowntree, the role of Quaker school education was 'fitly to blend the intellectual, spiritual, and physical training of the child, and to educate for a liberal citizenship its unformed mind'.[87] Spiritual training was especially important to the Society in the wake of the educational reforms of 1870 and 1902: whereas many schools were narrowly Anglican, in the non-denominational Board Schools religious teaching was 'necessarily colourless and often mechanical',[88] a fault which it was hoped Quakers would avoid through their emphasis on individualism and the Divine Seed. Nevertheless, it was recognised that the religious teaching in their schools was often inadequate, and John Wilhelm envisaged a role for a 'scheme of special scholarships' at Woodbrooke or elsewhere for Quaker teachers who could thus be trained in this side of their work.[89] Quaker schools were themselves shifting in focus by the end of the war: Joseph Rowntree warned in his memorandum to the JRCT in 1919 that many non-Quakers who could afford the fees were using the schools at the expense of Quakers who could not,[90] and he and the Trust established scholarships to improve access for able young Friends. By 1929 E. B. Castle (a young Quaker educationalist and newly-appointed headmaster of Leighton Park School) was arguing in *The Friend* that the new challenges posed by this influx of non-Friends must be met by a re-connection of the schools with the ideals of service, and another Friend was wondering: '[h]ave the schools, like the monasteries in the Middle Ages, made themselves an end in themselves instead of a means for the service of mankind, thinking of the schools apart from the Society to which they belong, and the Society as something which is not the servant of humanity?'[91] Already in the 1900s The Mount School had established a Scholarship and Training Department in which girls could stay for a year and gain experience of teaching;[92] and at a Trust meeting in June 1914 Joseph Rowntree floated the idea of donating a further £4,000 to the JRCT to be used to help female Friends train for social work at The Mount.[93] Arguably the educational settlements represented an extension of these ideas into the sphere of adult education, and the links are emphasised by the fact that Gerald Hibbert, warden of the Swarthmore settlement in Leeds, left this post in 1919 to become Headmaster of Ackworth School. In 1922 the JRCT supported a scheme for two girls from The Mount to spend a year at the Letchworth educational settlement;[94] while there were a number of suggestions to encourage school teachers to attend settlements or, preferably, Woodbrooke, to enhance the spiritual power of their teaching or simply to enjoy a sabbatical.[95]

Woodbrooke itself remained chronically short of funds and reliant on the Rowntrees and Cadburys for periodic injections of funds to help it to steer itself through the most difficult years and to do some of the work of the socially concerned Quakerism which John Wilhelm Rowntree had wanted it to do. There were some notable developments in the post-war period. From 1919 Woodbrooke was confederated into the Selly Oak Colleges,[96] together with Fircroft, Kingsmead (a Friends' college for the training of foreign missionaries), Carey Hall and Westhill (a Nonconformist college for the training of Sunday School teachers and work with boys' and girls' clubs). The creation of a central council and the establishment of a 'Central Staff' helped the colleges to pool their teaching resources and to appoint lecturers who carried out some work at all five institutions. Woodbrooke managed to expand in the 1920s, especially through the gift by Elizabeth M. Cadbury of the new George Cadbury Hall in 1925, which became the venue for most of the lectures centrally organised by the Selly Oak Colleges. An extra common room was provided, a Biblical Museum established; and through the initiative of Sturge as warden, the governance of Woodbrooke was adjusted to allow for regular staff meetings and the provision of a male and a female student representative to improve communication between students and staff. Nevertheless, the Rowntrees were frequently critical of Woodbrooke and its apparent failures to achieve as much as had been hoped for the benefit of the Society of Friends. Seebohm Rowntree, a member of the Woodbrooke Council from its inception, was especially critical. In particular, the college seemed to be failing to provide the service to English Quakers and the Quaker schools that had been envisaged by its pioneers. There had been some successes: at a crisis meeting of the JRCT in April 1921, at which Sturge (not yet a trustee) was present by invitation, it was emphasised that Woodbrooke had been important in 'establishing an organic connection between English and American Quakerism ... [and] in spreading the Woodbrooke spirit and method in other European countries', on top of its importance within the Selly Oak College system.[97] Yet Woodbrooke was failing as a central resource for the wider schemes of education which it was intended to serve. John Wilhelm Rowntree had envisaged Woodbrooke as a 'settlement' that, through its residential element, would supply an extra dimension to Quaker education that none of the existing institutions could provide:

> In the noisy rush of modern life we need periods of quiet when the soul may feed in peace on that which shall nourish it for action. We need that type of character which, in earlier days, by its calm strength, its transparent truthfulness, and its spiritual depth, worked as a leaven of righteousness in the land. Neither a sound education, nor Quaker Sunday Schools, nor a settlement for Bible study can give us all this, but they will contribute to 'an intelligent grasp of Christian truth, and the shaping of Christian character in the mould of a strong manhood and womanhood.'[98]

Sturge hoped that the college would play a part in training individuals to teach 'Bible and Theology' lessons in the Quaker schools,[99] while other trustees hoped it might be able to play a greater role in training educational settlement wardens.[100] It was also partly envisaged as a resource for adult school teachers,[101] who did not always live up to what was expected of them in terms of Bible knowledge or pedagogic skills.[102] Altogether, Woodbrooke did not live up to these expectations, and although affiliated to the ESA, its links with the educational settlements remained undeveloped throughout the interwar period.

Integral to John Wilhelm's vision of Quaker educational provision was the idea of the guest house, and the idea was taken up by his surviving relatives after his death. At the time of his death in 1905 he was in the process of establishing Friedenstahl, the guest house at Scalby, as a centre for residential courses and conferences. In its first season it had over 300 residents, and it was at Scalby in September 1905 that the plans for 'Quaker tramps' were agreed by Arnold and Arthur Rowntree and Wilfrid Crosland.[103] In 1919 the guest house was moved, thanks to the agency and money of Arnold Rowntree, to Cober Hill, at Cloughton near Scarborough, and the administration was taken over by the JRCT. There was space to house seventy people, plus another thirty at nearby Court Green, and although intended primarily as a holiday venue for members of the Yorkshire Adult School Union, it also catered for for groups of schoolchildren, a conference of Wesleyan ministers and attracted well-known speakers including Albert Mansbridge, Ramsay MacDonald and George Bernard Shaw.[104] Working-class adult scholars could go, inexpensively, on holiday with their families for a period of physical recreation and spiritual contemplation: perhaps a better version of John Wilhelm's proposed 'Way-side Inn' which had also found institutional expression at Woodbrooke.[105] (John Wilhelm had proposed that the 'Way-side Inn' be established in 'some favoured resort':[106] whether Birmingham could really be included in this category is perhaps questionable.) Although the strictness of the regime at Cober Hill strikes the modern reader as unconducive to the holiday spirit – the long-serving manageress Helen Andrews remembered with sadness 'two tragedies with drunkenness and insincerity' but more hopefully that 'we have never had a bathing accident'[107] – the institution did provide much-needed holiday accommodation for a favoured few families near a popular holiday destination. The curriculum echoed the eclecticism found in many of the educational settlements: the winter school for women held in 1926-7, for example, included literature, 'Home-making', citizenship, folk-dancing, religious study, committee work and fourteen different kinds of handicrafts.[108] With its Quaker Meetings and adult school services, Cober Hill aimed at what Andrews called 'the deeper side of life' and at fostering the 'art of holiday-making'.[109] The guest house's own publicity described it as 'an ideal centre for men and women … to meet together in fellowship to compare ideas and to gain fresh strength, both intellectual and physical, for their work'.[110]

No less important to the members of the JRCT was the Yorkshire 1905 Committee (renamed the Yorkshire Friends Service Committee in 1928), which continued to receive regular support, and which had had a direct influence on much of the early educational settlement work. In the early 1920s the Trust was supporting the Committee to the extent of £200 a year, plus the cost of a rail season ticket for the field secretary;[111] and it still had to be helped out with occasional additional sums.[112] The Committee was clearly taking on more responsibilities than were justified by its resources: Stephen Rowntree told the JRCT in 1924 that it had made a 'decision to concentrate effort on certain areas and meetings'.[113]

In the later 1920s Stephen found himself able to give more of his time to the Committee, and the Trust agreed to fund the cost of additional secretarial assistance for him if required.[114] The Quaker histories were also brought up to the present in this period, Rufus Jones's two-volume *Later periods of Quakerism* appearing in 1921. The trustees were eager to support other Friends' literature: for some years they had been concerned about *The Friend*, which had been struggling to maintain its circulation for some time but which was beginning to find its feet by the 1920s, perhaps strengthened by the appeal of the Quaker peace testimony among a wide range of first world war pacifists.[115] Other Friends' periodical publications were less eagerly endorsed, however: awarding a grant to the Friends Home Service Committee, the trustees expressed ambivalence about its publication *The Wayfarer*, arguing that the proliferation of periodicals serving a small Society was probably unhelpful.[116] On the other hand, the Swarthmore lecture did not become fully self-financing until the 1930s, and even then help was sometimes required,[117] but the Trust consistently supported what had already become an important occasion for the airing of matters of concern to Friends. Indeed, it has been suggested that from around 1913 and for 'the next few years' the JRCT took 'a much closer interest than before in the choice of the lecturers'.[118]

A very different strand of Trust funding was the research work of Seebohm Rowntree. Seebohm has figured little in this chapter – although he was involved in many of the activities it has described, for example as a member of the Woodbrooke Council – partly because his work in the early 1920s has been described elsewhere,[119] but partly because his interests took him away from York and away from JRCT activity for much of this period. He usually attended trustees' meetings, but much of his research work centred around the cocoa works itself and around wider questions of national importance on which he collaborated with other leading political and administrative figures of the period. The JRCT supported the research and publication of *The human needs of labour* (1918), in which Rowntree revised his poverty line of 1901 to take account of nonessential expenditure, and which later formed the basis for his second social survey of York carried out in 1936, and *The human factor in business* (1921), based on conditions in the cocoa works, which formed a plea to employers to take more account of factors other than wages which made for industrial unrest. Although not an enemy of trade unionism, Rowntree was anxious that industry should not be paralysed by the strikes and lockouts that were an unprecedentedly significant feature of the period in which he was writing. Although maintaining that he wished to avoid '[a]ny rash procedure [which] might lead to a serious lowering of business efficiency',[120] he suggested that shorter hours, paid holidays, the establishment of works' councils and profit-sharing schemes, and the provision of more workplace social amenities could all improve the efficiency, productivity and general happiness of an industrial workforce. Although his advocacy of many of these initiatives was based on an economic rationalism that was arguably rather unquakerly,[121] and in some respects distanced his perspective from that of other members of his family, he was nevertheless advocting a vision of industrial partnership to which Joseph Rowntree also came to subscribe towards the end of his life.[122] Seebohm's denunciation of the attitude prevalent among many industrialists that was epitomised by the use of the word 'hands' as a synonym for 'employees' or 'workers'[123] was met with a determined insistence on the importance of the self-development of the individual that transcended his or her economic role: 'A just community ... will endeavour to distribute work, and wealth, and chances of development justly ... [and] among its units there will exist a real sense of equality as children of one nation, and as men and women who ... are not tools but ends in themselves'.[124]

These ideals were realised in practical terms through the establishment of regular conferences of employers, held at Balliol College, which grew out of a Quaker employers' gathering at Woodbrooke in April 1918.[125] The Oxford conferences were intended to further a progressive view of industrial relations among employers and foremen, and thirty-three such gatherings were held, until in 1936 the responsibility for their organisation was passed to the Institute of Industrial Management.[126] Here, then, is an example of the JRCT, through one of its trustees, supporting a new initiative which later came to be the province of a different body, and emphasising the pioneering role that the trustees envisaged for themselves. From the Oxford conferences developed the idea of the 'Management Research Group', another initiative to which Seebohm attached much importance.[127] Seebohm did not confine his attention to those in work: he also involved himself in inquiries into the condition and prospects of that large number of his countrymen who were unemployed. Unemployment had not been of great significance in determining the proportion of the population living in poverty at the turn of the century, but it was to become the most important domestic political issue of the inter-war period. He had already carried out a study of unemployment in York, published in 1911,[128] but he took this further in the early 1920s, when registered unemployment reached a million (a figure below which it was not to fall until the second world war). He was involved in various committees which investigated the problem, most notably one convened by J. J. (later Viscount) Astor, which produced the influential multi-authored book *Is unemployment inevitable?*, and drew on the findings and expertise of skilled social investigators such as Arthur Bowley and leading economists including A. C. Pigou.[129] Large questions of immense national importance were addressed. As Rowntree explained to the JRCT in December 1923, shortly before the publication of the report, '[t]he committee is concentrating on the question [of] how far this country can hope to maintain the whole of her population in work at satisfactory wages under ordinary conditions or whether some fundamental change in the method of doing trade must be sought'.[130]

Nevertheless, for all Seebohm's research into the great problems facing the nation, and the forewarnings that much of his work contained of the problems that were to be experienced on a national scale in years to come, such work remained for the JRCT essentially ancillary to its main purposes. Seebohm was usually given money to do largely what he wanted with, and although he delivered regular reports on his progress, these appear to have been brief. The items most regularly discussed at JRCT meetings were the activities of Edward Grubb, Herbert Waller, the Yorkshire 1905 Committee and other regular recipients of the trustees' support, as well as the distribution of scholarships to the Quaker schools. Concern for the educational, social and personal welfare of members of the Society of Friends and citizens of York was paramount among the trustees. Thus, for example, £1,000 was given to the Bootham School centenary fund in 1922;[131] in the following year the Trust made a one-off grant of £250 towards the improvement of Clementhorpe Park (later renamed Rowntree Park);[132] while at around the same time £100 was given to Herbert Waller and his family 'to enable them to have a good continental holiday'.[133] By contrast, the trustees were relatively unwilling to support groups, such as the National Council for the Abolition of the Death Penalty, the National Christian Council of China and the Wayfarers' Benevolent Institution (all of which applied unsuccessfully for JRCT funding in this period), which they knew little about and could not oversee or assess.[134] Significantly, when Joseph Rowntree died in 1925, the trustees remembered him in the following terms:

> the surviving trustees expressed their gratitude for the opportunity given to them by the generosity of the Founder to assist important religious and educational work in connection with the Society of Friends, the Adult School and other similar movements, as well as in the application of Christian ideals to industry, the promotion of Peace at home and abroad, of Temperance, and the publication of literature. Special reference was made to Joseph Rowntree's long personal connection with the Boarding Schools at Bootham and the Mount; also to the large part he took in the shaping of the more modern literature of the Society of Friends. His interest in Woodbrooke increased year by year, and he took constant pleasure in hearing of the pioneer work done at the non-residential Settlements.[135]

It was the educational work which the trustees emphasised, and for his educational endeavours, conducted within the Society of Friends and within the city of York, for which they remembered the Founder's public life. (As if to emphasise Rowntree's provincialism, his funeral was reported in detail only in the northern press.)[136] Joseph Rowntree's death, however, preceded a partial change of focus in the activities of the JRCT. As a deeper sense of national crisis, along with forebodings of international conflict, entered the consciousness of the nation and the trustees in subsequent years, the local objectives of the JRCT, while never being abandoned, would increasingly be supplemented with grants made in recognition of a wider range of pressing national and international concerns. In addition, as the next chapter will show, the position of the Founder's last great interest, the interest that had given his philanthropy a more national focus – the educational settlement movement – was also being called into question, while the Society of Friends as a whole was entering yet another period of reassessment of the nature of its social concern and the proper field of its social service.

NOTES

1. Lucy Fryer Morland, *The new social outlook*, 1918.
2. Ibid. 32-4.
3. Ibid. 34-5.
4. Ibid. 39-40.
5. *The Friend*, 31 May 1918, 333.
6. The statement is reprinted in Adams, *Far-seeing vision*, 45.
7. Ibid. 23.
8. Kennedy, *British Quakerism*, 384.
9. *The Friend*, 9 August 1918, 491. (The article is unsigned; however, a typescript copy appears in JRF JR93/VIII/1, and it may be inferred that Rowntree was too modest to put his name to an article that referred to his own private benevolence as a model for what other Friends ought to be doing.)
10. Ibid. 492.
11. Wagner, *Chocolate conscience*, 138ff.
12. Joseph Rowntree, memorandum of 16 April 1919, inset in JRCT minute book, no. 1, pp. 241-2.
13. On Cober Hill see *Cober Hill, Cloughton 1920-1986*, York 1986; on Friedenstahl see Allott, *John Wilhelm Rowntree*, 95ff.
14. Arnold Rowntree, memorandum of 13 May 1920, inset in JRCT Minute book, no. 1, pp. 273-4.
15. Ibid.
16. *The Friend*, 9 August 1918, 492.
17. Quoted in *Arthur B. Gillett 1875-1954: memories from some of his friends*, Gloucester [1955]. This pamphlet was printed for private circulation only. In the British Library catalogue, Gillett is mistakenly referred to as Arthur Barington Gillett. For Further information on his brothers see George M. L. Davies (ed.), *Joseph Rowntree Gillett: a memoir*, 1942.
18. Kennedy, *British Quakerism*, 390.
19. *Arthur B. Gillett*, 15. Original emphasis.
20. Note in JRF JRCT93/I/10 (f).

21. See below, p. 70.
22. Ernest F. Champness, *Adult schools: a study in pioneering*, Wallington 1941, 19-20; Rowntree and Binns, *History of the adult school movement*, 35.
23. Helen M. Sturge, *Personal religion and the service of humanity*, 1923, 20-1.
24. *The Friend*, 9 August 1918, 492.
25. Champness, *Adult schools*, 51. Bevin, however, did not attend the meetings of the Committee and did not sign the final report.
26. *Ministry of Reconstruction: Adult Education Committee final report*, Parliamentary Papers 1919, Cmd. 321, 177.
27. Allaway, *Educational centres movement*, 17; Pimlott, *Toynbee Hall*, 281-2. These figures include the residential colleges which were also affiliated to the ESA, and Pimlott's figure also includes 'centres in association', mostly settlements in the Special Areas which were pending full affiliation. The Lemington-on-Tyne settlement was established in 1913 as an adjunct to the adult school work of Dr. Andrew Messer, and the JRCT later took over the freehold of the land, leasing it to Messer at a peppercorn rent (JRF JRCT93/IV/4; JRCT minute book, no. 2, minute nos. 105, 121, 186). However, although it was founded a year earlier than Beechcroft it is not usually considered as one of the pioneering educational settlements, possibly owing to Horace Fleming's desire to inflate his own role in the history of the ESA. Fleming did not mention Lemington-on-Tyne in his history of Beechcroft at all. Kelly, *History of adult education*, 264, points out that the Homestead, Wakefield, was also established in 1913.
28. See Allaway, *Educational centres movement*; Mark Freeman, '"No finer school than a settlement": the development of the educational settlement movement', *History of Education* xxxi (2002), 245-62; Jonathan S. Davies and Mark Freeman, 'Education for citizenship: the Joseph Rowntree Charitable Trust and the educational settlement movement', *History of Education* xxxii (2003), 303-18; and for a later perspective K. T. Elsdon, *Centres for adult education*, 1962. There are brief references to educational settlements and the ESA in J. F. C. Harrison, *Learning and living 1790-1960: a study in the history of the English adult education movement*, 1961, 311-12; Kelly, *History of adult education*, 263-5, 277-8; John Lowe, *Adult education in England and Wales: a critical survey*, 1970, 60-5; Roger Fieldhouse and associates (eds), *A history of modern British adult education*, Leicester 1996, 261-3 (with incidental references at 49-50, 54, 81).
29. 'Educational work in York', JRF ROWN.FAM.L/93/3.
30. 'Joseph Rowntree and adult education', article from *Common Room*, June 1925, copy in JRF JR93/VIII/2.
31. Ibid.
32. Grubb, *What is Quakerism?*, 176-7.
33. Kelly, *History of adult education*, 265. See above, p. 39.
34. W. Arnold Hall, *The adult school movement in the twentieth century*, Nottingham 1985, 51-2.
35. Martin, *Adult school movement*, 345-6.
36. Hall, *Adult school movement*, 213.
37. JRCT minute book, no. 1, p. 212.

38. Michael Rose, '"A microcosm of cultivated society": education, the arts and the social settlements', unpublished paper, University of Manchester, 2001.
39. See R. A. Evans, 'The university and the city: the educational work of Toynbee Hall', *History of Education* xi (1982), 113-25; Brian Simon, *Education and the labour movement 1870-1920*, 1965, 78-85.
40. *Ministry of Reconstruction: Adult Education Committee final report*, 226-33.
41. Ibid. 227-8.
42. Ibid. 229-30.
43. Allaway, *Educational centres movement*, 7-8.
44. David Englander and Rosemary O'Day 'Introduction', in Englander and O'Day, *Retrieved riches*, 21ff.
45. Picht, *Toynbee Hall*, 36-7.
46. Ibid. 88; Meacham, *Toynbee Hall*, 124-7.
47. Yeaxlee, *Lifelong education*, 85.
48. Picht, *Toynbee Hall*, 235 and passim.
49. Allaway, *Educational centres movement*, 10.
50. Picht, *Toynbee Hall*, 209-45.
51. Fleming, *Beechcroft*, 13.
52. Meacham, *Toynbee Hall*, ch. 2.
53. Ibid. 39.
54. Ibid. 49.
55. Rose, 'Microcosm', citing Meacham, *Toynbee Hall*, 171-81; Lawrence Goldman, 'Intellectuals and the English working class 1870-1945: the case of adult education', *History of Education* xxix (2000), 294.
56. See for example Taylor to Crosland, 18 April 1923, JRF JRCT93/IV/3 (e), on the new draft constitution of St. Mary's, in which Taylor queries what exactly was to be the definition of 'the members of the Settlement'.
57. Picht, *Toynbee Hall*, 31-3.
58. JRCT minute book, no. 1, pp. 59-60.
59. Allaway, *Educational centres movement*, 10-11.
60. Martin, *Adult school movement*, 351.
61. JRCT minute book, no. 1, p. 263.
62. See for example Jones, *Later periods*, ii. 956-8; Briggs, *Seebohm Rowntree*, 13; Allott, *John Wilhelm Rowntree*, 13-14. See above, p. 16.
63. Horace Fleming, *The lighted mind: the challenge of adult education to Quakerism*, 1929, 57.
64. 'Report of conference of extension secretaries held at Colwyn Bay, 25-7 May 1912', JRF JRCT93/VI/1 (a).
65. Harrison, *Learning and living*, 307.
66. Yeaxlee, *Lifelong education*, 85, 115-16.
67. W. E. Williams, 'The educational settlements: a report prepared for the Joseph Rowntree Charitable Trust', October 1938, 69, 78, 101, JRF JRCT93/IV/2.
68. *Common Room* xxviii (1932), 10.
69. John Ormerod Greenwood, *Quaker encounters, volume III: whispers of truth*, York 1978, 188.
70. Horace Fleming, 'Interim report on the Society of Friends, etc.', 1928, 33, JRF JRCT93/VI/1 (e).

71. Ibid. 33-4.
72. Rowntree, *Essays and addresses*, 146.
73. Fleming, 'Interim report', appendix C, JRF JRCT93/VI/1 (f). The appendices are archived separately from the main body of the report.
74. Fleming, *Lighted mind*, 58-9.
75. Ibid. 58.
76. Fleming, *Beechcroft*, 78-80.
77. Henry A. Mess, *Industrial Tyneside: a social survey made for the Bureau of Social Research for Tyneside*, 1928, 8; *Common Room* xxii (1930), 4.
78. Williams, 'Educational settlements', 36-7; *Common Room* xxvii (1932), 13, xxviii (1932), 11.
79. Report on autumn term [1921], JRF JRCT93/IV/3 (d).
80. Quoted in Williams, 'Educational settlements', p. 147.
81. Pimlott, *Toynbee Hall*, 260-1.
82. Ibid. 260.
83. Horace Fleming, *Education through settlements, being an address delivered at the tenth annual conference of educational associations, University College London, on January 6th 1922*, ESA papers, no. 4, 1922, 3.
84. ESA, *Settlements and their work, from the point of view of the Educational Settlements Association*, ESA papers, no. 2, n.d., 3.
85. *Settlements and their outlook: an account of the first international conference of settlements, Toynbee Hall, London, July 1922*, ed. Basil A. Yeaxlee, 1922, 82, 96.
86. Ibid. 161.
87. Rowntree, *Essays and addresses*, 190.
88. Ibid. 182.
89. Ibid. 148.
90. Joseph Rowntree, memorandum of 16 April 1919, inset in JRCT minute book, no. 1, pp. 241-2.
91. [E. B. Castle,] *Quaker education and the Society of Friends*, 1929, 5, 7 (quoted). The pamphlet was reprinted from *The Friend*.
92. H. Winifred Sturge and Theodora Clark, *The Mount School, York, 1785 to 1814, 1831 to 1931*, 1931, 214-17.
93. JRCT minute book, no. 1, pp. 140-1. There is no record of this idea having been put into practice, although further support was given to various initiatives in the Quaker schools in subsequent years.
94. JRCT minute book, no. 2, minute no. 78.
95. Ibid. minute nos. 142, 159 (b), 204 (a); 'JRCT conference, York, 24-26 February 1928', inset in JRCT minute book, no. 2 (at relevant date).
96. The following account is drawn from Rowntree, *Woodbrooke*, and Wilson, 'Post-war conditions'.
97. JRCT minute book, no. 2, minute no. 3.
98. Rowntree, *Essays and addresses*, 150. The quotation is not attributed.
99. JRCT minute book, no. 2, minute no. 204.
100. JRCT minute book, no. 1, pp. 252-3.11
101. Martin, *Adult school movement*, 345-6; Rowntree, *Woodbrooke*, 26.
102. Joseph Rowntree, 'Decline of the membership of the adult schools', n.d., 1-3, JRF JR93/V/18 (b).

103. Allott, *John Wilhelm Rowntree*, 109ff.
104. *Cober Hill*, 1-2.
105. Rowntree, *Essays and addresses*, 145.
106. Ibid.
107. *Cober Hill*, 28.
108. Ibid. 3.
109. Ibid. 30, 7.
110. Ibid. 23. In 1926 the income tax authorities decided that the operation at Cober Hill was not legally charitable, and the responsibility was taken over by the JRSST.
111. JRCT minute book, no. 2, minute no. 22.
112. Ibid. minute no. 7.
113. Ibid. minute no. 224. There was a complete reorganisation of the Committee towards the end of 1926, when a new chairman, A. B. Searle, was appointed (minute no. 324 (b)).
114. Ibid. minute no. 338 (e).
115. On the increasing circulation of *The Friend* in wartime see memoranda in JRF JR93/V/20.
116. JRCT minute book, no. 2, minute no. 392 (b).
117. JRCT, 'Review of operations for the year 1935', 10, JRF JRCT93/I/11 (a).
118. Janet Scott, 'The making of an institution: the Swarthmore lecture 1907-1913', *Journal of Quaker Studies* i (1995): typescript copy in Friends House Library, shelved with *Quaker Studies*.
119. See Briggs, *Seebohm Rowntree*, esp. chs 7-8.
120. B. Seebohm Rowntree, *The human factor in business* (1st edn 1921), 1925, 177.
121. Jonathan S. Davies, 'Grounding the work of the JRCT: the Rowntrees and political and economic democracy'; unpublished paper, University of York, 2001.
122. Vernon, *Quaker business man*, ch. 16.
123. Rowntree, 'Labour unrest', 374. See above p. 55.
124. Rowntree, 'Labour unrest and the need for a national ideal', 498.
125. Briggs, *Seebohm Rowntree*, 268ff.
126. Rowntree, 'Report on the work done by the JRCT 1905-1939', 12-13.
127. Briggs, *Seebohm Rowntree*, 272ff.
128. Rowntree and Lasker, *Unemployment*.
129. J. J. Astor (ed.), *Is unemployment inevitable? An analysis and a forecast*, 1924; JRCT minute book, no. 2, minute no. 241. The JRCT contributed a one-off grant of £250 especially for the purpose of investigation into unemployment (minute no. 88).
130. JRCT minute book, no. 2, minute no. 176.
131. Ibid. minute no. 84.
132. Ibid. minute nos. 147, 151.
133. Ibid. minute no. 179.
134. Ibid. minute nos. 243, 348, 397 (e). The last two of these refusals came some time after Joseph Rowntree's death.
135. Ibid. minute no. 245.
136. Vernon, *Quaker business man*, 9.

CHAPTER 4

Widening fellowship and new forms of service: the JRCT after the Founder's death

AFTER JOSEPH Rowntree's death, the JRCT remained primarily a family concern (no new trustees were appointed for a further eleven years), but it began to operate on a somewhat more regularised basis. The number of unsolicited applications for grants continued to increase, as public knowledge of the Trust, especially within the Society of Friends, grew, and some paid secretarial support was taken on to assist with the demanding tasks of dealing with applications and maintaining a watching brief over the various initiatives the Trust supported.[1] The largest element of the Trust's expansion was the development of the new educational settlements: because many were far from Yorkshire, and were administered through the ESA, it was impossible to deliver the guidance that was still exercised at times over the Yorkshire 1905 Committee and the JRCT employees who worked mainly in Yorkshire. Having said this, the trustees themselves were actively involved at an individual level in many of the schemes which the JRCT funded. Stephen Rowntree was secretary and treasurer of the 1905 Committee, while Arnold Rowntree remained president of the ESA, and Frank Sturge was still warden of Woodbrooke. The diverse, if often interlocking, interests of the trustees were reflected in the decision made in 1925 to devolve areas of the Trust's grant-making to particular trustees; thus, although all decisions were made collectively, Arnold Rowntree and Ernest Taylor took particular reponsibility for adult education, Sturge for Woodbrooke, Stephen Rowntree and Ernest Taylor (again) for Friends' literature, and Seebohm Rowntree for social and economic work.[2] This last category was a relatively low priority for the trustees in this period, forming an average of less than eight per cent of total expenditure in the 1920s, and only climbing above ten per cent in the second half of the 1930s. The main area of Trust expenditure in the second half of the 1920s was still adult education, which was given a block grant each

89

year, separately administered, and mostly given to the ESA and then distributed to the different settlements. This grant represented about half the expenditure of the JRCT every year until 1933 (when it stood at £7,696), falling to around a third in the later 1930s. The Rowntrees themselves, based in York, unsurprisingly gave the bulk of their attention to the local settlement, St. Mary's, and to the Swarthmore settlement in nearby Leeds. Their philanthropy may have shifted to an extent from individuals to institutions, but the conception of individual service that had underpinned Joseph Rowntree's attitude to philanthropy remained of central importance to their work. The late 1920s were a time of profound soul-searching among members of the Society of Friends, and a period in which Quakers reasserted their social concern in the wake of political and social changes, and the JRCT, bereft of the personal leadership of its Founder, had to find new ways to respond to these changes without abandoning the central tenets of its approach to philanthropic giving.

Twenty years after the establishment of St. Mary's and Swarthmore, the educational settlements had reached what one observer called 'the healthy stage of having "growing pains"'.[3] Much of the pain arose from differences that had arisen over the internal governance of the settlements. Although the pioneers were justly proud of their achievements in helping to bring about a new (if unspectacular in terms of size) institutional provision of adult education in many parts of Britain, some of their claims for their work do not always stand up to close scrutiny. In particular, the claim that the settlements themselves were governed democratically, in line with their stated aim of promoting an educated democracy at large, was frequently contested. For all the rhetoric of 'citizenship', 'democracy' and 'fellowship', the governance of the settlements, at least in their early years, was in the hands of their patrician founders rather than their 'members'. For example, St. Mary's in York was governed by a committee, on which the students had no elected representatives until 1920, when the Students' Association was founded; the Association was entitled to send four representatives to the governing body. The Students' Association, as well as contributing to the sense of corporate life in and around the settlement (for example by publishing the settlement magazine), advanced the interests of all types of settlement student, although as there was an annual membership fee of a shilling it only included, in the early 1920s, about a quarter of the student body.[4] In 1923 a new constitution was agreed, in which the interests of the students and the paymasters were equalised on the committee to the extent that the Students' Association directly elected twenty members, the four officers of the settlement (the warden, the sub-warden, the treasurer and the secretary) sat *ex-officio*, and sixteen further members were co-opted from other interested bodies. At Beechcroft a council was established in 1917, consisting of representatives of the University of Liverpool, the local education authority, the

Birkenhead Trades and Labour Council, the WEA and the Mersey District Adult School Union and other interested bodies, but even at this most supposedly democratic of settlements it was an advisory council only until 1924, when the somewhat dictatorial founder Horace Fleming retired from the wardenship.[5] From 1921 the Students' Association was entitled to appoint three members to the council. As Fleming later recalled, this arrangement 'provided a satisfactory method whereby the council was kept in touch with the wishes of students';[6] but it ultimately gave those students only a limited degree of control over the settlement's activities.

Fleming, whose commitment to the democratisation of settlements remained equivocal throughout his life, feared that the establishment of a council and 'the emergence of the settlement as a public institution' would mean 'the institutionalizing of its work'.[7] Such an institutionalisation of the settlement's activities would compromise the spirit of 'fellowship', a development which must be guarded against even at the expense of giving the members of the settlement a full democratic say in its organisation. As the extension secretaries' conference at Colwyn Bay in 1912 implicitly recognised, the establishment of a continuous programme of educational activity in a single building might 'overshadow' the very spirit of 'fellowship' that they were anxious to promote.[8] Indeed, wherever there was a building, and wherever a sense of settlement identity was actively encouraged by the founders and the wardens, conflicts were likely to arise over the governance of the institution. Thus at St. Mary's the Students' Association repeatedly clashed with the executive committee, perhaps most notably when they protested at the methods used to appoint the new housekeepers in 1925, an appointment over which they felt they should have a say.[9] In 1921 Ernest Taylor, who in addition to his many other activities was chairman of the settlement's executive committee, had ruled that the students at the settlement had no automatic right to know the salaries paid to the warden and sub-warden;[10] and concern was expressed in 1923 that the propagandist activities of the Plebs League, inside and outside St. Mary's, had succeeded in 'shaking the faith of students in the Settlement itself'.[11] St. Mary's in particular was tainted with the suspicion that financial reliance on the Rowntree family prevented it from developing along genuinely democratic lines.[12] The JRCT trustees were ambivalent about the concession of democratic control to the settlement: Ernest Taylor explained ambiguously in 1923 that he feared 'that we may be so much in haste to label ourselves democratic without being able to achieve true democracy that we may risk the loss of vital things by the way'.[13] In any case, it was arguable that in terms of the development of the curriculum, the value of internal democracy was limited: one observer pointed out in 1938 that '[i]t is the function of Settlement leadership to persuade students to adopt a programme which has been thought out by an authority more competent and more aware of the difficulties and objectives than any student-body can possibly be. It is not fair to play at a democratic control which can have no real validity in such matters'.[14]

When political ideas with which the pioneers were uncomfortable did penetrate the settlements, attempts were speedily made to reassert control, often couched in the rhetoric of democracy and fellowship. In 1924 the executive committee of the ESA censured the Sheffield settlement, and its flamboyant warden Arnold Freeman, for allowing a communist Sunday school to meet on its premises, and the ESA was distinctly uneasy about the prospect of allowing the socialistic National Council of Labour Colleges to run courses on settlement premises.[15] Even Woodbrooke briefly came under socialist influence in the immediate post-war period.[16] The JRCT noted in 1924 that there was 'a real danger of ill-considered economic theories and proposals being encouraged in some of the Settlements', and the trustees were glad to hear that the ESA was giving the matter its urgent attention.[17] This problem was bound up with the wider question of the role of the settlements in educating for democratic participation, and the fact that it was viewed as a problem at all contributed to the perception among their critics that the educational settlements were essentially institutions aimed at defending capitalism against its socialist opponents. The charge that the Rowntrees and their colleagues were attempting in the most cynical way to 'educate their masters' was compounded by some of the statements they made, such as Arnold Rowntree speaking to the Co-operative Educational Conference in 1921:

> The aristocratic control of industry was easier than democratic control, but the more democratic that control became the more necessary was it to cultivate the virtues of patience, understanding and tolerance, and to have knowledge at the back in order to reach the wisest decisions. They must let their great universities know that democracy and industry needed their help with that object in view, and when they had settled on their reforms they must devote attention to teaching the workers to use their increasing leisure to higher purpose than at present.[18]

If they were not educated, the workers might fall foul of 'ill-considered economic theories'; and the ESA explained rather comically in 1938 that 'Settlements are not places to stave off revolution ... [but] Folk dances keep the earnest Marxist human, and Christian and Atheist are able to meet together in a community which is salted with humour'.[19] Unsurprisingly, then, the settlements were open to criticism from socialists, including many in the WEA. The WEA in York was especially suspicious of St. Mary's: as A. J. Peacock has explained, '[t]he Settlement was [established] to help the adult school movement, and the adult schools were equated with middle-class concepts and attitudes on fundamental social issues'.[20] Thus although WEA tutorial courses were held at St. Mary's from 1912, the settlement never managed wholly to free itself from 'the prejudice which exists against it, based on the idea that it is capitalist in origin and control'.[21]

The relationship between the ESA and the WEA remained uneasy throughout the interwar period; and, for example, in Leeds the long connection between the WEA and the Swarthmore settlement was eventually ended after the second world war.[22] WEA students were not attracted to settlements as places of study; and from the settlements' point of view, WEA classes, although held on settlement premises, were not thought to contribute to the spirit of fellowship that the settlements existed to promote. One commentator even suggested that it should be made clear to the WEA and other outside bodies that 'if they remain impervious to the notion of the Common Room they should be excluded from the Settlement altogether';[23] while in terms of the curriculum, there was a marked divide between the WEA students with their taste for economics, industrial history and similar subjects on the one hand, and the settlement students with their preference for 'aesthetics' (literature, music, art and drama) on the other.[24] Matters were not helped by the dependence of the settlements on voluntary or under-paid tutors and lecturers, who only taught at the settlement when they were available; this resulted in a poorly unified and inconsistent curriculum. There was little unity among the students either: when the St. Mary's Students' Association tried to instigate a course on 'civics' in 1925, it failed to attract the interest of the body of students as a whole, and had to be abandoned.[25] The failure of the common room to act as a unifying body was representative of the inability of most educational settlements to develop, and adhere to, a clearly delineated range of activities, and hence of their failure to achieve what was expected of them by their founders. As one critic described it in the 1930s, 'there is often revealed in the Settlement a neglect of the activities which the Common Room symbolises, a very inadequate attempt to cross-sectionalise the interests of the Settlement, to weld its rivalries of activity, to disperse differences of outlook and preoccupation in a sense of fundamental unity'.[26] For example, the development of drama and musical groups often took settlement members away from educational work, and created a faction – 'a sort of Settlement *Samurai*'[27] – that had little to do with the rest of the institution's activities. These groups also sometimes acquired a distinctive political identity: at St. Mary's the representatives of the Settlement Community Players at first refused to meet John Hughes, the new warden, in 1921, and appeared to resent the warden's right to veto any play they might choose to perform, a right reserved 'so that the good name of the Settlement is maintained'.[28] In many settlements, the religious content of the curriculum, or perhaps rather the religious atmosphere that sometimes pervaded the institutions, was the target for criticism: settlements were sometimes viewed as 'an Adult School dolled up',[29] while the warden of Swarthmore Hall, Plymouth, admitted ambiguously that the involvement of Quakers in the foundation of his settlement had both 'its dangers and its advantages'.[30]

Yet it was clear to most observers that the quantity of religion in settlement curricula was decreasing, and although this broadened the appeal of the settlements, it was unsettling for the Quakers themselves, who had seen in the movement an opportunity to strengthen the Society by training able social leaders who could go on to work in adult schools or participate in the vocal ministry. This was symptomatic of the spiritually impoverished state of the Society in this period, which was frequently commented on in the Friends' periodicals. Even at Woodbrooke, one lecturer recalled that during the 1920s '[t]he number of students who had enough interest to take at least one or two Biblical courses was decreasing; the idea was often prevalent that adequate human planning could construct the good world we all desired, without divine help ... it seemed as if the spiritual side of life was almost forgotten'.[31] Closer to home, the Yorkshire 1905 Committee was also struggling to maintain its previous position, and was heavily reliant on JRCT money, about which the trustees were uneasy, believing that the Committee should be the responsibility of the whole Quarterly Meeting.[32] The increasing difficulty in attracting recruits to Quaker voluntary service, and the apparent torpor of much of the Society of Friends in this period, in contrast to the flurry of post-Manchester, pre-first world war activity, bred a concern that British Quakerism might stagnate and even retreat into a modern equivalent of its eighteenth-century 'quietism'.

As at so many points in their history, Quakers were looking for a new, or at least a reinvigorated, spiritual and social purpose. Membership of the Society was in decline, and, perhaps more significantly, membership of the adult schools – still one of the most important avenues of connection between the Quakers and the wider society which they sought to serve – was also continuing to fall.[33] In the hope of encouraging wider participation in the vocal ministry, the practice of 'recording' ministers was abandoned by Yearly Meeting in 1924, and four years later saw the first substantial revision of the Friends' 'advices and queries' since those that had followed John Stephenson Rowntree's criticisms of the Society in 1859.[34] Nevertheless, it was felt, with much justification, that the optimism of 1895 had by this time been lost in the wake of the tribulations of the first world war and the decline of active social involvement among Quakers. Put simply, the Society was looking for a cause to attach itself to. The generation which had been so inspired by John Wilhelm Rowntree at Manchester was now growing old. Many of those whose eloquence had sent the Manchester delegates into their search for and fulfilment of a new

94

social purpose were dead, including William Braithwaite and Joseph Rowntree himself, who had strongly supported his son's efforts in the wake of the 1895 conference. John S. Hoyland, the JRCT-supported lecturer in modern history at Woodbrooke where he was also warden of Holland House, writing in the *Friends Quarterly Examiner* in 1930, remembered that the previous generation had experienced a great awakening and unleashed an outburst of energy into 'various enterprises of social hygiene in the immediate home-environment' and hoped for a similar response to the problems of his own period;[35] while the veteran American Quaker Rufus Jones saw the need for 'a new spiritual adventure'.[36] Jones saw the period as a kind of 'Dark Ages', in which the 'sufferings of humanity' had brought the inward spirituality, on which Quakerism was predicated, to a low ebb among mankind, and believed that people were looking for some kind of fresh vision that could lead them out of their profound confusion.[37]

Jones's proposal for the new spiritual adventure typified the uncertainties that bedevilled Friends on both sides of the Atlantic in the later 1920s. He recommended the establishment of a 'Wider Quaker Fellowship', to bring some of the principles and practices of Friends to seekers who may not have had easy access to a Quaker Meeting. This fellowship would, in the words of one biographer, be a 'looser, less completely organised group than the Society itself, which these people could join';[38] and unsurprisingly it attracted the criticism of conservative critics within the Society (in both Britain and America) because of the implied suggestion of a 'two-tier' membership, which was anathema to the doctrine of the inward Christ. Jones, never one to prevaricate, retorted that the 'wider fellowship' of which he spoke already existed (although Jones did not refer to them, attenders already had a somewhat anomalous position in Friends' Meetings), and that the problem facing Quakers was how to co-operate with it and potentially incorporate it into the Society.[39] As he explained to a joint meeting of the Friends Service Council and the Home Service Committee in 1929,

> There would be no conditions of membership in this fellowship except a readiness to dedicate oneself to the way of love, and a faith that man is a candle of the Lord and can become a center of radiance, an organ of the Spirit, just where he lives ... I am not interested any more in just clinging to the Society of Friends and preserving it ... We stand at a crisis and we can be bearers of the torch as our fathers were or can carefully husband a little flame and keep it from going out a little longer.[40]

This vision inspired some members of the Society, including the JRCT, who granted Jones up to £200 a year for two years in 1929 to advance his cause;[41] however, the vision remained inchoate and vague. Jones had to admit that he had 'no ready-made proposal of a method or a technique or a plan of organisation' for the wider fellowship,[42] and when it was eventually formed the Wider Quaker Fellowship (which is still in existence) was a small body built primarily around informal correspondence and the circulation of literature.[43] This kind of organisation would appeal to trustees who were trying to further Joseph Rowntree's philanthropic purposes, but the trustees themselves recognised that it was not enough: when they signalled their agreement to support Jones's plan, Seebohm Rowntree pleaded for a '[c]onference primarily devoted to the question of what Quakerism really does stand for, and how our faith is to be made an integral part of our life'.[44]

For Rowntree, as for many other Quakers, faith went hand-in-hand with social action, and he developed this point at more length in an article for the *Friends Quarterly Examiner* in 1927. Reiterating his father's insistence on the futility of 'superficial remedies' for social problems, Seebohm argued that the Church, 'as a corporate body' should be concentrating on the spiritual teaching of individuals and the community, as ultimately this was 'the only lasting means of curing our social and industrial ills'.[45] The Church's pastoral and philanthropic responsibilities had to be viewed within this over-arching necessity, and Rowntree recognised that the 1918 Yearly Meeting statement on the 'Foundations of a True Social Order' had clear implications for the industrial policy in which he was especially interested, as it suggested that the distribution of wealth should be arranged in the interests of 'the highest ends of the community'.[46] However, Rowntree insisted on the limitations of this duty in the political sphere, arguing that 'the Church will make a fatal error if it attempts to declare, in its corporate capacity, by what methods existing systems should be altered'.[47] In particular, and especially significantly in the context of the general strike the previous year, the Church should not intervene in industrial relations. This unambiguous statement of political neutrality was made in the context of a fresh challenge to the Society of Friends which had resulted in a division between the more conservative 'quietists' and the ambitious radical 'go-aheads'. The latter, influenced by socialism and inspired by Lucy Fryer Morland's Swarthmore lecture in 1918, appeared to want to ally the Society with the Labour party and to embrace wholeheartedly the policies of nationalisation of industry which many individual Quakers personally endorsed.[48] The election of the first Labour government in 1924 provided temporary encouragement to the collectivism supported by this wing of Quakerism, and it could be argued that the demise of the Socialist Quaker Society in the same year may have reflected no more than a growing acceptance of socialistic ideas within the mainstream of the Society, seen in the adoption of the 'Foundations of a True Social Order' in 1918.[49]

Whatever the political stance of the individual Quaker, it was recognised that the growth of state intervention in the economic and social life of the nation had far from obviated the responsibilities of, and far from diminshed the opportunities for, philanthropically-minded people, especially Quakers, to involve themselves in voluntary work. (Helen Sturge had made this point in her Swarthmore lecture in 1923.)[50] While it was a matter of debate whether Quakers should embrace the socialist revolution or not, it was clear that the involvement of members of the Society in practical philanthropic endeavour was not as great as it could be. There were many reasons for this, one being that their economic circumstances did not allow as many Quakers as formerly the opportunity to engage in voluntary work, either overseas or domestically: the JRCT noted that 'business is absorbing the energies of a greater proportion of our able men and women than formerly'.[51] More seriously, the dearth represented a more general decline in Quakerism, as addressed by Rufus Jones. In 1930 John S. Hoyland expressed the problem historically, linking spirituality, Bible knowledge and social involvement in much the same way as John Wilhelm Rowntree had done three decades earlier in his 'Plea for a Quaker Settlement':

> The current phase [of Quaker history] appears to be marked, on the one hand, by little interest in or knowledge of the history of Christian revelation: and on the other hand, perhaps as a consequence, by little desire to share in philanthropic activity ... there is ... growingly in evidence a tendency to stay away from meetings altogether, a motor-picnic in the country being felt to be more genuinely conducive to spiritual welfare than attendance at public worship, where unedifying ministry may be inflicted upon one.[52]

Unsurprisingly, then, many non-Friends saw the Quakers as 'intolerably self-centred and conceited', disinclined to social action.[53] Hoyland's solution to this problem was re-connection with Christ as the first step towards the re-establishment of 'a dynamic Quaker fellowship': this must be based on prayer and Bible study, firstly in the Quaker home and secondly in the Quaker school. If this was not achieved, then neither Rufus Jones's hoped-for 'revitalisation of our own membership' in the interests of the wider fellowship,[54] nor the reinvigoration of Quaker philanthropy, would be possible. In 1930, warned Hoyland, thirty-five years after the high point of the Manchester conference and its aftermath, 'we have reached a low spot: and ... the prospects ahead are none too bright'.[55]

The educational settlement movement remained at the centre of the wider conception of Quaker philanthropy, and the uncertainties over the future of the Society were echoed in the various attempts at re-evaluation undertaken within this movement in the later 1920s. The JRCT trustees, conscious of their pivotal role in the development of the educational settlement movement, and all with an interest in Quaker boarding schools, fostered this re-evaluation through a series of conferences and commissioned reports. In April 1926 a conference was held at Cloughton, attended by five of the six surviving trustees,[56] plus Herbert Wood of Woodbrooke, Horace Fleming, Basil Yeaxlee (who continued as secretary of the ESA until 1928), Frederick Gillman, at the time a vice-chairman of the NASU Council, and Dr. Charles Hodgson, warden of the Swarthmore settlement in Leeds and a former master at Bootham. Already aware that the JRCT was due to be wound up in thirteen years' time, the trustees engaged in a general discussion of the Founder's aims, and how they could be advanced given the present position of the Society of Friends. They were reminded that Joseph Rowntree and his fellow trustees 'largely provided the means for starting the non-residential Settlements and for developing them to their present point [and t]hey felt that the Educational Settlement was the natural method of growth of the principles animating the Adult School and Summer School movements'.[57] However, as we have seen above, the movement was not developing along the lines hoped for by many of the trustees, and several problems were identified that required further investigation. In particular, attention was drawn to the 'disappointing' effects of extension work at Woodbrooke and on the part of the Yorkshire 1905 Committee, and to the questionable role and effectiveness of the Quaker boarding schools. Not only were fewer volunteers able to give their time to adult education, but, just as importantly, despite the shortening hours of labour in much industrial and other employment in this period, the concomitant expansion of leisure-time opportunities was drawing many potential consumers of adult education into other pursuits; and in any case the educational settlements, the adult schools and the Workers' Educational Association appeared to be largely limited to 'the intellectuals only of labour'.[58] Adult learners were still dominated by the 'labour aristocracy' and lower-middle-class groups such as clerical workers: as the annual report of the Yorkshire North district branch of the WEA pointed out in 1922, '[m]en and women cannot be expected to show marked enthusiasm for education if they do not know where their next good meal is to come from or how the rent is to be paid.'[59]

For Quakers, Woodbrooke remained a particular area of concern. It did not appear to be strengthening the Society of Friends by providing able leaders, teachers and settlement wardens, and it was felt by some that even the diploma in social study may have outlived its usefulness by the 1920s. As Horace Fleming pointed out, the work of the Society and other bodies had 'shifted from social amelioration to the more constructive work of developing individual personality',[60] and, as Joseph Rowntree had repeatedly emphasised, this necessitated the training of strong and influential individuals for the work of personal service both to the Society

itself and to the wider community.[61] Woodbrooke, it was felt, was manifestly failing in its duties at the centre of the educational web that was
designed to deliver these trained individuals to the Quaker (and the wider)
community. During this period attendance at the college was 'encouraging' in terms of numbers,[62] but as Frank Sturge told the trustees some
years later (in 1934), of 47 students at Woodbrooke in a fairly typical term,
only a third were Quakers. About the same proportion were overseas students, and two-thirds were female.[63] A large group was taking the diploma
in social study; and it was remarked that there tended to be a substantial
divide between those taking this course and those engaged on more distinctively Quaker projects (as well as those taking the teacher training
course).[64] The director of studies, Herbert Wood, remarked in 1930 that
even the Bible study aspects of the college were failing to meet the needs
of the Society, Woodbrooke having failed to arrest 'a growing ignorance
of the Bible even among Friends'.[65] Moreover, the amalgamation of
Woodbrooke into the Selly Oak Colleges federation had further marginalised the role of Quakerism within the college. One commentator thought
that, while Woodbrooke was valuable, it was not producing people who
would 'leaven' the Society of Friends, at least not outside Birmingham.[66]
Although many who went to Woodbrooke in this period remembered a
powerful spiritual side to its work, and spoke with affection of the personalities and activities of the wardens and lecturers, many of the joys to
be found there were far removed from the visions of its founders. Although,
as Wood recalled, the establishment of a permanent 'Quaker settlement'
was intended to overcome the 'holiday spirit', which at summer schools
was found to be not always conducive to serious study,[67] many residents
appear to have concentrated on matters other than their work. One student, funded by a JRCT bursary,[68] who took the diploma in social study
in the late 1920s (under Sturge's wardenship) enjoyed the regular late-
night conversations in the common room, and took full advantage of the
favourable female-to-male ratio: he recalled his first meeting with a
'ravishing dewy-eyed young woman … [with a] particular brand of middle-
class accent', later 'fell violently in love' with a young Norwegian, and
soon afterwards found himself 'in love somewhat uncertainly with a beau-
tiful madonna-like Swiss girl'.[69] Although this particular resident eventually found himself a position as a warden of an educational settlement,[70]
his experience at Woodbrooke suggests that many students were not being
prepared for their future service in quite the way the pioneers had envisaged: this was one reason behind the repeated conferences between the
Rowntrees and other concerned Friends.

Following the Cloughton conference, it was agreed that 'an enquiry
into the teaching of religion in the Settlements' would be undertaken by
Horace Fleming, and funded by the JRCT under the direction of Arnold

Rowntree and Ernest Taylor.[71] This investigation soon acquired a wider remit, and, as eventually carried out from Fleming's temporary base at Woodbrooke, included the whole question of Quaker educational provision. Fleming's report drew attention to the problems of the Birmingham college, especially the perceived danger that the Selly Oak Colleges affiliation might marginalise the peculiarly Quaker character of Woodbrooke.[72] The pedagogical skills of the lecturers, he thought, were poor – one reason, perhaps, why the JRCT supported the employment of the inspirational teacher John S. Hoyland in 1928[73] – and few adult school teachers had availed themselves of the opportunity to improve their own teaching by attending Woodbrooke for a time.[74] For Fleming as for Joseph Rowntree, the personal direction of students and the development of leadership skills in an atmosphere of fellowship were the cornerstones of all Quaker education; and the difficulties in which some of the institutions found themselves caused him to wonder 'whether personal concern is becoming less operative in the Society than formerly, and if so, whether one of the causes is that the machinery of the institution is becoming too elaborate'.[75] Although the complexity of modern industrial organisation itself complicated the duties of citizenship in the modern world, the way to train for this new kind of citizenship was through an even more intensively individual type of education firmly grounded in the doctrines of the Inward Light.[76] Thus what Fleming saw as the failures of the ESA were due to the lack of 'leaders of the right type',[77] while Friends' Meetings themselves ought to become at least 'centres of a partial training' for this kind of leadership role.[78] Although individual connection was of the essence in this educational vision, Fleming nevertheless emphasised the importance of the permanent institution of education – as opposed to the itinerant teachers and missionary workers whom the JRCT sometimes supported – in the aim of 'the leavening of the local community life'.[79] Essentially, this vision, although it embraced the work of bodies such as the WEA, local authorities and the universities (all of which had been involved in the establishment of Fleming's own settlement in Birkenhead), was a Quaker vision, and entailed a Quaker conception of fellowship. As we have seen,[80] Fleming identified three stages in the education of the individual: the adult school, the educational settlement and, the most fulfilling of all, the Quaker Meeting.

However, the frequent complaint of Quaker educationalists was that the first two stages did not bring many recruits to the third stage, and into membership of the Society of Friends. It was difficult to translate Fleming's high-minded aspirations into a practical programme for the development of Quaker educational initiatives, and this was reflected in the fact that the result of Fleming's report was another conference, this time at York, in February 1928, which considered a wide range of topics but still expressed its conclusions largely in the form of further questions rather than answers. Attended by the JRCT trustees, Fleming himself, Gerald Hibbert and Herbert Wood, and with Fleming's report as its terms of reference, this conference was keen to promote greater co-operation between the adult schools, the educational settlements, the Quaker boarding schools and other institutions, although it was concerned about 'the dangers which exist of over centralisation of effort, with the paramount necessity of personal initiative and responsibility'.[81] Again the hope was expressed that both adult school teachers and, even more importantly, prospective settlement wardens, could be induced to spend some time at Woodbrooke, although it was recognised that few of the latter would be able or willing to do this without the guarantee of a job at the end of it.[82] Quaker school teachers, it was thought, would also benefit from a sabbatical, hopefully spent at Woodbrooke; while adult schools might be encouraged to take a further role in the development of educational settlement work.[83] Thus the essential interlinkage of all Quaker educational work, as expressed by Fleming, was endorsed wholeheartedly by this conference, which considered (but, typically, postponed for further discussion) a 'Programme of Evangelistic Education' put forward by Gerald Hibbert, which involved a cut in the number of Quaker boarding schools, more educational support for Quaker parents, the establishment of educational hostels aimed at children in areas where there were no Quaker schools, and more support for Woodbrooke as a Friends' institution.[84]

Whatever the hopes held by these leading Quaker educationalists, the practical results of the Cloughton and York conferences were negligible; and the same might be said for further events staged along similar lines during the next few years. One of the main recommendations of the York conference was (yet) another conference to consider Fleming's report as it would be amended after York, and this call was repeated at a meeting of the JRCT a few months later.[85] Further conferences were held during the next few years, including an inter-Trust meeting in July 1929, chaired by Colonel Mitchell of the Carnegie UK Trust, who appealed to the Rockefeller Trust to lend its support to the ESA, the NASU and other educational bodies;[86] and two meetings took place at Jordans in Buckinghamshire in 1929 and 1930, attended by a wider range of Quakers including Carl Heath (who spoke on the international dimension of Quaker education), Sir George Newman and Horace Fleming, who told delegates that, although brought up as a Congregationalist, he saw his Beechcroft experiment as 'the expression' of practical Quakerism.[87] However, the inter-Trust conference had hit on the real problem of the educational settlements in its plea to the Rockefeller Trust: there was insufficient money available, and if the settlements wished to be independent of the state and local authorities, alternative sources of funding had to be attracted. The JRCT had recognised this soon after the first world war, attempting without success to establish a new trust for adult education which would draw in other funding bodies.[88] The JRCT already had heavy demands on its comparatively small resources (a particular concern for a trust which was only expected to last until 1939 and which needed to make pension provision for its ageing group of employees) and as early as 1924 the trustees admitted that 'a larger sum of money than was justified by their income' had already been spent on the ESA.[89] The ESA itself was worried about overstretch: in 1923, soon after the flurry of new settlements in the optimism of the early post-war years, some pioneers were beginning to doubt 'whether it was wise to encourage the setting up of additional settlements in view of the needs of those already existing'.[90]

Running through all these discussions in the 1920s was the insistence among members of the JRCT that the most important task for the future was to bring gifted and committed people (Friends or otherwise) into the adult schools and the educational settlements, and the focus of the Trust's grant-making in this period was on the provision of salaries to those who, like Edward Grubb and Herbert Waller and other long-standing Trust employees, would graft their personalities onto the movements in which they worked and inspire others to do the same. This could be reinforced by appeal to Joseph Rowntree's 1904 memorandum, which exhorted the trustees not to spend money on buildings, but rather to 'strengthen the hands' of those who were doing the necessary work.[91] Rufus Jones, present by invitation at a JRCT meeting in 1923, thought that 'the chief problem [for the Society of Friends] was the want of inspired persons',[92] while at the York conference in 1928 it was agreed that '[p]ersons matter most'.[93] As early as 1905 Joseph Rowntree had insisted on the need 'to train leaders',[94] and in 1919 he had reiterated this point by insisting that it would be 'quite in accordance with my wishes that the Settlement work should be helped; the money given not to be available for bricks and mortar or for the rent and care of the rooms, but towards the remuneration of those who direct the Settlements or assist locally in their establishment'.[95] Training was essential: in 1923 the JRCT was glad to note that the Thomas Wall Trust had agreed to contribute to the 'Training of Wardens of Settlements', and in later years attempted to draw other bodies into this area of funding.[96] This kind of work was just as important within the Society of Friends itself: the York conference considered 'how to help men and women who have the larger gifts in visitation to carry out this work carefully and systematically and on a living concern. At every step the effort should be made to discover individuals likely to become "pillar" Friends in their districts.'[97] The successors to Edward Grubb and other inspirational leaders needed to be sought; and this aim emphasises the importance of the conception of personal service to the philanthropic and educational traditions in which the JRCT was operating.

As these discussions were taking place, a new experiment in educational settlement work was beginning, one which would have profound implications for the development of the movement in the subsequent decade, and which the JRCT was anxious to support as far as possible. The story of the new settlements and other educational ventures of the second half of the 1920s and the early 1930s have been told elsewhere, but the broad outlines bear repeating here.[98] The miners' lockout of 1926 precipitated the nine-day general strike between 3 and 11 May, and Yearly Meeting, convening in the same month in Manchester – a city with great resonance for socially concerned Friends – was acutely conscious of the distress caused by the industrial depression and intensified by the lockout, which in the case of the miners continued until the following winter. Although it was arguably contrary to the spirit of Quakerism to support one side or the other in the industrial conflict itself, members of the Society could be expected to sympathise with the sufferings of the unemployed and poorly paid; and some Quakers, from the 'go-ahead' wing of the Society, worked hard in support of the strikers.[99] Unemployment remained high in the coalfields throughout the remainder of the interwar period, and it was widely agreed that distress was at its worst in the Rhondda valleys in south Wales.[100] In some respects the acute social problems of the Rhondda gave the Society of Friends a cause worth supporting, and a Coalfields Distress Committee was established, co-chaired by Joan Mary Fry and the ubiquitous Horace Fleming. In 1928 Meeting for Sufferings authorised a general appeal by the Committee for financial and personal help.[101]

As with so many Quaker initiatives, however, independent activity by members of the Society pre-dated this officially-sanctioned appeal. When Horace Fleming visited the Rhondda in the course of preparing his report on education for the JRCT in 1926, in the course of his research into the position and prospects of Quaker adult education, he found that Friends were involved in the distribution of various forms of material relief at the request of the Ministry of Health, using the voluntary work of unemployed men and women in the process. People were grateful for the 'entire absence of religious or institutional propaganda' that went with the provision of this relief – a long-standing feature of Quaker philanthropy, and one which had been praised in the past[102] – and there was plenty of opportunity for educational endeavour on top of this work.[103] Early visitors to the Rhondda included Arthur Gillett's brother Joseph Rowntree Gillett,[104] A. D. Lindsay (A. L. Smith's successor as Master of Balliol, who was married to a Quaker, although not a Friend himself) and Roger Cowan Wilson, an Oxford undergraduate, Quaker and socialist, who supported the general strike.[105] As we will see, Wilson was later to join the JRCT and become its chairman and its most influential trustee. However, the most prominent recruit from within the ranks of Quakerism was Emma Noble,[106] who in June 1926 answered Yearly Meeting's call and went to lodge with a mining family at Tonypandy to learn about conditions at first hand. Noble's husband William was president of the Engineers' Union branch in the Great Western Railway works at Swindon, and was himself working half-time as a result of the industrial depression; he was soon to follow her to the Rhondda. As a result of the time they had spent at Ruskin College, Oxford, the Nobles were friendly with the Gillett family, and in due course joined the Society of Friends themselves. As a result of the Gillett link, in combination with Fleming's report and other personal contacts, the Rowntrees became associated with the south Wales work at an early stage, albeit indirectly. As early as 1926 the JRCT awarded a small grant of £5 towards a trip by the editor of the *Northern Echo*, Luther Worstenholme (who was simultaneously preparing a biography of Joseph Rowntree, also supported by the Trust), to the Rhondda to 'study mining conditions';[107] and the trustees in subsequent years made an annual grant of £100 towards the Nobles' educational work.[108] The JRCT took notice of what was going on in south Wales and other districts, and the trustees sought ways of assisting the relief effort, preferably in ways that would strengthen the educational work of their Trust and the Society of Friends as a whole. Thus in 1928 the York conference was exhorted to '[r]emember Friends can inspire movements with their spirit just as they have inspired individuals'.[109]

The support for these ventures was not given wholly in the cause of disinterested relief and educational work: it had a political and industrial purpose as well. The Rowntree family were uneasy at the escalation of industrial discontent after the first world war, and at the accompanying growth of industrial and political militancy – much of the educational and social work of the settlements was directed towards the modification of such militancy – and Seebohm in particular feared the communist threat in the 1920s. He was involved in negotiations to bring the miners' lock-out to an end in 1926, and although he gave a much stronger endorsement to the principle of trade unionism than had his father, he mistrusted the militancy that was on display in the mid-1920s.[110] Other family members shared his concern; thus at the JRCT meeting held immediately prior to the York conference Arnold Rowntree

> spoke of the very serious condition of the mining areas in this country and expressed the fear that things were being allowed to drift. It was resolved that if B. S. Rowntree should see any way in which further work for industrial peace could be done in relation to this question, the Trustees would receive favourably an application for help.[111]

It was as important to maintain 'industrial peace' as it was to distribute relief, and it was felt that adult educational initiatives were one of the best ways to advance this cause. Horace Fleming, reporting on educational opportunities in the Rhondda, was similarly concerned that the National Council of Labour Colleges had gained a strong foothold in the area, 'with its condemnation of existing economic conditions and its doctrine of the class war'; and the failure of the strong Nonconformist infrastructure to shore up its position in the valleys with tangible relief measures or the provision of educational opportunities led him to the conclusion that 'the clergy's failure has meant the demagogue's gain'.[112] Fleming found cause for optimism, though, in the Nobles' educational work, based on what he rather vaguely termed 'simple groups ... without labels', which he hoped would exert its influence along existing vectors of community life if the JRCT or some other body could nurture it by providing premises and support for employees or volunteers.[113] Fleming's vision was to be of central importance to the future of the educational settlement movement: within a few months of the delivery of his report the Nobles had been appointed wardens of a new settlement, Maes-yr-Haf, in Trealaw, a mile from Tonypandy.

Maes-yr-Haf – the name means 'Summer Meadow' – grew from a committee established in January 1927, originally comprised of Henry and Lucy Gillett of Oxford, Joseph Rowntree Gillett, Robert Davis (the Woodbrooke Extension Secretary), Joan Mary Fry, A. D. and Erica Lindsay, and George Peverett, a leading figure in the adult school movement. With the exception of A. D. Lindsay, all were Quakers; and they were joined in the following year by four more Friends, including Fleming himself and Basil Yeaxlee, who resigned the secretaryship of the ESA in 1928.[114] In the words of Yeaxlee's successor William Hazelton, the aim of Maes-yr-Haf was to create 'a hearth and a home of adult education', and to foster 'fellowship wider than sect, party or class': language very similar to that used by the early educational settlement pioneers.[115] Much of the early organisation was directed from Oxford, where the Gilletts and Lindsays were based, and as such there are parallels with the early social settlements of the 1880s; indeed, Barrie Naylor (a veteran of Quaker work in the Rhondda) points out that there was some local nervousness, not to say antagonism, to be overcome before the work of the settlement could be carried on efficiently and free from opposition.[116] As an early ESA report noted, a settlement 'must spring out of the needs and desires of the neighbourhood where it is situated, and ought not to be planted down from outside merely because people at a distance think they would like to see a Settlement there'.[117] The fact that Maes-yr-Haf was, unavoidably, partly residential probably reinforced the sense of middle-class patronage which any such settlement venture was likely to evoke during this period. In 1928, in another reinvention of the settlement idea, at the behest and through the organisation of Roger Wilson, groups of earnest young men from the Oxford University Labour Club made weekend and vacation visits to the coalfield.[118] Similarly, the establishment of the Malthouse in 1932, a Cober Hill-type residential centre near the Glamorgan coast under the wardenship of George M. L. Davies, where unemployed miners could go for periods of intensive physical training, also provoked some opposition.[119]

The settlement, and Quaker relief in south Wales in general, was intended to be organised on the self-help principle, and it was envisaged that the main work of Maes-yr-Haf would consist of occupational training, the enjoyment of rational recreation, and adult education activities which aimed at the longer-term welfare of the unemployed miner and his family rather than the meeting of immediate material needs. However, the sheer scale of the social problems encountered by the Quakers in the Rhondda meant that somewhat inevitably the settlement came to take on much of the short-term relief work that pioneers such as Emma Noble had engaged in during the dark days of the strike. As one early relief worker recalled, '[a]lmost unawares and in spite of itself, [the settlement became] the base of relief operations covering a population of over 160,000 in the two Rhondda Valleys, and stretching out to outlying districts beyond.'[120] To borrow Joseph Rowntree's words, it was all very well to seek out the 'underlying causes' of social problems and to eschew remedies for their 'superficial manifestations', but with a problem of this magnitude it was impossible to address matters without first handing out some kind of material relief. For example, Maes-yr-Haf was involved in the provision of a soup kitchen, distributing heavily subsidised refreshment.[121] Nevertheless, as time went on the relief work was gradually scaled down, and adult education and various cultural activities were foregrounded: especially popular were lectures on philosophy and political theory, and on economics, 'because men wanted to know why they were out of work'.[122]

Another successful educational experiment at Maes-yr-Haf was the women's citizenship class, established in 1929 and taught by Emma Noble herself,[123] a particularly challenging and useful class for women whose geographical and socal horizons had hitherto been limited, and timely given that women had finally achieved political equality with men in 1928. This class helped to overcome the reluctance of miners' wives, with their traditionally home-centred lives, to attend classes.[124] Maes-yr-Haf affiliated to the ESA in 1930; and in 1931 began in earnest the extension work for which it became best known. By the following year, ten unemployed clubs had been established in the district surrounding the settlement; these clubs gave unemployed men the opportunity to learn new skills, such as

106

shoe-repairing, carpentry and metalwork, to engage in cultural activities such as drama and music, and to keep themselves physically fit through organised training.[125] Eventually the number of such clubs reached forty, not all under the control of Maes-yr-Haf;[126] and some clubs, such as the Community House at Brynmawr (started by the Coalfields Distress Committee) and the unemployed men's club at Dowlais, both established in 1928, later evolved into educational settlements.[127] As if to emphasise the conception of citizenship and social leadership that lay behind the south Wales institutions, no less than the older educational settlements, William Hazelton pointed to the role of Maes-yr-Haf as 'a place of vantage from which the whole social scene in the Rhondda could be closely observed and studied';[128] and in the 1930s some of the settlements would involve themselves in social survey work.[129] The education received by many of the unemployed men enabled them to gain a new vantage point on their situation in the valley and hence to reassess their own lives. Some successful students graduated to courses at residential colleges, including Fircroft in Birmingham and Coleg Harlech in Snowdonia (founded in the same year as Maes-yr-Haf, 1927), and many of these students 'returned to give valued leadership in their own club and district'.[130] Others, realising the limited opportunities that were likely to come their way in the declining staple industries of south Wales, moved away 'to places like Birmingham, Coventry and Slough',[131] where new industries, above all automobile manufacture, afforded more secure and generally better remunerated employment.

The experiment at Maes-yr-Haf was followed by similar ventures elsewhere, some involving Quakers from the beginning and others with only a more distant connection with the Society, but all growing from the same kind of concern that had lain behind the establishment of the first educational settlements in York, Leeds and Birkenhead. Settlements in south Wales followed at Merthyr Tydfil (1930), Risca (1931), Rhymney and Bargoed (1933), Pontypool (1934), Dowlais (1935), Aberdare (1936) and Pontypridd (1937), each serving a population of around 70,000.[132] The Risca settlement, known as Oxford House in another echo of the establishments of the 1880s, was set up by 'members of the City and University of Oxford'; while in another distressed area, the extreme northwest of England, a settlement at Maryport was established by the Cumberland Friends Unemployment Committee.[133] The new settlements were less dependent on Rowntree money than most of their predecessors – they sought and received support from the Carnegie UK Trust, the Pilgrim Trust, the Ministry of Labour and other sources – but many of the ideals they shared were very similar. Like the early ESA settlements, they were keen to become recognised adult education providers and hence to receive official funding; but they did not wholly abandon a religious and voluntary conception of adult education. Thus D. E. Evans, one south Wales settlement pioneer, remarked that

> The work of a Settlement is permanently needed. The aims are comradeship, social service and research ... The Settlement enterprise needs to be regarded as the extra-mural work of the church[,] the university and the state. Of the state, financially through voluntary organisations; of the university, educationally; of the church, morally and spiritually.[134]

It is unnecessary to describe here in any detail the work of the settlements in the distressed areas, but it is worth quoting the assessment made by the historian of the Merthyr Tydfil settlement, which summarises the achievements and failings of the institution, noting also the problem of democratic governance which it shared with the settlement at York:

> At a time of great economic distress the Settlement had met a particular problem with courage and vision. It had become for the more mature and balanced section of the population a haven, a focal area within which their creative energies could be channelled. It did not achieve the place it deserved in the life of the local community partly because of the lack of local representation on the committee and partly because it appeared initially as the manifestation of the tail-end of Victorian patronage, a salve to uneasy consciences. Nevertheless, the Settlement, despite its deficiences and financial struggles, recognized a need and within its limitations attempted to remedy a desperate situation.[135]

The new settlements were taken under the wing of the ESA very quickly. Although the JRCT was unable to take as close an interest in the development of Maes-yr-Haf and its successors as it could in the Yorkshire settlements, the trustees retained close contacts through their relationship with the Gillett family and their connections in the ESA. They broadly welcomed the extension of the model they had themselves done so much to create. Thus, six years after the establishment of Maes-yr-Haf, Seebohm Rowntree confidently 'drew particular attention to the discriminating nature of the education given in these Settlements [in the distressed areas] ... and to the evidence ... of the success of the effort made to enlarge the outlook on life'.[136] Nevertheless, the pioneers were beginning to lose their control over the settlements they had created, and new settlements were being established under different forms of concern from that which had animated the Edwardian originators of Swarthmore, St. Mary's and Beechcroft. As we will see, the Quaker dimension of the education these bodies provided would soom be subsumed under a more secular adult education which more clearly met the demands of a mass audience, whose political consciences had been stirred into greater activity by the general strike and the coming of mass unemployment.

NOTES

1. Arnold Rowntree to Mrs D. Hartwell, 8 November 1933, JRF JRCT93/I/13 (c), refers to the death of E. Remmer, secretary of the JRCT from 1925 to 1933. Remmer's appointment was evidently not full-time.
2. Untitled memorandum [1925], JRF JRCT93/I/10 (g).
3. *The Friend*, 11 January 1929, 40.
4. Hughes to Taylor, 15 May 1925, JRF JRCT93/IV/3 (e).
5. Fleming, *Beechcroft*, 83-4.
6. Ibid. 84.
7. Ibid.
8. 'Report of conference of extension secretaries held at Colwyn Bay, 25-7 May 1912', JRF JRCT93/VI/1 (a); see above, pp. 73-4.
9. Hughes to Taylor, 7 April 1925, JRF JRCT93/IV/3 (e).
10. Crosland to Taylor, 23 December 1921, JRF JRCT93/IV/3 (e).
11. 'Memorandum on democratic control of settlements', JRF JRCT93/IV/3 (d).
12. See Peacock, 'Adult education in York', 286ff.
13. Taylor to Hughes, 25 January 1923, JRF JRCT93/IV/3 (e).
14. Williams, 'Educational settlements', 74.
15. Allaway, *Educational centres movement*, 25.
16. Wilson, 'Post-war conditions', 53-4.
17. JRCT minute book, no. 2, minute nos. 185 (b) (quoted), 203.
18. *Yorkshire Herald*, 29 March 1921, press cutting in JRF ROWN.FAM.L/93/6.
19. ESA, *Community education, being a description of the work of residential and non-residential colleges for adult education*, 1938, 8.
20. Peacock, 'Adult education in York', 287.
21. 'Memorandum on democratic control of settlements', 2.
22. Harrison, *Workers' education in Leeds*, 24-5.
23. Williams, 'Educational settlements', 139.
24. Report on autumn term [1921], JRF JRCT93/IV/3 (d).
25. Minutes of executive committee, 26 November 1925, JRF JRCT93/IV/3 (c).
26. Williams, 'Educational settlements', 69.
27. Ibid. 68.
28. Hughes to Taylor, 19 December 1921, Baines to Taylor, n. d., JRF JRCT93/IV/3 (e).
29. Williams, 'Educational settlements', 118.
30. *Common Room* xxvii (1932), 12.
31. Wilson, 'Post-war conditions', 71.
32. JRCT minute book, no. 2, minute nos. 45, 233 (d).
33. Membership stood at 51,917 in 1924-5, and fell to 48,116 in 1928-9; however, the new practice of recording junior members as part of the total masked a much greater decline, of about a third among men and more than 10% among women (Hall, *Adult school movement*, 213).
34. Alastair Heron, *Quakers in Britain: a century of change 1895-1995*, Kelso 1995, 42-4.
35. John S. Hoyland, 'The present need of the Society of Friends', *Friends Quarterly Examiner* lxiv (1930), 43-4.
36. *The Friend*, 8 November 1929, 994.

37. Hinshaw, *Rufus Jones*, 205-6.
38. Vining, *Friend of life*, 267.
39. *The Friend*, 8 November 1929, 993.
40. Quoted in Vining, *Friend of life*, 267.
41. JRCT minute book, no. 3, minute no. 43 (a).
42. *The Friend*, 8 November 1929, 994.
43. Hinshaw, *Rufus Jones*, 207; there were 100 members in 1937, and the numbers reached 4,000 in 1952 (Vining, *Friend of life*, 269).
44. JRCT minute book, no. 3, minute no. 43 (a).
45. B. Seebohm Rowntree, 'The function of the Society of Friends with regard to social and industrial questions', *Friends Quarterly Examiner* lxi (1927), 266, 268.
46. Ibid. 270-1.
47. Ibid. 271.
48. John Pease Fry, 'The function of the Society of Friends with regard to social and industrial questions', *Friends Quarterly Examiner* lxi (1927), 273-9. The article had the same title as Rowntree's piece in the same volume.
49. Adams, *Far-seeing vision*.
50. See above, p. 66-7.
51. JRCT conference, Cloughton, 17-18 April 1926, visitors' memorandum, JRF JRCT93/VI/3.
52. Hoyland, 'Present need', 44-5.
53. Ibid. 45.
54. *The Friend*, 8 November 1929, 994.
55. Hoyland, 'Present need', 46.
56. Seebohm Rowntree was absent.
57. JRCT conference, Cloughton, 17-18 April 1926, visitors' memorandum, JRF JRCT93/VI/3.
58. Ibid.
59. Quoted in W. E. Styler, *Yorkshire and Yorkshire North: the history of the Yorkshire North district of the Workers' Educational Association 1914-1964*, Leeds 1964, 15.
60. [Horace Fleming], memorandum 'For discussion by the JRCT', n.d. [1926], JRF JRCT93/VI/3.
61. Founder's memorandum, 2-3; memorandum of 16 April 1919, inset in JRCT Minute book, no. 1, pp. 241-2.
62. JRCT minute book, no. 2, minute no. 339 (a).
63. JRCT minute book, no. 3, minute no. 334 (a).
64. Fleming, 'Interim report', appendix C, JRF JRCT93/VI/1 (e).
65. Herbert G. Wood, 'Woodbrooke and the Society of Friends', *Friends Quarterly Examiner* lxiv (1930), 143.
66. Castle, *Quaker education*, 11.
67. Herbert G. Wood, 'The first director of studies', in Davis, *Woodbrooke*, 27.
68. JRCT minute book, no. 3, minute no. 6 (a).
69. W. David Wills, 'A sense of vocation', typescript memoir [1976], pp. 105-6, JRF JRCT93/VII/10.
70. Oxford House, Risca.
71. JRCT minute book, no. 2, minute no. 309.

72. The Young Women's Christian Association joined the Selly Oak Colleges in 1926, and Avoncroft residential college in the same year; the College of the Ascension joined in 1929 and Overdale College in 1931 (John S. Hoyland, 'Woodbrooke and the Selly Oak Colleges', in Davis, *Woodbrooke*, 169-84, and list of Selly Oak Colleges (omitting Avoncroft), at 191).

73. See items on Hoyland in file on Trust servants, JRCT basement archive, box 45.

74. Fleming, 'Interim report', appendix C.

75. Ibid. 9.

76. Ibid. 29ff.

77. Ibid. 36.

78. Fleming, *Lighted mind*, 65.

79. Fleming, 'Interim report', 33-4; see above, p. 75.

80. See above, p. 75.

81. JRCT conference, York, 24-26 February 1928, inset in JRCT minute book, no. 2 (at relevant date).

82. Ibid.

83. Ibid.

84. Ibid.

85. Ibid.; JRCT minute book, no. 2, minute no. 410.

86. JRCT minute book, no. 3, minute no. 29.

87. Jordans invitation conference, 12-13 Oct. 1929, second Jordans conference, 13-15 June 1930, reports in JRF JRCT93/VI/3.

88. JRCT minute book, no. 2, minute nos. 37, 47.

89. Ibid. minute no. 185 (d).

90. Ibid. minute no. 120.

91. Founder's memorandum, 3.

92. JRCT minute book, no. 2, minute no. 138.

93. JRCT conference, York.

94. Joseph Rowntree, 'The problems of bridging the gulf between the adult schools and the church, and of the creation of a vigorous Quaker church: some general considerations' (1905),10: privately circulated pamphlet, copy in JRF JR93/V/18 (a).

95. Joseph Rowntree, memorandum of 16 April 1919, inset in JRCT minute book, no. 1, pp. 241-2.

96. JRCT minute book, no. 2, minute no. 157; no. 3, minute no. 403 (b).

97. JRCT conference, York.

98. See esp. Naylor, *Quakers in the Rhondda*; Allaway, *Educational centres movement*, ch. 4; J. Elfed Davies, 'Educational settlements in south Wales, with special reference to the Merthyr Tudful settlement', *Transactions of the Honourable Society of Cymmrodorion*, session 1970, part 2, 177-98; William Hazelton, *Maes-yr-Haf 1927-1952: an account of 25 years of work and friendship in the Rhondda valley*, Rhondda [1952]; Alan Phillips, *Maes-yr-Haf: the time – the place*, Rhondda [1996]; *Common Room* xxx (1933). Hazelton's pamphlet can be consulted in Friends House Library, box 045: Maes-yr-Haf Settlement annual reports, etc.

99. See for example Fred Brown, *The making of a modern Quaker: Roger Cowan Wilson 1906-1991*, 1996, 15-18.

100. There are two Rhondda valleys, Rhondda Fach and Rhondda Fawr.
101. *The Friend*, 12 October 1928, 906.
102. See Helen E. Hatton, *The largest amount of good: Quaker relief in Ireland 1654-1921*, Montreal 1993, esp. 167, 252.
103. Fleming, 'Interim report', appendix E (dated 25 November 1926), JRF JRCT93/VI/1 (f).
104. For an account of Gillett's involvement see Davies, *Joseph Rowntree Gillett*, 57ff. Gillett had been president of the NASU in 1925-6 (Hall, *Adult school movement*, 108, 150-1).
105. Brown, *Making of a modern Quaker*, 15ff.
106. The following account of Emma and William Noble is drawn mainly from Hazelton, *Maes-yr-Haf*; Naylor, *Quakers in the Rhondda*; Phillips, *Maes-yr-Haf*; and Davies, *Joseph Rowntree Gillett*.
107. JRCT minute book, no. 2, minute no. 332 (c).
108. Ibid. minute no. 392 (c); no. 3, minute nos. 24 (b), 56 (c), 258 (c).
109. JRCT conference, York.
110. Briggs, *Seebohm Rowntree*, 255ff; Davies, 'Grounding the work'.
111. JRCT minute book, no. 2, minute no. 393.
112. Fleming, 'Interim report', appendix E.
113. Ibid.
114. For a full list, see Naylor, *Quakers in the Rhondda*, 109, 113ff.
115. Hazelton, *Maes-yr-Haf*, 3; quoted in Allaway, *Educational centres movement*, 30.
116. Naylor, *Quakers in the Rhondda*, 33.
117. ESA, *Settlements and their work*, 3-4.
118. Brown, *Making of a modern Quaker*, 19-23.
119. Naylor, *Quakers in the Rhondda*, 57.
120. Lucy M. Hawkins, *Maes-yr-Haf*, n.d., 3. This pamphlet was reprinted from the *Common Room* and the pages are not numbered: the first page of text has been taken as page 1.
121. Ibid. 3-4.
122. Hazelton, *Maes-yr-Haf*, 4; Naylor, *Quakers in the Rhondda*, 33, 36 (quoted).
123. Naylor, *Quakers in the Rhondda*, 35-6.
124. *Common Room* xxx (1933), 13-14.
125. See Naylor, *Quakers in the Rhondda*, 43, for an example of the varied activities of such clubs.
126. Ibid. 47.
127. Davies, 'Educational settlements in south Wales', 182-3.
128. Hazelton, *Maes-yr-Haf*, 5.
129. Davies, 'Educational settlements in south Wales', 188.
130. Hazelton, *Maes-yr-Haf*, 9-10.
131. Naylor, *Quakers in the Rhondda*, 36-7.
132. Davies, 'Educational settlements in south Wales', 182-5.
133. Allaway, *Educational centres movement*, 31.
134. Quoted in Davies, 'Educational settlements in south Wales', 181.
135. Ibid. 198.
136. JRCT minute book, no. 3, minute no. 258 (a).

CHAPTER 5

Quaker service, mass unemployment and the problem of leisure: the JRCT in the 1930s

ALTHOUGH INTERNATIONAL issues were foregrounded in the public mind as the 1930s progressed, and although the problem of mass unemployment generated new schemes of philanthropy and new strategies of social investigation, during these years the JRCT remained firmly attached to its Yorkshire roots and still aimed above all else at the strengthening of Quakerism. Even in August 1936, when attention was focused on the International Peace Campaign, the outbreak of the Spanish civil war, the end to the war in Abyssinia and the rearmament debates, all of which had serious ramifications for the nation and for the Society of Friends, Ernest Taylor could still refer to the JRCT as 'the York Trust'.[1] The majority of the expenditure still went on educational settlements and Quaker ministry, with a smaller amount on social investigation, including Seebohm Rowntree's follow-up poverty survey of York, also carried out in 1936. As a small trust, certainly in comparison with such bodies as the Rockefeller Foundation and the Carnegie Endowment for International Peace, the JRCT could not expect to be able to make a significant impact on the large-scale projects demanded by the national and international problems that forced themselves onto the political agenda of the 1930s. The remit of the Trust, therefore, remained localised and the trustees were still reluctant to diversify their grant-making beyond what they could realistically oversee to some extent themselves. Indeed, only two new trustees were appointed in the whole period between 1922 and 1947: Christopher Rowntree, Arnold's son, and John Wilfred Harvey, Arnold's brother-in-law, both in 1936. Before the appointment of these two, the trustees were Seebohm, Arnold and Stephen Rowntree, Ernest Taylor, Arthur Gillett and Francis Sturge, all of whom, as it were, had grown old in the service of the Trust and all of whom brought their own interests and preconceptions – and arguably prejudices – to their views of the directions the Trust's grant-making ought to take. Therefore, as will be seen, the Trust's activities lacked coherence in the 1930s, perhaps inevitably given the apparent scale of the social and political problems that both the state and the voluntary sector were called upon to face, but intensified in the York context by the activities of a group of trustees who were signally failing to appoint enough younger trustees with direct experience of the kind of work they were trying to fund, and watching the institutions they had helped to create appear increasingly obsolete in the face of new economic and social imperatives and new sources of state and municipal financial support. It was only at end of the decade, as the initial thirty-five year lifespan of the Trust came to an end, that trustees began to take stock of what they had done and to develop strategies for the expenditure of the income of a re-founded Charitable Trust.

The main domestic political issue of the period was undoubtedly mass unemployment. During the interwar years registered unemployment never fell below a million, and in the trough of the depression in the early 1930s it topped three million, much of which was concentrated in the 'distressed areas', later re-labelled 'Special Areas' – South Wales, Tyneside, West Cumberland and industrial Scotland – under the Special Areas Act of 1934. These officially designated areas in no way encompassed all the places which experienced high unemployment, but they entailed a recognition on the part of the National government (which had come to power following the defection of Ramsay MacDonald and other Labour leaders and the fall of the minority Labour government in 1931) that special efforts needed to be made to fight the economic and social problems of regions in which declining staple industries provided the bulk of employment opportunities. The problems of these areas were brought to public attention in books such as Ellen Wilkinson's *The town that was murdered* (1939) – the story of Jarrow – and *The problem of the distressed areas* (1937) by Wal Hannington, leader of the National Unemployed Workers' Movement, which at its peak in 1931-2 commanded a membership of between 50,000 and 100,000. This was only a small proportion of the unemployed, but a particularly visible portion, represented in mass demonstrations and hunger marches across the country, some of which ended in violence and provoked coercive responses from a somewhat bewildered and ill-prepared state. The concentration of long-term unemployment in the regionally specific staple industries intensified the contrast between the high-employment economy of the south of England, characterised by new industries, for example automobile manufacture in Oxford, Coventry, Luton and elsewhere, and the depressed heavy industrial sector. Britain was divided into two nations, one enjoying the fruits of the consumer revolution, the other living on bare subsistence incomes provided by the Unemployment Assistance

Board. A weakened Labour movement, whose party was heavily defeated in the general election of 1935 by the incumbent National government, found itself unable to provide the leadership that working-class communities required.

The apparent inability of the existing state machinery to deal with distress on the scale experienced during the depression necessitated the mobilisation of the voluntary sector in the provision of short-term relief, and a reassessment of the contribution the sector needed to make in order to help ensure the social regeneration of the depressed areas. Education played a key role in this: the educational settlement model was transferred to the Special Areas and the new institutions enjoyed statutory support for their vocational and non-vocational adult education provision. Although it is a matter of debate whether voluntary provision for the unemployed was given in a disinterested charitable spirit or whether it was simply a means of 'keeping the jobless occupied' with meaningless tasks to deflect their attention from political demagogery, there is no doubt that it was given on an immense scale and that it did make a substantial difference to the lives of many of the unemployed men in the Special Areas and their families. It also entailed new vectors of partnership between voluntary bodies and statutory authorities. Thus the National Council for Social Service (NCSS), established in 1919, was involved in the formation of centres for the unemployed in which training and recreational opportunities were provided (and which sometimes developed into educational settlements or, more commonly, community centres); and these centres were supported by grants from the Special Areas Commissioners, appointed by the Act of 1934. One such commissioner, it should be mentioned in passing, was George Masterman Gillett, a Labour MP and brother of Arthur and Joseph Rowntree Gillett. Another important source of funding for these projects came from bodies such as the Carnegie UK Trust, the Ratan Tata Foundation (an Indian foundation which had supported the establishment of the Department of Social Administration at the London School of Economics before the first world war) and the new Pilgrim Trust, founded in 1930 by E. S. Harkness.[2] The Nuffield Fund for the Relief of Distress in Special Areas, of which Seebohm Rowntree became a trustee in 1936, also devoted a lot of attention and money to the problem of mass unemployment, although Rowntree found the work frustrating and continued to press for further scientific investigation of social problems. The point about all these endeavours, statutory and voluntary, was that they were endowed with substantial funds, with which the limited assets of the JRCT could not compete. They aimed at large-scale measures to combat the problems of the Special Areas, whereas a trust like the Rowntrees' could achieve genuine influence only within a smaller and more localised sphere of operation.

115

The coming of mass unemployment was a source of particular concern to the Society of Friends. Yearly Meeting was understandably reluctant to take a firm stand on an issue that had clear party political implications; and the two most obvious routes to the creation of work – greater consumption and production of luxury goods and, especially, the intensified manufacture of armaments – were viewed with suspicion or hostility by most British Quakers. Moreover, the problem seemed to many to be simply too great in extent for anything other than large-scale organised state intervention to make any significant difference. Traditional Quaker voluntarism, expressed either through model employment practices or through ventures such as the work at Maes-yr-Haf, could not hope to meet a situation where three million people stood idle, many of them the victims of a structural unemployment whose underlying causes transcended the more predictable vicissitudes of the trade cycle. Unsurprisingly, many Quakers followed large groups of their contemporaries and demanded wholesale adjustments or even revolutionary changes to the existing industrial and social order. However, violent revolution – be it on a Russian or Italian model – was distasteful to most members of the Society; and as Shipley Brayshaw explained in the Swarthmore lecture for 1933, following the principles set out by Bertrand Russell in *The practice and theory of Bolshevism* (1920), '[a] change that came by violence would outrun the bounds of justice and reason, and assuming extreme forms, would establish injustices which might be as great as those it abolished.'[3] Brayshaw, asking rhetorically how the problem of unemployment could be resolved without recourse to luxury or military production, endorsed economic planning to some extent,[4] but could only end rather vaguely with a plea for the establishment of a 'right social order', organised along the lines of 'national rationalization'.[5] It is doubtful whether many listeners came away from the lecture with a very clear scheme in their minds. As it was, the Quakers – limited in numbers and in the availability of time to give to relief work – tended to approach the relief of unemployment in the 1930s much as they had approached similar problems in the past; the experiment at Maes-yr-Haf in the later 1920s provided the model for much of what was to happen later.

The Rowntrees, inheritors of Joseph Rowntree's belief in the importance of personal service and the human touch, responded to domestic distress by endorsing and financially underpinning the employment of individuals to undertake such work in distressed communities. They placed great faith in the itinerant Quaker ministry of John A. Hughes, formerly warden of the St. Mary's Settlement, and now employed by the Trust in much the same way as Edward Grubb had been in earlier years, to travel to Meetings, lecture, preach and generally involve himself in Quaker and non-Quaker social work. Nevertheless, it was not until 1936 that Hughes threw himself into Special Areas work. During the trough of the depression in 1931, the trustees advised him to concentrate his attention on the Quaker schools at Bootham, The Mount and Ackworth, and especially on the older scholars, whom Ernest Taylor wanted to be taken on 'tramps' to the fell country to study the origins of Quakerism.[6] In 1935, Taylor and Arnold Rowntree were still emphasising this aspect of Hughes's work, although he was also by now involved in crisis conferences about the performance of Woodbrooke with Taylor, Rowntree and Jack Cadbury.[7] Hughes viewed his role as one of 'husbandry in the Society', seeing in 1931 no signs of an imminent spiritual revival: it was rather a 'preparative time'.[8] However, by 1935, at the age of 59, he was clearly becoming restless, and anxious to have a hand in the increasingly urgent project of rejuvenating the Special Areas. He asked Taylor if he might be allowed to undertake a tour of Meetings north of the Tees, which Taylor supported on account of Hughes's 'rather special appeal to youth': he clearly saw an evangelistic role for him.[9]

Nevertheless, when Hughes finally visited the Durham coalfield in 1936 – and it is notable that he visited the depressed area that was geographically closest to York and the centre of the JRCT's activity – he quickly involved himself in the work of multifarious schemes that had been established to deal with the problems of mass unemployment. By September he was in the mining village of Stanley (a village which Arthur Bowley had shown had a high proportion of poverty among out-of-work mining families in the 1920s),[10] where he had held meetings with representatives of the Women's Institute, the Labour party, a local chapel, a men's meeting, the Women's Co-operative Guild and other groups, and was helping in the production of a play at the community centre. He saw himself as 'a living focus of interest in the community', remarking that '[i]f a person like myself comes into a district under special concern it acts as a stimulus and challenge to co-operate'.[11] Central to his – and the trustees' – conception of this work was its Christian element: Hughes spoke admiringly of the work of a local Methodist preacher and school-master who had arranged a host of educational and recreational activities, including adult school and WEA classes, and regretted that too many local activists were wasting their time on organising whist drives and dances, and not using the community centre to full advantage.[12] He identified 'a *crying* need for leadership – the local outside committee consisting of too many parsons and such like who take on the place merely as *one more committee* and do not see the place these [community] centres ought to occupy in the social life of the place'.[13] At least some of the Charitable Trustees concurred with his view, and sought to fund more of this kind of work. Following a meeting between Hughes and Ernest Taylor in November 1936, it was reported that

The results of [Hughes's] work suggest a new form of useful activity ... There are other districts where exactly the same kind of useful work can be given, provided that we have the right kind of people available, and careful consideration needs to be given to the question as to whether some of the effort now directed to bolstering up very small, and perhaps decaying Meetings, could not now be given to more individual work like this. We need not care so much about membership figures but the mere fact of getting to know people in the midst of distress will, if undertaken, bring its fruitful results.[14]

Indeed, when Taylor retired as Trust secretary in 1936, he emphasised the importance to the Trust's grant-making priorities of the support of men like Hughes, referring to the section of the Founder's memorandum on the value of 'strengthening the hands of those who are effectively doing the work that need to be done':[15]

I have a strong feeling that J[oseph] R[owntree]'s central concern in founding these Trusts has been fruitful especially as we have remembered his desire that men and women with a definite concern for religious and other work should be assisted to do that work by removing from their minds anxiety regarding material ways and means. I sincerely hope that those who follow us in this Trust may feel drawn to spend a good deal of time in considering how they may be able to assist individual Friends in the wisest way.[16]

When Hughes had finished his work in Durham, he embarked on a similar venture in the South Yorkshire coalfield in the early months of 1937, receiving similarly positive testimonials.[17] He was later invited to carry out similar informal itinerant work in Bradford, Lancashire and Ireland.[18] However, the latter two ventures were likely to be viewed with suspicion by the trustees, who still had an eye to the importance of the local, which they could more easily oversee personally: at one meeting in 1936, referring to another long-standing Trust servant, it was 'noted that only a small proportion of [Herbert] Waller's time had been spent in Yorkshire and he is to be encouraged in making his arrangements to keep in close touch with [Stephen] Rowntree'.[19]

Others helped by the Trust in this period included Frank Sturge (still a trustee himself), following his retirement from the wardenship of Woodbrooke in 1932 until his death in 1948: his job was to maintain contact with the 'Joseph Rowntree' scholars at Bootham and The Mount, and he also had a continuing oversight brief for the activities of Woodbrooke, which remained a cause for concern to the trustees throughout the 1930s. Sturge and his wife also joined the executive of the Yorkshire Friends Service Committee, of which Stephen Rowntree was still the honorary secretary.[20] Their activities were directly aimed at the strengthening of Quakerism, as envisaged in the Founder's memorandum: a trustees' meeting in 1934 noted the importance of the Sturges' work, 'especially perhaps of that which deals with small groups and with individuals. If only in every Meeting, annually, three or four new people were to become keen Quakers, considerable results would follow.'[21] In the same hope, the trustees continued to pay part of Herbert Waller's salary, £365 per annum in 1938, after he had given up his part-time secretarial work at Bootham School at the age of 57 in the previous year; they maintained their support for the Yorkshire Friends Service Committee, which received an annual grant of £250 from 1916, increased to £350 in 1941 and to £500 in 1948; and they supported the individual educational activities of H. W. Locke (£75 a year from 1934 for educational work at New Earswick, the cocoa works, and among York Friends), Mrs. E. Tawell of Malton (£2 7s. 6d. a week from 1934 for '[p]astoral work in Malton and Pickering and Hull'), and others.[22] The veteran Friend Neave Brayshaw, who reached the age of 70 in December 1931, was employed until his death in 1940 for his work with older boys at Bootham, with those who had recently left Bootham and the other Quaker schools, and with Friends at the universities.[23] Horace Fleming, who had taken up the wardenship of the Mary Ward Settlement in London in 1929 and held it until 1934, continued to receive support, as did local projects such as the purchase of the York Nursery School from Arnold Rowntree in 1938 and the subsequent provision of substantial annual grants.[24] The Rowntrees themselves were still frequently the recipients of grants: Michael Rowntree, son of Arnold, received one of the 'Joseph Rowntree' scholarships at Bootham in 1932, and Margaret Rowntree, eldest daughter of John Wilhelm, received £100 in connection with educational work in 1939.[25] In addition, the Rowntree and Cadbury Trusts between them supported a young Friend, Stephen Porter, through an agriculture degree at Aberystwyth University;[26] and in 1933 Joseph Brayshaw, son of that year's Swarthmore lecturer, was given £100 towards his attendance at the University of Manchester, in the hope that he would be able to train as a Quaker lecturer.[27]

The theme of personal service that lay behind these grants also underpinned much of the work of the educational settlements during the depression, including the new settlements in the Special Areas, which were not (except in the case of Maes-yr-Haf) funded directly by the Rowntrees but received state support in the form of grants from the Special Areas Commissioners, and support from the Pilgrim Trust. In November 1934 a grant of £12,000 from the Pilgrim Trust for the next three years was noted by the JRCT;[28] and in total the ESA spent £30,000 of Pilgrim Trust money on the Special Areas settlements between 1931 and 1941.[29] The government, through the Special Areas Commissioners, gave around £100,000 in the 1930s.[30] As we have seen, these new settlements were better funded, more professionalised and necessarily larger-scale operations than their predecessors at York, Leeds and elsewhere, but they retained much of the educational ethos of the older institutions. They still intended to minister as much to the spiritual and cultural needs of the population, an ambition that went beyond the mere provision of material assistance through a period of crisis, necessary and proper though this was. As William Hazelton, secretary of the ESA and a veteran of the Coalfields Distress Committee, explained in 1932, unemployment benefit satisfied (arguably) the basic material needs of the unemployed,

> but it does not and it cannot stay the subtle process of mental, spiritual, and physical deterioration which accompanies continued unemployment ... People permamently out of a job are in danger of regarding themselves as social outcasts, and of losing this deep sense of the goodness of life unless somehow and by some means they can be shown a way whereby their whole social life may be given a new orientation.[31]

This was to be done, as in the earlier ventures, through the provision of a 'hearth and home for adult education', and with it an opportunity for social, cultural and religious self-expression and self-fulfilment.[32] In the particular context of south Wales and the other Special Areas, the new settlements were at first primarily engaged in the provision of relief and amenities for the unemployed, but as the 1930s progressed, it was found that they had 'outgrown many of their emergency functions' and that there was no essential difference in purpose between them and the original educational settlements.[33] Indeed, it was even argued that 'no more impressive or authentic manifestation of the Settlement idea exists than the growth of [the] South Wales Settlements'.[34] The main difference was simply that they were much better funded than the older institutions.

The older educational settlements and residential colleges also responded constructively to the needs of the unemployed. For example, Beechcroft started woodwork classes, and a magazine 'partly to keep typists in practice'; at the John Woolman Settlement in London unemployed men were admitted as members on payment of only a quarter of the usual subscription; and at Avoncroft College in 1933 a summer residential course taught a hundred unemployed men from Birmingham techniques of fruit and vegetable growing 'to equip them for allotment work'.[35] At St. Mary's in York the classes the unemployed were admitted free of charge to classes, although this did not entitle them to membership of the settlement.[36] The Youth Hostels Association – the secretary of which, E. St. John Catchpool, was a Quaker veteran of the Friends Ambulance Unit and a former assistant warden of Toynbee Hall – also co-operated with the settlements, making 'special arrangements for parties of unemployed people'.[37] It was recognised that the problem of unemployment, while catastrophic to the individual and the family affected, nevertheless represented a great opportunity for the educational settlement movement. The *Common Room* announced in 1933 that

Thousands of men and women throughout the country have reached that state for which the educationalist has been longing – the state in which there is time to learn and to do those things which concern the mind and the spirit. Thousands now have leisure, but it is aimless leisure, and is slowly but surely destroying their bodies, their minds, and their spirits.[38]

The objectives of the educational settlement movement, then, were carried enthusiastically and ambitiously into the distressed areas, and many of the ventures were undoubtedly successful in bringing hope to the communities they touched. Certainly the Rowntrees endorsed the activities, although they were unable to involve themselves actively. Arnold Rowntree visited south Wales, staying with the Nobles,[39] and regular formal and informal reports were received on the work of the new settlements. Direct support of the unemployed was confined to York, where the JRCT funded schemes to help local unemployed men, and received regular reports back: again, Arnold Rowntree was the most active trustee in this respect.[40] Three clubs were established in the city in 1935, one a self-governing group, one under the auspices of the Unemployed Workers' Association and one organised by the NCSS; however, the membership was small, and probably more transient than might be expected in the Special Areas, where long-term unemployment predominated in the staple industries.[41] This naturally undermined the cohesion of the clubs, as men left when they found work and the membership frequently changed. In the case of the JRCT, it is not entirely clear to which of the institutions the financial support was directed,[42] but it reinforces once more the importance of the localism of the Trust's grant-making focus.

Mass unemployment was one feature of interwar Britain, but a tendency no less important was the development of new suburban housing estates to accommodate a growing population, living mainly in the south and midlands of England and tending to work in the new light industries or in the expanding service sector. The promotors of adult education, and the Society of Friends, devoted a great deal of attention to the very specific needs of these areas, and attempted to apply some of the models developed in other contexts to the problems that the new estates posed. An educational settlement had been established in Letchworth, the first of the garden cities, in 1920, and in 1928 the NCSS established a New Estates Community Committee, chaired by Sir Ernest Barker, on which the ESA was represented; this was renamed the Community Centres and Associations Committee in 1935.[43] An early venture, involving Duncan Fairn (later warden of St. Mary's, York, deputy governor of Strangeways prison and eventually head of the national prison service),[44] was at Dagenham, where a large working-class population, concentrated in the car industry, lived in council housing, and where social opportunities were limited. Sir Wyndham Deedes, at the ESA summer conference in 1929, 'described the economic situation of these new "dormitory" suburbs, which often suffered from unemployment, high travelling expenses, and a marked absence of community life'.[45] Even in a high-employment area, the limited social and recreational opportunities of the new estate offered an opening for various kinds of voluntary social work. Horace Fleming was also concerned for the new estates, 'those frightful twentieth-century alternatives to our old English town and village life … brick boxes all almost identical, with no background of culture and no social amenities', and wondered '[w]hat can the effect be on the huge aggregations of population but that of the herd mind[?]'[46] The JRCT also to some extent subscribed to this view, and the trustees were glad to record that in 1937 John Hughes, having visited Bradford, was about to go to a new estate, Wythenshawe, outside Manchester, to carry out personal visitation and promote Quakerism and social work.[47]

The altered industrial conditions that spawned the new estates also generated the new 'problem' of leisure: if the unemployed man suffered from having too much leisure time and not enough money to spend to enable him to occupy it wisely, the higher earnings and shorter hours for those in work (coupled with the increase in paid holidays, which became more widespread following legislation in 1938) gave people in work more leisure time and a small but significant margin of income to spend on leisure pursuits. It was considered important that the educational settlements equipped themselves to meet this need by providing more trained wardens and staff: Seebohm Rowntree told the JRCT in 1936 that 'the larger leisure enjoyed by the population and the many schemes now being advocated to occupy that leisure worthily, suggest that the [ESA] should do more than it is doing now to train men and women for educational leadership'.[48] The developments also forced religious bodies, including the Society of Friends, to question their role. Delivering the Swarthmore lecture at Bristol in 1937, Caroline Graveson told the Society that

> Nowadays even the narrowest life of ill-paid toil offers choices of which the monotonous existence of a village Hampden fifty years ago knew nothing. The library, the daily newspaper, the cinema, the wireless, the motor-bus all bring the power of saying 'Yes' or 'No' to this and that new opportunity. Life is not the habitual round it used to be.[49]

Although education was one important way in which these wider opportunities could find fulfilment, Graveson warned: '[g]ive the masses more and more education and their gaze will turn from heaven to earth.'[50] There was no doubt that the place of religion within the curricula of adult education institutions was in decline, and that secular concerns were coming to dominate the leisure pursuits of the 'masses'. The early educational settlement pioneers had seen the provision of training for the active and useful employment of leisure time as an important feature of their work, but the expanding leisure needs of the population in the 1930s seemed to demand a more widespread and highly coordinated response from the voluntary sector, in partnership with statutory and municipal authorities.

It was largely to meet these new leisure needs that the community centres movement developed rapidly in the 1930s. Growing from the work of the New Estates Community Committee, local community associations, with the financial support of the NCSS, established centres which had much in common with the educational settlements, but lacked their educational focus. Community centres tended to be located in new residential areas populated by families displaced from large towns and cities by slum clearance and lured by the promise of affordable privately owned or local authority housing. The Housing Act of 1925 enabled local authorities to build community centres, but it was really only through the Physical Training and Recreation Act of 1937 that the real impetus to the construction of such centres was given. Grants were available from the National Fitness Council under the Act, supplementing the resources that could be claimed for youth sections of centres from the Board of Education. The declared rationale behind the community centres was very similar to that invoked by the supporters of the adult schools and the pioneers of the educational settlements. Flora and Gordon Stephenson, introducing a report commissioned early in the second world war by various interested bodies,[51] recalled that

Community life has changed fundamentally in the past century ... Before this country changed from an agricultural and commercial economy to a highly industrialized capitalism, the forms of community life were simple and easy to understand. The towns spread about the central market place which, with the town hall, guild halls, churches, and inns were centres of life. The link between the towns and the tilled fields outside was simple.[52]

By contrast, the greater complexity of modern life, especially post-first world war conditions in the new estates, necessitated a reappraisal of the social life of urban communities:

In these expensive new [suburban] communities, peopled by families who had formerly lived in crowded towns, there was seldom even a low standard of community facilities. The residents, unaccustomed to their more spacious and polished surroundings, found it harder to make acquaintances where there was less opportunity for door-step gossiping. Active community life, in fact, was at a low ebb, and provision for any activities outside the home or in addition to work was seldom to be found except at the cinema, the public house, or in church. Conditions like these inevitably foster the tendency to passive or mass entertainment at the dog races or football matches and are a negation of neighbourhood spirit.[53]

Like the educational settlements, the theory of the community centres aimed at a partial restoration of the supposedly superior social relationships associated with the pre-industrial economy, albeit within a newly democratised organisational framework. The nineteenth-century preoccupation with 'rational recreation' is still discernible; as is the concern over 'national efficiency', reflected in the intention to provide physical training, at a time when the nation was manifestly preparing for war.

Although the community centres movement (like 'adult schools' and 'educational settlements', 'community centres' was regularly suffixed with the word 'movement') remained ill-defined, in terms of both its function and its relationships with other community institutions, its importance – and arguably the threat it posed – was acknowledged by the leaders of the educational settlements. Arnold Rowntree told the JRCT in 1936 that, in light of the tendency for the settlements in the Special Areas to be established and governed in collaboration with the NCSS, it was essential for the ESA and NCSS to maintain a close working relationship;[54] but the community centres posed an even greater challenge. W. E. Williams, secretary of the British Institue of Adult Education, in a long report on educational settlements commissioned by the JRCT and delivered in 1938,[55] maintained that although community centres shared many purposes in common with the educational settlements, which could be viewed as 'first cousins, in an older line of the family', to the new institutions, the vastly greater financial support available to community centres made a reassessment of the validity of the whole settlement project essential.[56] Unlike settlements, which enjoyed poor facilities, and were seen as 'the slums of adult education',[57] community centres were well-equipped, having access, for example, to new technologies such as film projectors.[58] Even in the better-funded settlements in the Special Areas, the equipment was often 'shoddy and defective'.[59] Nevertheless, the experiences of the settlements might help the new community centres, and it was manifestly in the interests of the ESA to press for greater involvement, in association with the NCSS, in the new movement.[60] The joint advisory committee, established in 1938, between the ESA and the British Association of Residential Settlements, included in its remit the consideration of community centres;[61] and in the same year Arnold Rowntree, addressing the ESA council but evidently aiming at a wider audience as well, echoed Williams's claims for a close relationship between the two types of institution:

> In order to foster the true democratic spirit in the running of the [Community] Centres it was necessary to bring together the members in the relationship of the family, of friends and of neighbours, and to help them to express themselves as individuals and as members of the community. That was of vital importance and was

what our Settlements had been seeking to do for the past twenty years.[62]

By 1939 the ESA council was hearing a plea from E. Sewell Harris – a former assistant to Horace Fleming at Beechcroft and now a leading figure in the Watling Community Association, one of the flagship associations of the New Estates Community Committee – for a series of educational settlements based in city centre locations to act as a central coordinating body for local community centres in the new estates.[63] That this function was never adopted by the settlements is not really surprising: as Harris recognised, the settlements ultimately served a much narrower purpose; and they barely had enough money to coordinate their own affairs, let alone those of community associations. To take one example, Harris's own association at Watling, whose centre opened in 1933, received a grant of £2,000 and a loan of £700 from the Pilgrim Trust, secretarial support from the Middlesex County Council Higher Education Committee, and was able to collect £500 and obtain a bank loan of £900 for the construction of the centre, as well as enjoying regular membership subscriptions.[64] Although, as Andrzej Olechnowicz has shown, the Watling community centre was poorly located, inappropriately constructed, failed to attract the active support of the London County Council, and in no way involved the whole community even on this relatively small new estate,[65] it was an important pioneering centre and served as the model for future ventures. Such centres received the support of large grant-making trusts and, later, local authorities. The community centres had the advantage of being new: W. E. Williams reported that large charitable trusts were more likely to support centres than settlements, as they were 'always following after some new thing, and are loth to reconsider the claims of a movement which has survived its first growth'.[66]

The community centres did not provoke the same degree of hostility that was aroused among some sections of the organised working classes by the activities of the settlements and unemployed clubs; and the more democratic governance of the new centres made them less open to the resentment of those with whom they came into direct contact. Radical critics of the NCSS unemployment centres saw them as 'trying to quieten the unemployed, and give the illusion that something was being done for them',[67] and Wal Hannington, secretary of the National Unemployed Workers' Movement, claimed that his members were refused membership of occupational clubs.[68] Percy Watkins of the NCSS recalled that the clubs did not receive the wholehearted support of the trade unions or the labour movement, which saw them as 'nothing more than an attempt to provide "dope"'.[69] From a different political perspective, George Orwell concurred with this view, seeing clubs as

125

simply a device to keep the unemployed quiet and give them the illusion that something is being done for them. Undoubtedly that *is* the underlying motive. Keep a man busy mending boots and he is less likely to read the *Daily Worker*. Also there is a nasty YMCA atmosphere about these places which you can feel as soon as you go in...[70]

(Nevertheless, Orwell had to admit that 'probably it is better that a man should waste his time even with such rubbish as sea-grass work than that for years upon end he should do absolutely *nothing*'.)[71] Some initiatives to help the unemployed seemed even more sinister: for example, George Davies's camps for unemployed miners in south Wales, held at the Malthouse, aroused suspicion among some of the men, who had read about 'concentration camps' in the press and tarred Davies's efforts with the same brush.[72] More than one observer pointed out that the reliance of the settlements in the Special Areas on outside control, often exercised from remote centres such as London or Oxford, did not encourage the settlement to take root in the local community, and made it seem distant from the real needs of the people.[73] By contrast, the community centre was rooted in local initiative and local aspirations. The Stephensons explained in their report the difference between the community centre and the settlement (not distinguishing between social and educational settlements): 'Whereas [community centres] aim at being democratic organisations secured and managed by their own Community Associations, settlements are planned and run by groups of charitable and socially-minded persons of a different class from those whom they hope to benefit.'[74] The atmosphere of the educational settlements did not encourage confidence in their aim of being 'neutral ground both to the working class and to the middle class':[75] for example, W. E. Williams remarked on how the origins of a settlement were frequently betrayed in its ambience:

> The relics ... are visible in many of the Settlements today; – the shadow of an evangelical purpose haunts the place, the mildly-musty aroma of an Adult School or the vestige of Quaker mysticism, or the echo of the traditional imposed by some great teacher, or the semi-political fervour of a social reformer, or the paternalism of some good Samaritan who created in some desolate area the first local habitation of adult learning and never let it pass out of his hands.[76]

To an extent the community centres were tarred with the same brush; they certainly drew fully on the precepts of the early educational settlement pioneers, albeit surrendering democratic control more quickly and more completely than their predecessor institutions. As Olechnowicz has shown, the community centres movement was inspired by the same ruralist ideology as the early social settlements, and embodied a vague sense of 'community', advancing a vision which, like the educational settlements, 'commanded wide respect, but little money'.[77] The New Estates

Community Committee was 'always rooted in the twin models of education and the settlements: the term "community centre" was borrowed from the educational settlements, who were the first to use it'.[78] Unsurprisingly, then, community centres attracted criticism for following the settlement model too closely.[79] The community centres were responses to the political threat apparently posed by the mass segregation of the working-class population onto new estates, and the NCSS, seeking a 'non-political' model for the community association, closely monitored the communist influence on the new estates, while at Watling the London County Council objected to the use of the community centre for a communist Sunday school.[80] The element of physical training associated with the early community centres, reflected in their endorsement by the Physical Training and Recreation Act, emphasised the potential for such ventures to be tools of social control; and Olechnowicz convincingly shows that a by-product of the spread of community associations was the intensification of class hostility in many districts. Nevertheless, the long-term viability of the community centres movement was more assured than that of the settlements, which were more evidently tainted by their Victorian heritage. The very word 'settlement' evoked unwanted memories of an era of patronage that was outdated and even offensive in the twentieth century: an 'old-fashioned – and to many people a rancid – title'.[81] If the ethos of personal service bequeathed by Canon Barnett and his collaborators was not to be abandoned, many of its trappings needed to be shed if the movement was to continue to reach out to those who were thought most in need of its ministrations.

Williams, therefore, concurred in his report that the patronage associated with the early settlements was by now outdated and dangerous: what was needed was 'the spirit of Abelard rather than the spirit of Canon Barnett'.[82] However, if the educational settlements were to avoid a metaphorical equivalent of Abelard's emasculation, they needed to carve out a distinctive niche for themselves within the complicated and diverse panoply of alternative educational and community endeavours with which they were faced.[83] Williams recommended a rationalisation of the diverse and still somewhat incoherent group of settlements that were represented in the ESA. He argued that it was pointless trying to make the Association's meagre resources stretch to cover the large number of settlements it supported, and that a few successful settlements should be retained, and remodelled on the Scandinavian principle of 'People's Colleges'. The relative success of the ESA-affiliated residential colleges (including Ruskin College and Coleg Harlech) encouraged the view that a rearrangement along these lines might prove effective.[84] The other educational settlements – those which had acquired a more social purpose and did not concentrate wholly on education – might develop into community centres and find financial support from elsewhere, or might be simply allowed to die. Williams recognised that there was virtually no chance of the settlements being saved by the state or by a large trust: he thought the only body able to provide sufficient funding was the Carnegie UK Trust, which was very unlikely to contribute anything.[85] (Pilgrim Trust funding was restricted to the Special Areas settlements.) For the JRCT, which had for some time been seeking to scale down its responsibilities for the ESA,[86] the streamlining of the educational settlement movement was an attractive proposal, the trustees agreeing in July 1939 that it was 'doubtful whether the Trust can make a serious contribution to the cause of Adult Education so long as its financial grants are spent in the form of comparatively small contributions to a large number of settlements'.[87] In any case, the trustees, as comparatively small players in the field, saw their 'function' as being 'to give adequate help to work of a definitely pioneer character',[88] rather than to support continuously a group of institutions that were struggling to maintain their precarious position as adult education providers. Williams's report confirmed the trustees in their opinion of the fruitlessness of continued large-scale investment in the movement they had done so much to nurture: it was reluctantly agreed in 1939 that 'whilst ... the ESA had developed a vitally important educational idea – a belief confirmed by Mr. Williams – the working out of that idea had been hampered by financial stringency', and to an extent now superseded.[89] The outbreak of the second world war delayed, but did not prevent, the abandonment of the educational settlements by the Trust.[90]

The one distinctive characteristic that some of the educational settlements did retain was the religious dimension of their work, but the demand for religious education was in a decline that members of the Society of Friends and other interested parties were unable to reverse. Nowhere was this more clear than in the continued waning of the influence of the adult school movement from which the educational settlements had initially emerged. Numerically, the decline was remorseless: whereas there were 1,450 adult schools with 50,000 members in 1927, the figures in 1935 were 1,200 and 34,000, while by 1942 there were only 696 schools.[91] Although it was noted in 1933 that Frederick Gillman's revised 'Fellowship Hymn Book' was expected to sell 50,000 copies in its first year, and that several Quaker Meetings had been 're-invigorated, and in some cases saved from extinction, by the results of Adult School work done by Friends',[92] the general outlook for the movement was pessimistic. In 1936 the JRCT sent Gwen Porteous, whose adult school work the trustees had long supported, to Woodbrooke to carry out an investigation into the future of the movement, and considered the endowment of a chair of adult education at Woodbrooke, which had always been seen (and almost never used) as a training centre for adult school teachers.[93] It was remarked that the declining membership was a result 'partly of the increased facilities for adult education provided by other organisations and the great change in the manner of spending Sunday';[94] and the long-time Trust servant Herbert Waller echoed this in the following year, when he told the trustees that Quakers' 'association with the adult schools is now very tenuous', largely because of the diminished interest in Bible study, even within Meetings.[95] In an attempt to arrest this long-term decline in the adult schools, the JRCT had for a number of years been working with the NASU to establish a panel of itinerant lecturers, of whom there were eleven by 1933, including Gwen Porteous and George Currie Martin,[96] but the general failure of such schemes – except for indirect successes such as the salvation of Keighley Monthly Meeting in the late 1930s[97] – shows the limitations of the appeal of the adult school movement to the interwar generation. Although some efforts were made to stimulate adult school activity along with Quaker Meetings on the new housing estates,[98] the heart of the matter was evident in Porteous's admission that 'I don't think folk want to be lectured to very much'.[99] Williams's verdict was even starker: the adult schools represented 'a movement which has fallen between the two stools of evangelism and education and which for all its merits is as incapable of surviving the pressure of modern educational needs as the magic lantern is of competing against the cinema'.[100]

This decline was symptomatic of a more widespread effacement of the religious element in adult education that Quaker service sought above all to promote. The JRCT was proud of the fact that so many individuals had been moved to join the Society of Friends through their work in educational settlements – Gerald Hibbert, Horace Fleming, John A. Hughes, Lettice Jowett of Bensham Grove, Arthur Gage of Swarthmore Hall, Plymouth, and Arthur Le Mare of Walthamstow among others[101] – but while the movement had provided a fertile recruiting ground for new Quakers capable of leading the Society in new directions, the movement itself was running away from Quakerism and quietly abandoning the religious study that lay at the centre of the early visions of the pioneers. A striking example concerns Wilfrid Allott, a lecturer at the Swarthmore settlement, Leeds, one of the ESA's flagship settlements,[102] describing his ideal 'all-round curriculum' for a settlement to the ESA council in January 1936. The content of this curriculum is valuable as a guide to what the progressive minds behind the education of adults in Britain were thinking in the mid-1930s, but its notable omissions must have disappointed many of those present:

It was time for the Settlements to put forward the idea of an all-round education and this, for him, consisted of four subjects – history, art, science and languages. History ought in one way or another to be the centre of the Settlement curriculum. There was a danger to-day in the doctrine of fresh starts, but history showed that there was nothing very fresh. Moreover the study of history led people away from lesser loyalties to a sense of universal humanity, often attracting pity and always reverence. Next to history came art, which became absolutely vital in middle life. It provided an outlet through poetry, painting, the drama and music by which people could get outside themselves and be absorbed in a seemingly infinite beauty. The third subject was science. Everyone should do some science or other. Economics was the most popular but political science was also very important. No Settlement could afford to neglect discussing such vital subjects as international law. It was just as important to educate the citizens of to-day as to educate the child – perhaps more important since many of the social sciences were not considered suitable for children still at school. Lastly there was the important subject of language. He was anxious to keep within the curriculum the English Grammar banished from the schools. It helped to give an idea of style. With grammar might be linked simple logic. At Trinity College, Dublin, every student did a term's logic, a term's astronomy, a term's ethics and so on, thus getting a wide survey of all the realms of knowledge.[103]

One realm of knowledge that Allott did not mention was religion. Even the Swarthmore settlement, which had been, according to its first warden Gerald Hibbert, 'definitely (though not narrowly) a Quaker organisation at the start', organising its curriculum around Bible study, religion, ethics and economics,[104] had reached a stage where almost every aspect of human life except the religious came within its educational purview. (Neither was the omission of religion simply a personal idiosyncrasy on the part of Allott, who was himself later employed directly by the JRCT for work connected with the Yorkshire Friends Service Committee, and who would contribute to the attempted reinvigoration of Quakerism during the second world war.) Only Woodbrooke appeared to be upholding religious education for adults in this period, under the wardenship of Henry and Lucy Cadbury, a time when something of a revival of religious study was taking place at the college, probably under the influence of Hibbert, the Reader in Quakerism appointed following his retirement from the headship of Ackworth School in 1930.[105]

If the decline in the religious element of the educational settlements' curricula was one cause of concern to the Rowntrees and their philanthropic colleagues in the 1930s, the descent of the Liberal party into the status of a bit-player on the national political stage was a no less disconcerting development, especially for Seebohm, who continued to advise what remained of the party on social matters. During the 1920s he had been involved in the study of the problem of unemployment, and turned his attention in particular to proposals for democratising industrial workplaces; but he was drawn into more active political involvement at the behest of Lloyd George in the early 1930s, when the second minority Labour government, led by Ramsay MacDonald, was failing dismally to contend with the onset of the depression and struggling to formulate a coherent and politically acceptable policy on unemployment. The Liberal party was in a period of decline from which it never recovered, being reduced – by a mixture of internal divisions, an unfavourable electoral system, the rise of the Labour party and the strength of the Conservatives under Bonar Law and Baldwin – to 117 seats in the House of Commons in 1922, 59 in 1929 and only 54 (separated into three distinct factions) in 1935. As Asa Briggs has shown, Rowntree remained loyal to the cause of Liberalism, although he was never a strong party man, and his personal attachment to the personality and politics of Lloyd George was resented in some quarters.[106] In the 1920s Rowntree was 'drawn more completely into Lloyd George's political research circle',[107] and it was '[l]ong before Lloyd George realised the political importance of unemployment [that] Rowntree had come to the conclusion that it would overshadow all else'.[108] His involvement in substantial studies of unemployment in the 1920s presaged the explosion of research into the issue in all quarters in the subsequent decade. The political dimension of much of this work arguably compromised its charitable status in law; nevertheless, the JRCT continued to pay a significant annual sum in support of Seebohm's office and secretarial costs throughout the 1930s.

As unemployment in Britain fell from its peak of over three million to below two million in 1936, however, Rowntree's thoughts turned to the issue with which he had announced his arrival as a social investigator more than three decades earlier: the problem of poverty, and more specifically the problem of poverty in York. He also returned to his old interest in agriculture;[109] but his best known venture of this period was the second social survey of York, carried out in 1936 and published in 1941.[110] Although it was difficult to draw meaningful comparisons between the economic and social condition of the people of the city at the end of the nineteenth century when the first poverty survey was undertaken, and the conditions in the 1930s, Rowntree's second survey was in its own right a valuable social study, carried out in a time when the very new conditions of working-class life seemed to necessitate new areas of investigation and new forms of social analysis. It was not the first follow-up survey: Arthur Bowley and M. H. Hogg had carried out a study entitled *Has poverty diminished?*, published in 1925 and investigating the five towns Bowley had studied in *Livelihood and poverty* in 1915; and the *New survey of London life and labour*, carried out under the direction of Hubert Llewellyn Smith at the LSE, had appeared in nine volumes during the first half of the 1930s, conceived as a sequel to Booth's *Life and labour of the people in*

London.[111] Moreover, the main thrust of *Poverty and progress*, the title chosen for Rowntree's study, was different from that of its Victorian predecessor. Whereas *Poverty* had ascertained the proportion in poverty through the impressionistic gleanings of a paid investigator, and then divided poverty into primary poverty (poverty due to insufficient earnings) and secondary poverty (poverty due to the misapplication of otherwise sufficient earnings), *Poverty and progress* did not rely on this distinction. (Secondary poverty was mentioned briefly, but it was not, at least outwardly, an important concept in the book.) Moreover, the stringent 'poverty line' adopted in the first survey and applied to ascertain the numbers living in primary poverty was modified in the second to allow a margin of expenditure on non-essential items, including the cost of a radio, a trade union subscription, a daily newspaper, and even a small amount for drink and tobacco. This more generous poverty line was based on a separate inquiry carried out for the purposes of Rowntree's book *The human needs of labour*, originally published in 1918 and updated in 1937. He did not use the impressions of visitors to decide whether households were living in 'obvious want and squalor', 'partly because the methods of doing this adopted in 1899 appear to me now as being too rough to give reliable results, and also because even had I done so the results would not have rendered possible a comparison with 1899, for ideas of what constitutes "obvious want and squalor" have changed profoundly since then'.[112] This did not prevent Rowntree from making a rough estimate of the proportion of the population in secondary poverty in 1936,[113] and he remained interested in secondary poverty until his death,[114] but the moral and cultural thrust of *Poverty and progress* was directed elsewhere.

Poverty and progress will not be discussed in detail here: many historians and social scientists have debated its importance, although it is as yet much less widely discussed than both the 1901 survey and Rowntree's third survey of York, carried out in 1950 and published in 1951. (This is partly explained by its untimely publication in 1941; the surviving archival material warrants much deeper investigation.) Put briefly, Rowntree's findings were that the proportion of the population of York living in primary poverty (as defined in the 1901 survey and updated to 1936 prices) had fallen dramatically, from 9.91% of the population to 3.9%; but, on the other hand, using the new poverty line, he showed that 17.8% of the population, comprising 17,185 individuals, lived below the *Human needs of labour* standard. In very general terms, there had clearly been an immense improvement in the economic condition of the people since 1901, seen in the diminishing proportion in primary poverty, as well as in improved standards of housing, health and education; but some startling facts were revealed, for example the findings that over half of all children under the age of one lived in a household that fell below the new poverty line,[115] and that the health statistics for the lowest-income groups

132

in the city remained a cause for concern.[116] Moreover, the survey implied that much could and should be done to improve the position of the people in other, perhaps less measurable ways. Of particular importance to this survey was the larger proportion of the book devoted to the leisure-time pursuits of the people of York: although the first survey had discussed a variety of topics including public houses, thrift, Friendly Societies, clubs, trade unions and religion, they were essentially ancillary to the main point of the investigation (relegated for the most part to a 'supplementary chapter'),[117] whereas in *Poverty and progress* they were central to the account of York and its life as Rowntree presented it. His final conclusion was that much had been achieved since 1899, although there was 'no cause for satisfaction in the fact that in a country so rich as England, over 30 per cent of the workers in a typical provincial city should have incomes so small that it is beyond their means to live even at the stringently economical level adopted as a minimum in this survey';[118] but more importantly:

> we must not rest content with raising to a higher level the physical standard of those who are living in poverty. The survey ... reminds us how much greater to-day than in the past is the temptation to seek fullness of life by indulging too largely in forms of recreation which make no demands on physical, mental or spiritual powers. At the same time the influence of the Churches is weaker than at any time in the memory of those now living. To raise the material standard of those in poverty may prove difficult, but to raise the mental and spiritual life of the whole nation to a markedly higher level will be an infinitely harder task, yet on its accomplishment depends the lasting greatness of the State. Everywhere democracy is challenged. A totalitarian State does not demand high intellectual or spiritual standards from its people; on the contrary it can only function successfully when they cease to think for themselves and are willing to obey the command to worship false gods. But a democratic State can only flourish if the level of intelligence of the community is high and its spiritual life dynamic.[119]

For Rowntree, it was through institutions such as the educational settlement that these interests of the democratic state might be met – elsewhere in the survey he praised the 'sound teaching and congenial companionship for the more seriously minded citizens' that could be found in the 'good training ground for responsible citizens' that was St. Mary's[120] – and through the training of children and adults in the responsible use of their growing leisure time that the spiritual needs of the population could be served in the future. Central to his analysis was a distinction between 'active' and 'passive' leisure pursuits (reminiscent of the denunciation by the Stephensons of the 'passive or mass entertainment' that community centres were intended to counteract): for example, watching football was passive and should be discouraged, whereas playing football was active and should be welcomed.[121] Within these two spheres of recreation, outdoor pursuits – watching cricket (passive), playing cricket (active) – were privileged over indoor pursuits – reading (active), cinema attendance (passive) – and to avoid any confusion, 'religion' was separated from 'active' and 'passive' recreation. As we will see, the theme of leisure was one Rowntree would revisit in a separate survey after the second world war.[122]

Although Rowntree's survey was in many respects an important contribution to the study of poverty in the interwar period, it was becoming clear that many other groups were by this time usurping the former role of the wealthy private individual in social research. The very existence of more settlements encouraged the undertaking of comparatively small-scale social surveys, some of which the JRCT supported, including Hilda Jennings's notable study of Brynmawr in south Wales, published in 1934.[123] This study involved some of those associated with the Quaker settlement at Brynmawr.[124] More importantly, by this time the financing of social research was being taken much more seriously by government departments, and by universities, where the establishment of separate departments of sociology encouraged trained academics to undertake more sophisticated kinds of social inquiry. The immense achievement of the *New survey of London life and labour* was just one example of this: the University of Liverpool was also involved in a survey of Merseyside, the University of Bristol carried out a social survey of its own city, and John Boyd-Orr (a well-known nutritionist and advisor to the Ministries of Agriculture and Health, and later professor of agriculture at the University of Aberdeen) published studies of diet and income which drew on far more sophisticated nutritional research than had been available to Rowntree at the turn of the century.[125] The professionally conceived and executed social survey, using advanced techniques of statistical analysis, was, as Eileen Yeo has argued, '[d]isplacing the old-style local patriots', and 'put the local "amateur" who carried out a survey of his, or increasingly her, own locality into a different and eventually more subordinate position'.[126] It might be argued that the development of the British social survey, dominated by a tradition of 'social accounting' to which Rowntree's poverty surveys belonged, was a classic example of the absence of theoretical sociology in Britain,[127] but it did at least provide social reformers with ammunition for the presentation of their cases for change, and this had been one of the motives which prompted Joseph Rowntree to set aside some of his Trust money for this kind of work. Nevertheless, the collection and analysis of social statistics was undoubtedly a much more widespread activity in the 1930s than it had been when Rowntree delivered his memorandum to his trustees in 1904. Arnold Rowntree and Ernest Taylor noted in 1939 that far 'more qualified people are engaged in research work on matters of interest to ourselves than was the case' in

1904, instancing the International Labour Office, Chatham House (the Royal Institute of International Affairs, established in 1920) and the British Association for the Advancement of Science.[128] The interwar period, then, marked another new phase in the organisation of social research, one to which the JRCT, and other voluntary bodies that supported the social survey as a prelude to social action, had to respond.

Similarly, the scale of the relief operations mounted in the 1930s, coupled with the close working relationship between the government and the NCSS, marked a new phase in the relationship between the state and voluntary action. John Stevenson has pointed to 'the tendency for philanthropic groups to act as the pace-setters for official action';[129] and it was in the nature of bodies like the JRCT to seek to provide funds for the establishment of new initiatives in the hope that others would take on the responsibility later. In the context of educational settlements, Joseph Rowntree had told the trustees as early as 1912 that the JRCT would 'have to start the movement first and the money would come from others afterwards', although, as we have seen, this optimism was not entirely justified.[130] Similarly, ventures such as Maes-yr-Haf were initiated by voluntary groups, and came to receive state sanction and support as they proved their value in treating the problem of unemployment. Barrie Naylor has called the Maes-yr-Haf story 'a classical example of a small voluntary body working with the statutory';[131] while as Stevenson explains,

> there was no necessary contradiction between philanthropic effort and government activity ... It was entirely characteristic of the still strongly voluntarist and *laissez faire* attitudes found up to and beyond 1945 that private groups and institutions were called upon to supplement official efforts and, sometimes, act as semi-official agencies, receiving support and funds from central and local government. Bodies such as the [NCSS] represented an essentially voluntary organization which received official backing and funds. It was a form of compromise between state provision and private initiative which was to continue even after the greatly expanded welfare role of the state during the Second World War.[132]

The state-voluntary axis of the 1930s was simply the latest manifestation of a relationship that stretched back into the Victorian prelude to twentieth-century British philanthropy. It was only the scale on which social action was taken, along with the political strength of the working classes at whom it was usually aimed, that had really changed.

Nevertheless, voluntary groups were conscious of limitations to the effectiveness of state intervention, and strove to retain a distinctive place for themselves within the tapestry of relief and social initiative. Percy Watkins, himself a former civil servant, told an audience at Leeds in 1935 that great as has been the increase in the duties and responsibilities of central and local government in matters affecting the condition of life for the masses of the population, there still remains an enormous field of useful, and indeed essential, service that can be better rendered by voluntary bodies than by public authorities ... perhaps the main reason why the nation has more and more turned, quite naturally and instinctively, to voluntary effort during the past quarter of a century is that life is undergoing, nowadays, so many rapid and fundamental social changes, and that it is as yet too soon to hand over to public authorities the sole duty of dealing with many of them.[133]

Watkins endorsed the notion that voluntary pioneers had more room to try out new ideas than did the public servant, being engaged in 'activities ... too experimental to be stereotyped';[134] and as for civil servants, whatever benefits they might bring in terms of resources and professionalism, he would 'hesitate seriously to place in their hands any service which deals with the intimate affairs of human beings'.[135] Watkins was a product of the Welsh Wesleyan tradition, but the Quakers shared his views on the distinctiveness of the contribution of the voluntary sector, and continued to express this distinctiveness in religious terms. Thus Horace Fleming, in his capacity as chairman of the ESA executive, told the JRCT in 1933 that in light of increased official support for settlements to work with the unemployed and the apparent inadequacy for the purpose of the settlements affiliated to the British Association of Residential Settlements, there was scope for a further expansion of educational settlements, but that the distinctly religious purpose of the latter meant that the ESA and its affiliated institutions must remain independent of the state. In this context, despite evidence of demand for the contrary, there should be a more substantial religious element in the movement.[136] Fleming was writing with the typical zeal of the converted (or to use the preferred Quaker term, the 'convinced'), but his concern illustrates the importance to Quaker philanthropists of maintaining a position for themselves outside the confines of the state and municipalities, even though it was possible and desirable to co-operate with them. (Indeed, there was no guarantee that support would be forthcoming: the Glamorgan local education authority, for example, consistently refused to grant money to voluntary adult education providers in the 1930s.)[137]

Ultimately, what the Quakers saw as their distinctive contribution to British philanthropic endeavour was the personal dimension with which their manifestations of social concern were endowed. This feature remained embedded in the educational settlements, and served as a counterweight to the growing machinery of the state and the conceptualisation of social problems in essentially collectivist and structural terms. One contributor to the *Common Room* in 1929 argued that the advances made by the new 'scientific' understanding of poverty – to which Seebohm

136

Rowntree had made such a significant contribution – had 'in no way removed the need for friendly personal contacts', and that educational settlements could still play an important role in the mediation of future social conflict.[138] In this context it was significant that the Special Areas settlements which had come to dominate the field in the 1930s had developed under the inspiration of a settlement, Maes-yr-Haf, that had sprung from the awareness of distress generated among the Society of Friends by the general strike, perhaps the most spectacular manifestation of social conflict of the interwar period. The Quakers – even unashamed 'go-aheads' such as Shipley Brayshaw[139] – rarely advocated violent revolution, and their radicalism tended to express itself along the individual vectors of social concern that the JRCT was trying its best in this period to support. The fact that this work was being undermined by the immensity of the social problems that appeared to face British society in the 1930s represented a serious problem for the trustees, who as usual devoted much of their attention to the personal influence of their employees. It is therefore hardly surprising that for much of the decade the JRCT was trying to find other sources of funding for the educational settlements, from larger Trusts such as the Carnegie UK Trust and the Pilgrim Trust, in order that it might concentrate on the kinds of philanthropy in which the trustees thought themselves best employed.

The appointment of two new trustees, Christopher Rowntree and John W. Harvey, in 1936 gave the trustees an opportunity to consider some of the directions that their philanthropy might follow in the future. Christopher was chairman of Yearly Meeting's Young Friends' Committee, was 'interested in the visitation of Meetings, and ha[d] shown in many other ways that he is anxious to play his part in the future progress of Friends'.[140] It had originally been hoped that he would be employed part-time by the JRCT and, possibly, the JRSST, in a secretarial capacity, while he continued to spend the rest of his time in his job at the cocoa works.[141] Although this proposed arrangement did not eventually materialise, Christopher was appointed a trustee instead, and during the progress of this appointment, the existing trustees placed on record their conception of the role and duties of the Trust and its members:

> The essential qualifications for Trusteeship of the Joseph Rowntree Charitable Trust were ... a concern for Quakerism and for social progress from a progressive Quaker standpoint; vision, initiative, the open mind; and time to co-operate reasonably in the working of the Trust. The present Trustees expressed themselves as being willing to continue their work for a time, and until new and younger Trustees should become familiar with the operations of the Trust and the ideals of its Founder.[142]

Another young Quaker who seemed to fit this bill, Roger Wilson – who, as we saw earlier, had been working with striking miners in South Wales and was rapidly gaining a reputation as a promoter of 'social progress from a progressive Quaker standpoint' – was suggested as a possible additional trustee, but Ernest Taylor decided against approaching him at this time.[143] (He eventually had to wait until 1948 for his formal appointment, and would serve until 1977.) The second man who was chosen (the hoped-for appointment of a woman did not occur until 1950), John W. Harvey (1889-1967), was another product of Bootham, from where he had proceeded to Rugby and Balliol, then to the University of Birmingham as a lecturer in philosophy. At the time of his appointment as a trustee he was professor of philosophy at the University of Leeds, of which he would later be a pro-vice-chancellor. Harvey had been involved with the Friends Ambulance Unit in the first world war, and in Corsican relief work,[144] and was shortly to become active in the provision of relief for victims of the Spanish civil war.[145] Chairman and later president of the British section of the International Voluntary Service for Peace, Harvey would later work closely with the Friends Ambulance Unit in the second world war. Like his fellow trustees, Harvey was interested in Friends' education, serving for seventeen years as chairman of the committees of Bootham and The Mount Schools.[146]

Instead of appointing Christopher Rowntree to the secretary's post, the trustees eventually decided on J. Roland Whiting, a friend of the Rowntree family, whose children's education the Trust had previously assisted with at a time when the Leeds firm of Hotham and Whiting had been in difficulties.[147] Whiting (1884-1970), who took on the paid secretaryship on the resignation of Ernest Taylor from the honorary secretaryship (but not the Trust itself) in 1936, was in many respects a typical Trust employee, and the lightness of the duties required by the JRCT and JRSST meant that much of his time could be spent in the kind of personal Quaker service which the Trust desired to promote in the region of Leeds and York. Educated in the Quaker schools at Ackworth and Bootham, and the first chairman of the Young Friends Central Committee, Whiting had reached 51 years of age at the time of taking up the appointment, had three children, and as far as his business commitments allowed had involved himself in local Quakerism, being instrumental in the establishment of a new Meeting at Roundhay, of which Harvey was also a member. This reflected the 'lifelong concern for small meetings' he shared with his wife Evelyn.[148] Both Whiting and the trustees recognised the great opportunity that had been placed in his way, not only to earn a steady salary of between £500 and £600 a year in place of what appear to have been precarious earnings from his business activities, but also to work for the strengthening of Quakerism in Yorkshire. In particular, it was hoped that Whiting would be able to assist 'as a kind of unofficial secretary' to York Preparative Meeting, and that he could work with

Stephen Rowntree and the Yorkshire Friends Service Committee.[149] As he remarked himself in a letter to Ernest Taylor, '[t]he work ... really attracts me [and] I know that at this stage of life I shall "find myself" in it in a way that has been impossible during my recent years of business life'.[150] Although always a paid employee and never a trustee, Whiting, who was to serve as secretary until his retirement in 1949, and later wrote the biography of Ernest Taylor,[151] became one of the most influential people in the Trust; and his appointment is of some significance as indicative of the 'professionalisation' of a Trust which, although nearing the end of its thirty-five year remit, was nevertheless shaping itself for a much longer existence.

It was in the back of the trustees' minds throughout the 1930s that the original Trust Deed would expire in 1939, and that according to the memorandum circulated by Joseph Rowntree in 1904, the assets of both the Charitable Trust and the Social Service Trust should either be used to establish new trusts, or be handed over to the Joseph Rowntree Village Trust, which was a permanent institution. Alternatively, it could be arranged for the capital to be completely expended by the expiration of the thirty-five year lifespan. Seebohm Rowntree had corresponded with the Trust's solicitor G. B. Black about this matter as early as 1918, suggesting even then that it may be inappropriate for the assets to go to the Village Trust, given the likely growth of state involvement in the housing sector;[152] and meetings about the future of the JRCT and the JRSST had been held in the mid-1920s.[153] By 1935 Seebohm was convinced that the JRCT should continue beyond the thirty-five years, and that the amalgamation of the assets of the JRCT and the Village Trust would be 'unwise', although he expected that grants would continue to be made from time to time from the Village Trust to the JRCT for specific purposes.[154] Nevertheless, in accordance with what he saw as his father's wishes, he was wary of earmarking too much money to be held in perpetual trust, conscious of the Founder's belief that such funds were likely to end up being used for purposes that could not have been envisaged at the time of drawing up the Trust Deed, especially as new trustees might in time be appointed who had less knowledge of and sympathy with the Founder's wishes.[155] To counteract this possibility, there was some suggestion that a new Trust Deed would include a clause giving a veto over any expenditure to trustees who had been appointed during the Founder's lifetime (at this time all the trustees except for Harvey and Christopher Rowntree),[156] arguably another reflection of the conservatism of an ageing body of trustees.

There was little doubt that plenty of work remained to be done under the terms of Joseph Rowntree's memoranda of 1904 and 1919; and it is a nice irony that the thirty-five year lifespan of the Trust, one of the objectives of which was the promotion of peace, expired in 1939. The legal and technical aspects of the re-establishment of the Trust need not concern us here; but importantly, as well as general reflections on the role of such a grant-making body among the trustees and their friends, the end of the thirty-five year remit prompted a significant reappraisal by Seebohm Rowntree of the grant-making priorities of the Trust, based on a historical survey of grants already made. Rowntree was sure that the generally adopted practice of giving annual grants rather than substantial capital sums was fully in line with his father's wishes, allowing the trustees the sanction of withdrawing support from groups and individuals who did not spend the money in the ways the JRCT intended. The fact that Trust employees did not usually obtain their entire income from the JRCT allowed them a certain independence; but at the same time 'the trustees kept sufficiently closely in touch with them to satisfy themselves that the grants made were fully justified'.[157] Despite his personal reservations about the value of continued support for the educational settlement movement, Rowntree noted that the trustees 'regard the settlements as important and deserving of further help on a considerable scale'; and in October 1939 they agreed to give £4,100 for the next year and £3,000 per annum for the following five years.[158] Rowntree fully recognised the limitations placed on the Trust's activity by its small income, and implicitly defended the trustees' moral right to make grants to their own 'pet projects':

> We must, of course, remember that we cannot put the whole world to rights through the JRCT and there will undoubtedly be activities which in the opinion of the trustees are not being very efficiently carried on but which nevertheless it may be well to encourage by making a moderate grant, without devoting effort to rendering them more efficient.[159]

Thus he was eager to endorse an extension of the kind of work carried out in the 1930s by John Hughes, and in the context of organised Quaker service he hoped for 'something on a more ambitious scale' than the activities of the Yorkshire Friends Service Committee or the Friends Home Service Committee.[160] Arnold Rowntree and Ernest Taylor believed that the Trust should be even more ambitious in this direction, suggesting greater emphasis on the Yorkshire work and the Quaker schools, as well as further consideration of the impact of Woodbrooke; they also hoped that more support might be given to *The Friend*.[161]

Considering future Trust support for social inquiries, Rowntree admitted that more support for such work was now available from other sources, but argued that there was still scope for inventive expenditure under this heading. By the time of writing this memorandum (1941) he was already working on a Liberal party committee on post-war reconstruction,[162] and although some trustees thought he should work independently rather than under party auspices, Seebohm defended his position on the grounds that he would be able to exercise more influence through the channels of party politics. He did not anticipate the forthcoming decimation of the parliamentary Liberal party, which was reduced to twelve seats in the general election of 1945.[163] Never an expert pundit, Seebohm told the trustees: 'I do not for a moment think that the political truce will be dissolved immediately the war is over and consequently the broad lines of reconstruction will be decided while a National Government is in power.'[164] In this context Liberal influence would be important:

> Pressure will probably be exerted by the Labour Party to adopt extreme socialistic methods, and there is a danger that a considerable proportion of the Conservative Party will oppose democratic legislation which will involve loss of power and wealth to those who now enjoy them. I think my co-trustees will agree with me that in the framing of the reconstruction policy it is important to avoid extreme policies leaning either to the right or the left.[165]

In the wake of the landslide Labour victory at the 1945 poll, the Quaker philanthropy that Rowntree and his fellow trustees represented would be subject to new challenges and would face another significant reassessment of its role in the context of a new phase in the relationship between the voluntary sector and an expanding state.

NOTES
1. Taylor to Cecil, 7 Aug. 1936, JRF JRCT93/VII/2.
2. John Stevenson, *British society 1914-1945*, Harmondsworth 1984, 317ff. For the histories of other grant-making trusts see Ronald William Clark, *A biography of the Nuffield Foundation*, 1972; William Robertson, *Welfare in trust: a history of the Carnegie United Kingdom Trust 1913-1963*, Dunfermline 1964; Asa Briggs, *The story of the Leverhulme Trust: for purposes of research and education*, 1991.
3. Shipley N. Brayshaw, *Unemployment and plenty*, 1933, 94.
4. Ibid. 113ff.
5. Ibid. 138, 65.
6. Memorandum of 24 July 1931, JRF JRCT93/VI/2 (a).
7. Memorandum of 15 July 1935 and other documents in JRF JRCT93/VI/2 (b).
8. Hughes to Taylor, n.d. [1931], JRF JRCT93/VI/2 (a).
9. Taylor to Amy Wallis, 17 June 1935, JRF JRCT93/VI/2 (b).
10. A. L. Bowley and M. H. Hogg, *Has poverty diminished? A sequel to* Livelihood and poverty, 1925.
11. Hughes to Whiting, 1 October 1936, JRF JRCT93/VI/2 (c).
12. Hughes to Taylor, 26 September 1936, JRF JRCT93/VI/2 (c).
13. Ibid. Original emphases.
14. Memorandum of 2 November 1936, JRF JRCT93/VI/2 (c).

15. Founder's memorandum, 3.
16. Taylor to B. S. Rowntree, 14 April 1936, JRF JRCT93/I/10 (i).
17. JRCT minute book, no. 3, minute nos. 434 (b), 446 (e)
18. Ibid. minute no. 459 (b).
19. Ibid. minute no. 434 (a).
20. For the commencement of this work see 'Review of operations of the JRCT for the year 1932', 2-3, JRF JRCT93/I/11 (a).
21. JRCT minute book, no. 3, minute no. 316.
22. Small ring binder, JRF JRCT93/VII/6.
23. 'Review of operations of the JRCT for the year 1932', 1; file on Brayshaw, JRCT basement archive, box 45.
24. The building was given to York Corporation in 1941.
25. Small ring binder, JRF JRCT93/VII/6.
26. Letters in JRF JRCT93/VII/3.
27. JRCT minute book, no. 3, minute no. 276 (f).
28. Ibid. minute no. 333.
29. Allaway, *Educational centres movement*, 31-2.
30. Rowntree, 'Report on the work done by the JRCT 1905-1939', 15. It was thought that around £135,000 had been raised by 'private subscriptions and donations'.
31. *Common Room* xxvii (1932), 14.
32. Hazelton, *Maes-yr-Haf*, 3.
33. Williams, 'Educational settlements', 30.
34. Ibid. 33.
35. *Common Room* xxx (1933), 9-11, 15, 4.
36. Paper on 'The settlement', Borthwick Institute of Historical Research, York, Rowntree Papers, PP/29/1-2, file on 'Active Recreation Out of Doors'. Although the catalogue lists items under PP/29/1 and PP/29/2, the items themselves are not separated out into two distinct files.
37. ESA council minutes, 10 July 1937, JRF JRCT93/IV/6.
38. *Common Room* xxxi (1933), 2.
39. JRCT minute book, no. 3, minute no. 333.
40. Ibid. minute nos. 328 (g), 351 (d) 367 (i), 393 (d), 449 (e); see Vipont, *Arnold Rowntree*, 94.
41. On the unemployed clubs in York see B. Seebohm Rowntree, *Poverty and progress: a second social survey of York*, 1941, 344-6.
42. Seebohm Rowntree referred to it as the York Unemployment Centre (B. Seebohm Rowntree, 'Report on the work and objects of the JRCT', 1939, 9, JRF, *Basic documents*, JRF library.
43. See Andrzej Olechnowicz, *Working-class housing in England between the wars: the Becontree estate*, Oxford 1997, ch. 5; Alan C. Twelvetrees, *Community associations and centres: a comparative study*, Oxford 1976, 1. Allaway, *Educational centres movement*, 33, dates the formation of the Committee to 1925.
44. On Fairn's tenure as warden of St. Mary's see Peacock, 'Adult education in York', 296ff.
45. *The Friend*, 19 July 1929, 656.

46. Horace Fleming, 'The Educational Settlements Association: retrospect', *Friends Quarterly Examiner* lxv (1931), 73-4; this article is wrongly attributed to Joseph Rowntree Gillett in Davies, *Joseph Rowntree Gillett*, in which this section appears at 146.

47. JRCT minute book, no. 3, minute no. 467 (spelt Withernshaw). The adult school lecturer Gwen Porteous also carried out some outreach work in the new estates. It should be noted that minute book no. 3, minute nos. 466 onwards are bound with minute book no. 4.

48. JRCT minute book, no. 3, minute no. 403 (b).

49. Caroline C. Graveson, *Religion and culture*, 1937, 8.

50. Ibid. 17-18.

51. The Leverhulme Grant Fund, the Community Centres Joint Research Committee, the Royal Institute of British Architects, the NCSS and the Housing Centre.

52. Flora Stephenson and Gordon Stephenson, *Community centres: a survey*, 1942, 1.

53. Ibid. 1-2.

54. JRCT minute book, no. 3, minute no. 403 (b).

55. The ESA 'welcomed' the appointment of Williams to this task (ESA council minutes, 3 January 1937, JRF JRCT93/IV/6).

56. Williams, 'Educational settlements', 151-2, 54 (quoted), 171, 150 and passim. According to Williams (151-2), the purposes of the community centres were '(a) to provide facilities for the development of the recreational, cultural and personal welfare of a community (b) to provide a meeting place for voluntary organisations'.

57. Ibid. 101.

58. Ibid. 105.

59. Davies, 'Educational settlements in south Wales', 195-6.

60. Williams, 'Educational settlements', 150, 151ff, 166-71.

61. ESA council minutes 8-9 January 1938, JRF JRCT/93/IV/6. There was, nevertheless, a growing division between the two kinds of settlements, reflected in the withdrawal of the Mary Ward Settlement from the British Association of Residential Settlements and of Toynbee Hall from the ESA, which provoked long discussions between the then warden J. J. Mallon and members of the ESA Executive.

62. ESA council minutes 8-9 January 1938, JRF JRCT/93/IV/6.

63. Allaway, *Educational centres movement*, 34; ESA council minutes 8 January 1939, JRF JRCT93/IV/6.

64. Stephenson and Stephenson, *Community centres*, 111; Olechnowicz, *Working-class housing*, 185-91.

65. Olechnowicz, *Working-class housing*, 189, 196-8.

66. Williams, 'Educational settlements', 55-6.

67. I. Tait, 'Keeping the jobless occupied: voluntary welfare and unemployment in 1930s Britain', in Ian Blanchard (ed.), *New directions in economic and social history: papers presented at the 'new researchers' sessions of the Economic History Society conference held at Edinburgh*, Avonbridge 1995, 63-4.

68. Ibid. 62.

69. Percy E. Watkins, *A Welshman remembers: an autobiography*, Cardiff 1944, 150.
70. George Orwell, *The road to Wigan pier* (1st edn 1937), Harmondsworth 1982, 74. Original emphasis.
71. Ibid. Original emphasis.
72. Naylor, *Quakers in the Rhondda*, 57.
73. Ibid. 33; Davies, 'Educational settlements in south Wales', 189-90, 194-5.
74. Stephenson and Stephenson, *Community centres*, 92.
75. Williams, 'Educational settlements', 88.
76. Ibid. 41.
77. Olechnowicz, *Working-class housing*, 137.
78. Ibid. 141.
79. Ibid. 143.
80. Ibid. 148, 198-9.
81. Williams, 'Educational settlements', 160.
82. Ibid. 127.
83. Ibid. 126-8, 64.
84. On the residential colleges, see *Common Room* xxxiii (1934), 11-16; Fieldhouse and associates, *History of modern British adult education*, ch. 9.
85. Williams, 'Educational settlements', 181-2.
86. JRCT minute book, no. 2, minute no. 185 (d); no. 3, minute nos. 29, 118.
87. JRCT minute book, no. 3, minute no. 558.
88. Ibid.
89. Ibid.
90. Ibid.; minute no. 565 shows that plans to investigate the possibility of obtaining money from other sources were held up by the additional problems visited on the settlements by the war.
91. Hall, *Adult school movement*, 128, 213; the number of members for 1942 is not given.
92. JRCT, 'Thirteenth annual report: adult education and settlements', 1933, 3-4, JRF JRCT93/IV/5.
93. JRCT minute book, no. 3, minute no. 435 (b).
94. Ibid.
95. JRCT minute book, no. 3, minute no. 468 (c).
96. JRCT 'Thirteenth annual report: adult education and settlements', 4-5.
97. JRCT, 'Eighteenth annual report: adult education and settlements', 1938, 6, JRF JRCT93/IV/5.
98. JRCT minute book, no. 3, minute no. 409 (b) (iv).
99. JRCT, 'Thirteenth annual report: adult education and settlements', 5.
100. Williams, 'Educational settlements', 114.
101. JRCT, 'Thirteenth annual report: adult education and settlements', 2; JRCT minute book, no. 3, minute nos. 105, 110, 296 (1) (c); Rowntree, 'Report on the work and objects of the JRCT', 8.
102. See Williams, 'Educational settlements', 33-6, 126-8, 150, 181-2 and *passim*, in which Swarthmore is considered as one of the few settlements likely to survive a radical overhaul of the movement. Allott was later to become warden of the settlement.

103. ESA council minutes, 4 January 1936, JRF JRCT93/IV/6. These typed minutes are erroneously dated 1935.
104. Quoted in Allaway, *Educational centres movement*, 10.
105. Wilson, 'Post-war conditions', 66, and 71 for the revival of religious education. There was also a succession of important 'Quaker Fellows', including Caroline Graveson, George M. L. Davies, Carl Heath, Gwen Porteous and Francis Pollard, who must have exercised a profound influence on the activities and atmosphere at Woodbrooke.
106. Briggs, *Seebohm Rowntree*, 193ff.
107. Ibid. 198.
108. Ibid. 202.
109. Ibid. 215ff; and see for example B. Seebohm Rowntree and Viscount Astor (eds), *Small holdings studies: reports of surveys undertaken by some agricultural economists*, 1939.
110. Rowntree, *Poverty and progress*.
111. H. Llewellyn Smith (director), *The new survey of London life and labour*, 9 vols 1930-5; Bowley and Hogg, *Has poverty diminished?*.
112. Rowntree, *Poverty and progress*, 461.
113. '[P]ossibly 7 or 10 per cent'. Ibid.
114. See below, pp. 184-5; Mark Freeman, 'Rowntree and poverty: the perspective of a century', Historical Association/University of York public lecture, 16 October 2001.
115. Rowntree, *Poverty and progress*, 156, 459.
116. Ibid. 290ff, 466.
117. See Freeman, 'Provincial social survey'.
118. Rowntree, *Poverty and Progress*, 476.
119. Ibid. 476-7.
120. Ibid. 373-4.
121. The distinction was first made in Rowntree, *Poverty and progress*, 329-30. For the Stephensons, see above, p. 123.
122. B. Seebohm Rowntree and G. R. Lavers, *English life and leisure: a social study*, 1951.
123. Hilda Jennings, *Brynmawr: a study of a distressed area*, 1934.
124. Pamela Manasseh, 'Quaker relief work and the Brynmawr experiment', *Woodbrooke Journal* vii (2000), 15-16.
125. D. Caradog Jones (ed.), *The social survey of Merseyside*, 3 vols Liverpool 1934; Herbert Tout, *The standard of living in Bristol: a preliminary report of the work of the University of Bristol social survey*, Bristol 1938; John Boyd-Orr, *Food, health and income: report on a survey of adequacy of diet in relation to income*, 1936.
126. Yeo, *Contest for social science*, 226, 228.
127. Raymond A. Kent, *A history of British empirical sociology*, Aldershot 1981, 107-10 and passim, which also demonstrates the crudeness of Rowntree's understanding of the science of statistics.
128. Arnold Rowntree and Ernest E. Taylor, 'Notes on B. S. Rowntree's memorandum', JRF JRCT93/I/11 (e).
129. Stevenson, *British society*, 319.
130. JRCT minute book, no. 1, p. 109.

131. Naylor, *Quakers in the Rhondda*, 9.
132. Stevenson, *British Society*, 319.
133. Watkins, *Welshman remembers*, 203.
134. Ibid. 204.
135. Ibid. 205.
136. JRCT, 'Thirteenth annual report: adult education and settlements', 12-13.
137. Watkins, *Welshman remembers*, 133-4.
138. *Common Room* xx (1929), 1.
139. Brayshaw, *Unemployment and plenty*, 92ff.
140. JRCT minute book, no. 3, minute no. 347 (c).
141. Ibid.
142. Ibid. minute no. 370.
143. Ibid. minute nos. 370, 383 (c).
144. *The Friend*, 8 December 1967, 1515-16.
145. JRCT minute book, no. 3, minute nos. 450, 463 (a); Greenwood, *Friends and relief*, 254, 277.
146. *The Friend*, 8 December 1967, 1515-16.
147. JRCT minute book, no. 3, minute no. 367 (f).
148. *The Friend*, 24 April 1970, 480.
149. JRCT minute book, no. 3, minute nos. 371, 389.
150. Whiting to Taylor, 7 March 1936, inset in JRCT minute book, no. 3, at 17 March 1936.
151. Whiting, *Ernest E. Taylor*.
152. Rowntree to Black, various, 1918-20, in JRF JRCT93/I/3.
153. Memoranda in JRF JRCT93/I/4.
154. 'The future of the JRCT and JRSST', 25 September 1935, JRF JRCT93/I/4.
155. Ibid.
156. Various items, JRF JRCT93/I/5.
157. Rowntree, 'Report on the work done by the JRCT 1905-1939', 2, 6 (quoted).
158. Ibid. 15.
159. Ibid. 18.
160. Ibid. 20.
161. Rowntree and Taylor, 'Notes on B. S. Rowntree's memorandum'.
162. See Briggs, *Seebohm Rowntree*, 310-17.
163. Eleven National Liberals were also elected.
164. Rowntree, 'Report on the work done by the JRCT 1905-1939', 22.
165. Ibid.

CHAPTER 6

The JRCT and peace between two world wars

JOSEPH ROWNTREE had made provision in the deed establishing the JRCT for expenditure in the field of peace, in particular the 'influencing of public opinion in favour of peace and the settlement of international disputes by arbitration or other pacific methods'.[1] However, apart from support for the Council for the Study of International Relations during the first world war, there was little large-scale funding for peace work during the early years of the Trust's history. It was indicative of the low priority given to this area that when particular trustees were given responsibility for different areas of the Trust's activity, no trustee was allocated the peace brief.[2] It was only as the threat from Nazism and Fascism became more apparent in the early 1930s that more serious consideration was given to applications for funding initiatives designed to promote peace, and even then expenditure under this heading did not total more than seven percent of the Trust's spending in any year between the two world wars. Even where money was spent, as we shall see, the projects supported tended to be similar in character to those helped in the fields of education or the local Quaker ministry. The trustees wanted to support individual service, something they valued especially highly in the context of the confusing and unhelpful fragmentation of British pacifism and the proliferation of anti-war bodies which varied widely in their ideological orientations and in their proposals for the encouragement of peaceful solutions to international problems. There were political pacifists, religiously motivated pacifists, and a variety of groups who, while not strictly pacifist at all – they adopted a more moderate stance which Martin Ceadel has categorised as 'pacificist'[3] – nevertheless aimed at the solution of international disputes by peaceful means and supported the development of institutional and other machinery to facilitate it. The League of Nations Union (LNU) was the best known and most significant of these internationalist bodies. Among members of the Society of Friends, there was no united stand on the issue of war: during the first world war the response of young male Quakers to the personal and religious challenge of compulsory military service varied from the 'absolutist' stance of men such as Maurice Rowntree, through the ambivalence of others such as Lawrence Rowntree, who began the war in non-combatant service but eventually saw combatant action at the Somme and was killed in 1917, to the large number of Friends who accepted combatant service from the start.[4] Nevertheless, Quakers, more than any other sect or denomination, had long been associated with opposition to war, and Friends had been involved in many peace campaigns before the first world war, including the opposition to compulsory military service in Australia and New Zealand, and in a variety of relief operations, including work with victims of the Balkan conflict in the early 1910s,[5] which illustrated the internationalist dimension of Quakerism and the importance to the Society of developing international links and mutual understanding as an essential prerequistite for the avoidance of conflict. Although damaged by the impact of the war, the Society would continue to play a distinctive role in the peace movement in the interwar years.

The peace movement had been shattered by the outbreak of the first world war, and in the 1920s the pacifist landscape was shaped by various peace societies that had grown out of the experience of the war.[6] Radical opponents of the war had quickly coaleseced into the Union of Democratic Control in August 1914,[7] while internationalists had established the League of Nations Society in 1915, which later merged with the newly-founded League of Free Nations Association in 1918 to form the LNU. From 1921, socialist pacifists were represented by the No More War Movement (NMWM), of which the absolutist conscientious objector and later Labour MP Walter Ayles was the organising secretary and the Quaker Harold Morland (clerk to Yearly Meeting from 1928 to 1933) the treasurer. The movement's journal *No More War*, edited by Fenner Brockway (a co-founder of the No-Conscription Fellowship who served a prison sentence during the first world war) was launched in 1922, in which year the JRCT made its only grant to the group, a one-off contribution of £25.[8] Martin Ceadel calls the NMWM 'truly the successor organisation to the [No-Conscription Fellowship]',[9] and most of its early leaders, like Ayles, had been absolutists during the war and were associated with the Independent Labour Party. After the election of 1929 the NMWM claimed the support of thirty Labour MPs[10] – including Ayles, who had been elected in that year – but a bitter internal dispute involving Ayles, who lost his seat in the election of 1931, resulting in the establishment of the inchoate and ineffectual British Commonwealth Peace Federation in 1932, was symptomatic of the fractured nature of the British peace movement in this period. The ineffectiveness in terms of campaiging that resulted from this divisiveness was noted by the JRCT as early as March

148

1927, when it 'was suggested that at a future Meeting careful consideration should be given to the work done by the different Peace Societies ...
[t]here is some reason to fear that serious overlapping of effort exists'.[11]
The following year Stephen Rowntree suggested a conference of fourteen
different peace societies, but although the other trustees were willing to
support such a venture, they thought it should be organised by somebody
else.[12] One body, the National Peace Council, sought to act as a coordinating committee for the other peace societies, but it was largely ineffec-
tive, as this very self-appointed role prevented it from addressing issues
of contention within the peace movement, especially the question of
economic and military sanctions in the 1930s.[13]

The Society of Friends contributed both to the proliferation of pacifist groups and to the divisions within the movement, although it would
be difficult to criticise the motives of those who continued to work in
Quaker relief endeavours overseas throughout the interwar period. The
Society had won some converts among other pacifists on the back of its
stand during the first world war, but as Ceadel points out, '[o]ne dis-
creditable motive which may have tempted officials of other peace societies to join was improved access to Quaker money, on which most such
societies relied to a certain extent.'[14] The JRCT certainly funded a dis-
parate group of organisations, and many others applied unsuccessfully for
grants. For example, the Friends Peace Committee (established in 1888)
was supported consistently from 1922, an association with the JRCT that
only came to an end seventy years later in 1992;[15] and another long-term
funding association was with the Northern Friends Peace Board (established in 1913): its pamphlets, propaganda and general educational work
were supported from 1929 until 1981. In addition, there were one-off
grants to the Commission on the Relation of the Individual to War (£25
in 1923), the National Council for the Prevention of War (£100 a year
for three years from 1924, on the condition that a trustee became a
member of the Council),[16] the Peace Society (£10 in 1926, to a society
that had been in existence for over a century but was by now '[m]ori-
bund'),[17] and the British Federation of Youth (£100 a year for three years
from 1926 for expenditure on peace-related work). Grants were also made
to individuals for peace work – the Rowntree trustees had been strongly
encouraged to support individuals who were 'effectively doing the work
that needs to be done', albeit in a different context[18] – including £256 to
Margaret Hirst in connection with the publication of her book *The Quakers
in peace and war*, which appeared in 1923,[19] and £150 in the same year
to the pacifist author (and member of the Union of Democratic Control)
Goldsworthy Lowes Dickinson for his book on *War: its nature, cause and
cure*.[20]

These grants reflect the central importance of education to the work of the JRCT, and most were directed towards the distribution of literature or other forms of educational material in the interests of the promotion of peace. Joseph Rowntree's founding memorandum had given the trustees little guidance on funding in the area of peace and international relations, and in any case his thoughts of 1904 were hardly likely to bear much relevance to the situation in the aftermath of a 'total war'. In fact, Rowntree saw the other activities supported by the Trust, especially educational settlements, as one of the most effective means of developing the '[i]nternational spirit';[21] and in any case, it might well have been argued that the JRSST was a more appropriate source of money for much of the propagandist work of peace, as one of its *raisons d'être* had been the purchase and management of newspaper and periodical publications as a counterweight to what Rowntree saw as the jingoistic warmongering of much of the Edwardian popular press. The JRCT had made its first small grant under the peace heading in 1913 (£18 to J. W. Graham for the distribution of Quaker peace leaflets), and supported some wartime publications including Margaret Hobhouse's influential pamphlet *I appeal unto Caesar* (1917), but except for the large wartime subsidies to the Council for the Study of International Relations the trustees made comparatively little expenditure in this area in the later 1910s and early 1920s. Indeed, although a separate JRCT International Fund was established in 1921, and £1,000 initially set aside for expenditure under this heading during the first year, only £392 was actually spent, much of it under the auspices of the Council for International Service, the official Quaker international relief body.[22] It had been hoped that some of the fund might be used to bring some German and Austrian students to Woodbrooke, but as Ernest Taylor explained to the trustees in 1922, the hyperinflated German economy had reached the stage at which 'the state of the exchange reduced their savings to a merely nominal figure'.[23] The International Fund was allocated only £350 for 1924,[24] and of this less than a hundred pounds had been spent by December of that year.[25] By May 1925, Arnold Rowntree was suggesting that some of the International Fund money might be used to pay for two or three overseas students to attend Yearly Meeting – he was clearly looking around rather desperately for something on which to spend the Trust's money – although in 1926 the trustees turned down an application for a grant from the NMWM, as well as a body called the Congregational Ministers Against War.[26] There was a clear reluctance to support socialist pacifism, and in the absence of other significant players in the field, the JRCT seemed content to fund only a limited amount of peace work.

Although the JRCT was not spending very much money directly on international work of this kind in the 1920s, it is important to bear in mind that there was a substantial international side to the work of the educational settlements, into which a lot of money *was* poured. The Quaker background of the majority of the early pioneers ensured that when, shortly after their foundation, the early settlements had to cope with the challenges of war, their members and staffs involved themselves in the support of refugees, the establishment of international relations study groups and even the holding of anti-war meetings such as those addressed by Arnold and May Rowntree in York.[27] Woodbrooke and other institutions housed conscientious objectors awaiting arrest; and in the immediate post-war years Quakers sought through their educational initiatives to rebuild bridges with enemy countries through the exchange visits of students and close educational collaboration, especially between British and German institutions. Indeed, from its foundation in 1903 internationalism was a key feature of the college at Woodbrooke and the Friends' conception of education in general. Although Woodbrooke was seen as something of a failure in a number of respects, its international dimension was frequently remarked on as a considerable success. The trustees noted in 1922 that Woodbrooke was by then 'giving more assistance to the International work of Friends than to the home work',[28] and one lecturer at the college later remembered that it was only the influx of foreign students, along with the establishment of the diploma in social study, that enabled Woodbrooke to survive its early years.[29] It was envisaged almost from the beginning that the curriculum at both Woodbrooke and the educational settlements would have an internationalist flavour: at a JRCT meeting in 1912 it was 'considered that the instruction given in these institutions must embody Norman Angell's view of international relations as set forth in *The Great Illusion*', and noted that Angell was preparing a textbook on the subject.[30] The war naturally fostered even greater interest in the study of international relations; and Horace Alexander was appointed as 'Lecturer on International Questions' at Woodbrooke in 1919, with financial support from the Quaker philanthropist and educationalist Frederick Merttens.[31] A year later William Braithwaite travelled to Germany for a conference on settlements, with the hope of developing the links between Woodbrooke and Warburg University, where the JRCT had already funded some scholarships.[32] There were also especially close links with Holland, where 'Old Woodbrookers', encouraged by the Dutch connections of their first director of studies J. Rendel Harris, were involved in the establishment of residential adult education institutions along the settlement or 'folk house' model.[33]

Such internationalism of outlook was also a feature of the educational settlement movement, which enjoyed close links with Woodbrooke and was seen as part of the same network of educational endeavours. The homeliness of the environment that the educational settlements tried to promote was echoed in the post-war international work of Friends. Both could be described as 'missionary' in the loosest sense, and both were certainly aspects of 'extension' work. Carl Heath, a Christian socialist and from 1909 secretary of the National Peace Council, who delivered the Swarthmore Lecture in 1922,[34] developed the idea of 'Quaker Embassies', or 'Quaker International Centres', which grew up in a number of large European cities, where it was hoped that conflicting parties could be brought together for mediation, and where Quakers could meet and discuss international problems in a supportive atmosphere. As John Ormerod Greenwood has explained, although Heath's conception of the role of the 'Embassies' may have been broader, many viewed them simply as 'at least a single room held in the name of the Society, with someone always in residence and a regular programme of activities';[35] and, significantly,

> The best of them know how to create the atmosphere of 'home'. This might be associated with residential accommodation and facilities for visiting Friends – whether travelling in the ministry, pursuing research or political contacts; for missionaries on leave or in transit, or even for holiday visitors ... And in time of emergency the centres provided help to refugees, political exiles, stateless persons; 'little islands of quiet spiritual resistance in a world of fear'.[36]

Such a description, with the exception of residential accommodation, could equally be applied to the educational settlement movement, and indeed Heath himself had briefly been a resident at Toynbee Hall. Moreover, while the Selly Oak Colleges of Kingsmead and Carey Hall had been established largely for the purpose of training Quakers and others for overseas missionary activity, it was felt after the war that Woodbrooke, with its international links, could also serve as a useful training centre for such service:[37] Ernest Taylor told the JRCT at a meeting in September 1918 that the Birmingham college 'should lay itself out to train for the Quaker Embassy work'.[38] A number of settlements, including St. Mary's in York, assisted European refugees in the 1930s, as they had done during the first world war.[39] Moreover, Arnold Rowntree envisaged a role for those returning from overseas relief work with the Friends Ambulance Unit, whom he hoped to be able to recruit (along with imprisoned conscientious objectors) as future settlement wardens.[40]

Partly because of commitments like this elsewhere, the JRCT did not start spending any significant sums on the promotion of peace until after the death of Joseph Rowntree, and their expenditure in the area grew during the later 1920s and early 1930s, as the international situation began to deteriorate. In part, this increased commitment reflected broader changes in the Society of Friends. A *Memorandum of future policy*, issued in 1925, bearing 'the impress of Carl Heath' and echoing 'the optimism of the moment', suggested the establishment of more 'Quaker Embassies' and greater contact between Friends in different countries, in the hope of promoting 'a wider service of national and international reconciliation'.[41] In the wake of this memorandum, and also, it must be added, in view of declining numbers of Friends engaged in active overseas missionary work, the Council for International Service (established in 1919 and sanctioned by Yearly Meeting the following year) merged with the older Friends Foreign Mission Association (sanctioned in 1917), to form the Friends Service Council in 1927.[42] At the same time Rufus Jones was campaigning for his amorphous 'Wider Quaker Fellowship', which entailed the closer collaboration of Friends and 'seekers' across the world.[43] These developments encouraged members of the Society to think even more internationally, and the Rowntrees and their philanthropic collaborators followed these lines of thought and began to contribute more to international and peace-related projects. In particular, there was a continued (and intensified) effort during these years to develop international links among the Quaker community, and the JRCT remained eager to endorse, and where possible to support, international activity. In 1935 Herbert Waller went as a visiting scholar to the Pendle Hill settlement in Pennsylvania, others followed in subsequent years, including John Hughes, who was acting warden in 1933 and 1934.[44]. Ernest Taylor was responsible for brokering many of these quasi-academic exchange visits;[45] he was also involved in the organisation of an Anglo-American conference of Quakers in Yorkshire, although this was replaced by a less ambitious scheme to hold a seminar in the USA prior to the second world Conference of Friends in Philadelphia in 1937.[46] The JRCT also fostered antipodean links through grants to the Friends' schools at Hobart in Tasmania and Wanganui in New Zealand.[47]

Most notably, the trustees began to support more projects aimed directly at the promotion of peace. Thus although the average expenditure under this clause of the Trust Deed during the first thirty-five years of the Trust's existence was £381 a year, it reached £680 a year in the period 1934-39.[48] The first serious long-term funding commitment was to the League of Nations Union, which as a moderate internationalist group had supplanted the more radical Union of Democratic Control as the foremost peace society during the post-Locarno optimism of the later 1920s. The LNU's universally acknowledged leader was Viscount Cecil of Chelwood, a member of Stanley Baldwin's Conservative government until his resignation in 1927, and the moderation of its leadership was crucial to maintaining the LNU's respectability and avoiding the accusations of crankiness that tainted many more fundamentalist pacifist groups in the public mind.[49] Although the LNU had a pacifist wing, in which many Quakers were represented, it was essentially an internationalist group that advocated collective security. The JRCT was keen to support the largest and most influential peace society: in 1927 the trustees agreed to find £500 a year for three years to support the Union, and during the following year donated a further £50 to the York branch.[50] The LNU peaked in size in 1931, when it recorded over 400,000 members; as such, it was probably in less need of JRCT money than many organisations, but the trustees were no doubt attracted to the moderation, political neutrality and internationalism of outlook (which contrasted with the isolationism of more militant bodies such as the Union of Democratic Control or even the Christian pacifist Fellowship of Reconciliation).[51] The JRCT was to continue to support the LNU, and its successor organisation the United Nations Association, throughout the interwar and postwar periods. However, as with most of their grantmaking, the trustees were unwilling simply to hand over money and allow the LNU to spend it as it liked. The additional support given to the York branch is illustrative of the continued localism of the trustees' outlook; while although the majority of their support for the LNU came in the form of block grants, they gave just as much consideration to smaller-scale initiatives, such as the establishment of children's essay competitions with prizes consisting of bursaries to attend the LNU's summer schools in Geneva.[52] Ernest Taylor in particular gave much of his time to the organisation of these competitions and the drawing up of itineraries for the children's visits.

This educational venture is a classic example of the localised and individualist (and arguably insular) nature of much the work funded by the JRCT in this period. In agreeing to support the scheme – in collaboration with Frederick Merttens – in 1927, the JRCT signed itself up to a decade of support (although the summer school was not held every year and in those years a smaller cash prize was substituted for the travel bursary). The venture only cost the trustees between £10 and £130 a year, and as such never represented a major funding commitment, but it typifies the brand of Quaker philanthropy in which the trustees felt themselves to be engaged in that it was educational, involved a considerable investment of time on the part of individuals, and emphasised the importance of broadening the mind through international travel.[53] Each Quaker school was allowed to send one pupil, or in the case of co-educational schools one pupil of each sex, to the summer school, which provided them with a comprehensive introduction to the League of Nations and its operations. The trip also involved some time spent in other parts of Switzerland. The broader educational importance of this scheme was emphasised by the stipulation that the children who attended should not be in their final year at their school, as 'it is important that the spirit of the Geneva gathering should be communicated to the School' on the pupil's return.[54] The JRCT, in particular Ernest Taylor,[55] took great personal interest in the administration of these small but important grants, and there was careful discussion about the itineraries that should be adopted. It is perhaps rather ironic that while the world was preparing for the greatest war in history, Taylor and his collaborators in the scheme were debating whether or not a small group of schoolchildren should be given the opportunity to spend a few days in the Swiss mountains after the summer school. (The first trip in 1928 featured a few days in the mountains after the conclusion of the summer school; but in the following year it was felt that this should not be attempted.[56] As a result, more time was made available in 1929 for exploring Geneva and the lake, but this itself appears to have caused some problems: as Taylor made clear later that year, '[f]uture Guides will do well to make it quite clear that no boating is allowed except under their supervision'!)[57] Nevertheless, the scheme was widely reported in both the Quaker and the non-Quaker press, and the idea was taken up by others, including a number of local newspapers in Yorkshire and beyond, which ran their own essay competitions with the same prize.[58] The summer schools were undoubtedly impressive: for example, the 1930 programme featured lectures by Alfred Zimmern, professor of international relations at Oxford, Mr. Sugimura, Under-Secretary General to Sir Eric Drummond (the first secretary-general of the League), Manley Hudson, professor of international law at Harvard, and H. J. Richardson, who worked at the International Labour Office but was shortly to take up a post as professor of international relations at the University of Leeds.[59] One attender recalled that as a result of the summer school, '[t]he League of Nations has become a living reality to us – we have met and talked with people who are actually doing its work. All who have shared the experience desire that they may be faithful in helping to spread and to foster these great ideals of international brotherhood and World Peace with which they have been brought into contact.'[60]

The support for the Geneva summer schools and other LNU ventures represented a growing interest on the part of the JRCT in the promotion of peace initiatives, not necessarily with the same objectives as the LNU; and this support sometimes developed into a longer-term funding relationship. The National Peace Council, the body which sought to coordinate the divergent elements within the peace movement, received support for the first time in 1933, and this support continued for the next 57 years (and Gerald Bailey, its secretary until 1948, later became a long-standing recipient of Trust support), while the Institute of International Relations was supported in the form of bursaries throughout the 1930s.[61] However, the most impressive venture supported by the Trust was the LNU's peace ballot, or 'The National Declaration on the League of

Nations and Armaments', to give it its cumbersome full title, carried out in 1934 and 1935. This exercise, which represented the largest private referendum ever carried out in Britain, was a controversial attempt by the LNU to show that the British people supported the League, and to influence foreign peace movements in the process. A strong element of political education also lay behind the ballot, although this could easily be interpreted as propaganda rather than education; moreover, it could be (and was) argued in some quarters that the reduction of complex issues to simplistic questions with 'yes'/'no' answers served a misleading and indeed counter-educational function.[62] The public was invited to respond to five questions, as follows:

1. Should Great Britain remain a member of the League of Nations?
2. Are you in favour of an all-round reduction of armaments by international agreement?
3. Are you in favour of the all-round abolition of national military and naval aircraft by international agreement?
4. Should the manufacture and sale of arms for private profit be prohibited by international agreement?
5. Do you consider that if a nation insists on attacking another, the other nations should combine to compel it to stop by
   (a) economic and non-military measures?
   (b) if necessary, military measures?[63]

All these were 'yes'/'no' answers, except for question 5, to each separate part of which the public were invited to respond 'yes', 'no' or 'I accept the Christian pacifist attitude'.[64] By the time the official account of the ballot was published, 11,640,066 individuals had responded, just over half the number who voted at the general election in the same year, and the result was even more one-sided than the election.[65] Over 80% of all those responding answered 'yes' to questions 1-5(a); and nearly 60% answered 'yes' to question 5(b).[66] The result represented a colossal victory for the supporters of collective security: as Lord Cecil crowed after the result was known, 'our people ... [b]y immense majorities ... have declared themselves ready to restrain an aggressor by economic action and, with more reluctance and by smaller by still important majorities, to follow this up, if it should prove essential, by military measures'.[67]

Martin Ceadel has called the peace ballot 'undoubtedly the most impressive single enterprise launched by any modern British "cause" or promotional group',[68] and its success in mobilising half a million volunteers and registering the responses of over a third of the adult British population is a tribute to the importance of international affairs in the domestic politics of the 1930s and to the attractions of a League of Nations which promised to prevent war through the firm, even belligerent, promotion of a policy of collective security. The fact that nobody was really sure what

156

collective security entailed did not immediately diminish its appeal. However, as the minor controversy over question 5 of the ballot shows, collective security posed a significant challenge to pacifists, and especially to the brand of Christian pacifism identified with the Society of Friends. In the 1920s, as J. A. Thompson has pointed out, pacifists 'could support the League, although it might possess "coercive" elements, because the use of non-moral sanctions was remote, and would remain so if pacifists helped strengthen the pacific techniques of the League and worked to create a new world outlook'.[69] Yet by the 1930s, and after Cecil had taken what for many was a step too far and endorsed the establishment of an international bombing force to enforce economic sanctions, many pacifists were finding it harder to accept the LNU's internationalist position. Indeed, organised pacifism was revived in the 1930s on the initiative of Canon Dick Sheppard, who, while the peace ballot was going on, called for an absolute pacifist 'peace pledge', which 'was interpreted as an absolutist challenge to the pro-sanctions Ballot'.[70] Although Sheppard eventually co-operated with the peace ballot, his own initiative grew into the Peace Pledge Union (PPU), formally established in 1936, which became the largest pacifist body of the period. Apart from some of its more quirky proposals – such as the strategic positioning of unarmed civilian volunteers between warring armies[71] – the PPU engaged in a variety of propagandist and educational work on an impressive scale.[72]

A number of prominent Quakers were associated with the PPU, including Maurice Rowntree and Corder Catchpool (both imprisoned as conscientious objectors during the first world war), who both served as treasurer. However, despite the family links, the JRCT did not finance the PPU.[73] Although it avoided militant tactics, the PPU clearly represented the more extreme wing of the peace movement, and the incorporation of the mainly socialist NMWM into the Union in 1937 intensified its perceived political militancy. Christian pacifism may have influenced the PPU and was certainly the prime motivation of many of its founders (the original 'sponsors' included Sheppard, George Lansbury and a number of other Christian pacifists; and the Quaker George M. L. Davies, warden of the Malthouse in south Wales, followed them in 1939), but it was 'essentially a secular pacifist organisation',[74] reflected in the endorsement of Harold Bing, Siegfried Sassoon, Ellen Wilkinson[75] and Arthur Ponsonby, a Labour MP and humanitarian pacifist. Pacifism had undergone a significant change in character in the early 1930s: in Pugh's words it was now more 'missionary', having undergone a 'process of politicization':[76] whereas in the 1920s most pacifist groups were small, 'basically old boys' clubs for C.O.s and their sympathizers', 'by 1931 this kind of village fraternity was no longer adequate to service the popular campaign for disarmament'.[77] For the Society of Friends, this development was difficult to handle: the focus of pacifism had changed from supporting individual conscience – which the Quakers were good at – to larger-scale campaigning – which they were much less good at – and the distinctiveness of the Quaker peace testimony was in serious danger of being undermined by the enormity of the issues which they now had to face. As a result many allied themselves tactically, albeit with some optimism, with internationalism, or pacificism: even where their pacifist convictions were maintained, they allied themselves to internationalist bodies, many Quaker Meetings affiliating *en bloc* to the LNU, for example.[78] The members of the JRCT, already anxious about the proliferation of peace societies, came to view these larger internationalist organisations as the most appropriate targets for their grant-making; but even this small and relatively homogenous group of trustees were by no means unanimous in their view of the peace movement, and in their efforts to maintain the distinctiveness of Quaker peace work they continued to support a wide range of minor pacifist societies as well.

The peace ballot had represented the last show of faith by mass public opinion in the conciliatory role of the League of Nations, but the ballot was 'swiftly rendered redundant' by the events of the following year, 1936, which initiated a major crisis within pacifist and internationalist ranks.[79] If the Manchurian crisis of 1931 and the German walk-out two years later had given powerful hints as to the impotence of a League of Nations lacking the power of military sanctions, the remilitarisation of the Rhineland, the outbreak of the Spanish civil war (which prompted a number of relief initiatives with which the Rowntree family was involved)[80] and the formal Italian annexation of Abyssinia finally laid this impotence bare. As an ongoing response to these crises, and to their organisation's diminishing role in British public life, several prominent members of the LNU, including Lord Cecil, were involved in the establishment of the International Peace Campaign (IPC). The IPC grew out of discussions between Cecil and continental internationalists in 1935, and was launched in 1936, with the aim of 'halting the arms race and restoring the authority of the League in the face of the fascist challenge':[81] in other words, it was based on the principle of collective security and did not reject military sanctions outright. Nevertheless, prominent Quakers were associated with the IPC, none more so than Philip Noel-Baker,[82] who had led the Friends Ambulance Unit during the first world war. Noel-Baker, who was to win the Nobel Peace Prize in 1959, had been educated at Bootham and Cambridge, and after the first world war had worked as an assistant to Lord Cecil on the committee which drafted the League of Nations covenant. Having worked for the League in various capacities, as well as occupying academic positions (most notably a chair in international law at the University of London) and being active in the Labour party (which he represented in the House of Commons, as member for Coventry during the second Labour government, and for Derby (later Derby South) from 1936 to 1970), Noel-Baker took a central role in the fundraising and propagandising side of the IPC. One of his first acts was to contact Arnold Rowntree, who in turn set up a lunch meeting which Ernest Taylor also attended; and through this triumvirate the funding relationship between the IPC and the JRCT was established.[83] Although the JRCT never gave very much to the Campaign – it appears to have received only a one-off contribution of £250 and to have been refused any further support – the trustees clearly viewed its work as important. Indeed, Ernest Taylor remarked to his colleagues that '[i]t is this year [1936] and next year which may decide the future of civilisation, and indeed, whether civilisation as we know it can continue to exist'.[84]

The aim of the IPC was to act as a coordinating body for existing bodies, not only peace societies, that were actively working for peace in countries across Europe, and indeed the whole world. Supported by the LNU (which gave the Campaign financial support matching that obtained from other sources), the IPC leaders aimed to establish premises in Geneva from which to organise the Campaign, and to employ one or two 'field secretaries'; by April 1936, national coordinating committees had been appointed in the UK, Belgium, Czechoslovakia, France, the Netherlands, Spain, Switzerland and the USA, and it was hoped that a 'World Peace Congress' could be held in Geneva just prior to the League's Assembly meeting in September. As it happened, this never took place; instead an 'International Peace Congress' was held at Brussels, attended by representatives of a bewildering array of existing associations, including the International Co-operative Women's Guilds, the New Education Fellowship, the International Federation of League of Nations Societies and the World Committee Against War and Fascism (to name a few taken almost at random).[85] The first British congress was held in London in October 1937; and the IPC attracted the support of influential internationalists such as A. D. Lindsay and Edouard Benes, the president of Czechoslovakia, to whose territory Nazi eyes were soon to turn. Unfortunately for the IPC, and for the LNU with which it was closely associated, it also attracted less welcome support, especially among continental communists, about which the LNU became extremely uneasy. Although intended as representative of a 'kind of popular front politics' – Leon Blum's short-lived Popular Front ministry in France was formed in the same year – in Britain at least the IPC failed, largely because of its supposed communist influence, to attract much Labour Party support.[86] The communist link also precipitated the resignation of Cardinal Hinsley as a vice-president of the LNU. In any case, the events of 1936 and subsequent years rapidly undermined public support for the League-based

159

collective security represented by the mainstream of the British peace movement. By 1939 the LNU was 'a mere shadow of what it had been – ignored in the corridors of power and abandoned by the public', one opinion poll as early as May 1936 recording less than four percent support for British membership of the League of Nations.[87]

In the face of the apparent impotence of collective security, the Rowntree trustees had stopped supporting large-scale peace campaigns and to an extent retreated into the support of the individual and small-scale educational initiatives with which they were more comfortable. At least two formal applications for funding by the IPC were refused, and the LNU itself was by no means guaranteed JRCT support.[88] However, Seebohm Rowntree disagreed with the direction of Trust funding, and was more critical of the tendency to support small peace bodies whose efforts inevitably overlapped. (As we have seen, Stephen Rowntree and other trustees had made this point in the 1920s.)[89] Seebohm was quite willing to alter the practices of the JRCT by concentrating resources granted under the peace heading among a few large groups. For Seebohm, the trustees' receipt of a report on the IPC's Brussels conference suggested the need for a complete re-examination of how the JRCT spent its peace grants.[90] The encouragement of the kinds of peace propaganda published by small Friends' peace societies would be a mere straw in the wind of European rearmament. At the end of November, the trustees met again, and Seebohm told them that 'as nearly everyone wanted peace, it was no use spending money in proclaiming its advantages. Generally speaking, the support of the Trust should go to the agency whose policy and activities are most likely to lead to the successful avoidance of war.'[91] The other trustees, however, did not wholly concur with Seebohm's proposals for the rationalisation of their grant-making strategy. Although they accepted in principle much of what he had said,

> it was agreed that the practical carrying out is difficult for the following reasons. The Trust has always desired to give support to individuals who are specially qualified to carry out concerns that it supports, and the small grants given in support of the work of Bertram Pickard [a Quaker journalist who had worked with Carl Heath in Geneva], Gerald Bailey (of the National Peace Council) and others have been fully justified. The work of interesting children in peace movements was recognised as being of great importance. It was felt that no drastic revision of the smaller items should be made.[92]

Hence the JRCT continued to give small grants to bodies such as the Friends Peace Committee and the Northern Friends Peace Board.[93] The work of individuals was also still supported into the late 1930s: Walter Ayles, for example, received funding for personal work in the cause of peace in Palestine, Corder Catchpool was helped with his personal peace missions to Germany and Czechoslovakia, and the Trust also supported Barrow Cadbury's initiative for a conference to promote better coordination of peace work among members of the Society of Friends.[94] Essentially, the support of large-scale initiatives such as the IPC remained unattractive to the Rowntree family and their associates, whose view of philanthropy, even in such a field as the promotion of peace, contiued to rest on an essentially individualistic conception of the value of charity. As with the religious and other education obtainable in the settlements, the real value of the political education they supported in the field of international relations lay in small-group teaching and personal influence, and even as the international crisis deepened in the 1930s there was a reluctance to move away from this educational vision.

Support of a large campaign to which the Trust would be a comparatively insignificant contributor would also compromise the influence the trustees hoped to exercise over the recipients of their benevolence. Whereas, for example, the Educational Settlements Association could not have continued without the annual grant from the Trust, the LNU, although it was beginning to struggle financially from the early 1930s, was an organisation attracting subscriptions from many thousands of people: even in 1939 it claimed nearly 200,000 members.[95] Similarly, although the IPC was grateful for the injections of cash that helped it to establish offices in Geneva, the size of the Campaign – which at its peak covered forty-three countries and involved affiliated groups representing something like 400 million people[96] – meant that the JRCT was unable to influence it to any significant extent. When it first applied for financial support the IPC was looking for between £30,000 and £40,000, whereas the average *total* annual expenditure of the JRCT in the second half of the 1930s stood only at just over £17,500.[97] A significant funding relationship with what in any case turned out to be a short-lived campaign would have been unlikely to benefit either side. Early in the negotiations with Lord Cecil and Philip Noel-Baker, Ernest Taylor made it clear that it would be more appropriate to look for support from 'a wealthy Trust' such as the Rockefeller Trust, rather than rely on the limited funds of 'the York Trust'.[98] The JRCT was content, even in the face of an imminent catastrophic war, to continue to organise its funding along the lines set down by its Founder; and it is likely that this kind of funding was more appropriate to a body of this kind. Certainly events of the three years following 1936 seem to bear out the decision not to pour more money into the support of peace campaigns; whatever the Trust did, it was hardly likely to stop the war. Nor, to be fair, did any of the trustees expect to stop the war. As Seebohm Rowntree admitted in 1939, '[e]ven I, who have been brought up as a Quaker and had all the teaching as to the wrongfulness of war, can see no way of dealing with Hitler except by the use of

161

superior force.'[99] It is easy to deride the notion that small grants made here and there could make a significant difference to the fate of a continent in the grip of dictatorship and conflict, but it is at least clear that the eager support given to essay competitions, international relations publications and personal peace initiatives all epitomised the distinctively Quaker version of philanthropy that Joseph Rowntree had outlined and that his successors sought to promote.

It was unfortunate for the Rowntree trustees that grants towards the promotion of peace did not easily fit into the conception of philanthropy that they inherited from the Founder. Joseph Rowntree had explained in *The Friend* at the close of the first world war that the growth of state involvement during the previous century (and accelerated during the war) into areas of economic and social life that it had never previously touched represented a challenge and an opportunity for 'private benevolence'; and he argued that the inculcation of the 'eternal verities', of which the Quaker peace testimony was one, depended on the development of education and literature, and 'above all' on 'highly qualified and competent teachers, instructors and writers'.[100] Regrettably, the implications of the failure to inculcate these eternal verities were, in the case of the promotion of peace, rather more serious for mankind as a whole on a material level, than were the implications of a spiritually moribund Quaker Meeting or the decline of Bible study in the adult schools and the educational settlements. Thus, although the lessons were learned the hard way, the priorities of the JRCT were by the late 1930s undergoing a process of modification that was to continue over the next two decades (although the issue of peace funding would remain a source of contention among a new generation of trustees after the second world war). In February 1938, ten different grants in the area of peace were agreed at a single meeting, none totalling more than £100,[101] but by September of the same year Stephen Rowntree, Francis Sturge and J. W. Harvey had agreed to investigate the possibility of rationalising this area of grant-making.[102] Although the immediate result of this investigation, which concluded unambiguously that 'there were too many such [peace] associations and that more concentration of effort was needed', was simply to put the concentration of effort off for another year,[103] it did signal a change in the way the trustees viewed their internationalist responsibilities. Writing in 1941, Seebohm Rowntree indicated some of the directions in which he expected the work of the peace movement, and by extension the funding priorities of the JRCT and similar bodies, to move in the future; and the agenda he sketched is worth quoting at length:

> Looking to the future I think those working for peace will have to change their tactics. There is no longer the same need – indeed I am not sure that there is any need – to carry on the old type of peace

propaganda. The fact is that the overwhelmingly [*sic*] majority of people throughout the world long for peace, but they seem powerless to prevent wars. It was hoped that the last war would 'end war', and to-day among all nations except Japan and the Axis Powers there is a determination to take steps which will render war impossible. To that end the Governments of every Allied country will bend their efforts, and I doubt whether events will be influenced in any way by the activities of Peace Societies. It is, of course, important that competent persons should be studying the best way in which peace can be maintained.[104]

This was, essentially, a research agenda – an agenda which the Trust did come to follow in the years after the second world war – and one to which, on this occasion, the other trustees did not demur, as they had done to Seebohm's suggestions of 1936.[105] After the war, as the trustees reassessed their priorities in the context of nuclear proliferation and the cold war, and as they began to spend a far greater proportion of their resources on the 'influencing of public opinion in favour of peace and the settlement of international disputes by arbitration or other pacific methods',[106] they showed a greater willingness to follow this kind of agenda.

NOTES

1. JRCT, Trust Deed, 3.
2. Untitled memorandum [1925], JRF JRCT93/I/10. Stephen Rowntree was the most active trustee in this area, working closely with the Friends Peace Committee and the Northern Friends Peace Board.
3. Martin Ceadel, *Pacifism in Britain 1914-1945: the defining of a faith*, Oxford 1980, esp. ch. 1; Martin Ceadel, 'Christian pacifism in the era of two world wars', in W. J. Sheils (ed.), *The church and war: papers read at the twenty-first summer meeting and the twenty-second winter meeting of the Ecclesiastical History Society*, Oxford 1983, 391-2, citing A. J. P. Taylor, *The trouble makers: dissent over foreign policy 1792-1939*, 1957.
4. On Lawrence Rowntree see Peacock, *York in the Great War*, 329-30.
5. Brock, *Quaker peace testimony*, 276-89; Greenwood, *Friends and relief*, 166-7, chs 8, 12.
6. The following account owes a great deal to Ceadel, *Pacifism*, esp. 60-1, 62ff
7. For the early history of the Union of Democratic Control see H. M. Swanwick, *Builders of peace, being ten years' history of the Union of Democratic Control*, 1924; Marvin Swartz, *The Union of Democratic Control in British politics during the first world war*, Oxford 1971.
8. JRCT financial records.
9. Ceadel, *Pacifism*, 73.
10. Ibid. 85.
11. JRCT minute book, no. 2, minute no. 344 (e).
12. Ibid. minute no. 412.
13. Ceadel, *Pacifism*, 318.

14. Ibid. 63.
15. For grants to the Friends Peace Committee, see for example JRCT minute book, no. 2, minute nos. 131, 194, 296 (c).
16. Ibid. minute nos. 219, 240. The other figures in this list are taken from the JRCT financial records, the amounts in which do not always tally with those recorded in the minute book. (For example, it appears that the full grant of £100 to the National Council for the Prevention of War was not actually given for each of the three years.)
17. Ceadel, *Pacifism*, 318.
18. Founder's memorandum, 3.
19. Margaret E. Hirst, *The Quakers in peace and war: an account of their peace principles and practice, etc.*, 1923.
20. Goldsworthy Lowes Dickinson, *War: its nature, cause and cure*, 1923. Dickinson was the author of a number of books and pamphlets that appeared during and after the first world war, and was a League of Nations enthusiast. See also Taylor, *Trouble makers*, 178-9.
21. Joseph Rowntree, memorandum of 16 April 1919, inset in JRCT Minute book, no. 1, pp. 241-2.
22. JRCT minute book, no. 2, minute no. 59. On the Council for International Service, see Greenwood, *Whispers of truth*, ch. 7.
23. JRCT minute book, no. 2, minute no. 111.
24. Ibid. minute no. 192 (b).
25. Ibid. minute no. 228 (a).
26. Ibid. minute nos. 255 (a), 320.
27. See above, pp. 51.
28. JRCT minute book, no. 2, minute no. 78.
29. Wilson, 'Post-war conditions', 64.
30. JRCT minute book, no. 1, p. 115.
31. 'The story of Woodbrooke: an account of a Quaker adventure' (filmscript, 1953), 6, JRF JRCT93/VI/9; JRCT minute book, no. 1, pp. 252-3.
32. JRCT minute book, no. 1, p. 287.
33. Barry J. Hake, 'The Dutch Woodbrookers movement and the development of residential adult education in the Netherlands 1903-1941', *History of Education* xxv (1996), 335-51.
34. Carl Heath, *Religion and public life*, 1922.
35. Greenwood, *Whispers of truth*, 239.
36. Ibid. 240.
37. Ibid. 203.
38. JRCT minute book, no. 1, p. 228; extract from minutes in JRF JRCT93/VI/1 (d).
39. ESA council minutes, 22-3 July 1939, JRF JRCT93/IV/6.
40. JRCT Minute book, no. 1, p. 207.
41. Greenwood, *Whispers of truth*, 275.
42. For a detailed description of the establishment and work of both the Council for International Service and the Friends Service Council see Greenwood, *Whispers of truth*, chs 7-9.
43. On the 'Wider Quaker Fellowship' and its implications, see Hinshaw, *Rufus Jones*, 203-9; Vining, *Friend of life*, 267-9; Rufus M. Jones, 'That wider fellowship', *The Friend*, 8 November 1929, 993-4. See above, pp. 95-6.

44. JRCT minute book, no. 3, minute nos. 238, 251, 281.
45. Platt to Brown, Gillett and Taylor, 18 October 1935, JRF JRCT93/VI/2 (b); Taylor to Platt, 31 March 1936, Platt to Taylor, 10 April 1936, JRF JRCT93/VI/2 (c).
46. Letters in JRF JRCT93/VI/2 (a) and (b).
47. Small ring binder, JRF JRCT93/VII/6. There are also a number of references in the minutes: for example, JRCT minute book no. 2, minute nos. 397, 422 (a), 408 (b), no. 3, minute nos. 547 (d)-(e).
48. Rowntree, 'Report on the work done by the JRCT', 20.
49. George Orwell delivered a perceptive and devastating critique of socialism, in which pacifism and Quakerism were implicated: 'One sometimes get the impression that the mere words "Socialism" and "Communism" draw towards them with magnetic force every fruit-juice drinker, nudist, sandal-wearer, sex-maniac, Quaker, "Nature Cure" quack, pacifist, and feminist in England.' He concluded with a simple wish, which if fulfilled would improve the prospects of socialism markedly: 'If only the sandals and the pistachio-coloured shirts could be put in a pile and burnt, and every vegetarian, tee-totaller, and creeping Jesus sent home to Welwyn Garden City to do his yoga exercises quietly!' (Orwell, *Road to Wigan pier*, 152, 195-6; see Ceadel, *Pacifism*, 83-4).
50. JRCT minute book, no. 2, minute nos. 380 (b), 394 (d).
51. Ceadel, *Pacifism*, 62-3 and passim.
52. JRCT minute book, no. 2, minute no. 369.
53. Similarly, the trustees saw considerable merit in the provision of overseas holidays with an educational content for members of educational settlements and adult schools: JRCT minute book, no. 2, minute no. 203; see also Joan D. Browne, 'The Toynbee Travellers' Club', *History of Education* xv (1986), 11-17.
54. Ernest Taylor, Donald Gray and Mary E. Hartley, circular letter, 31 January 1929, JRF JRCT93/VII/8 (b).
55. See Whiting, *Ernest E. Taylor*, 76.
56. Memorandum, 'Boarding schools' visit to Geneva', 26 November 1928, JRF JRCT93/VII/8 (a).
57. Memorandum, 'The boarding school visit to Geneva 1929', 15 October 1929, JRF JRCT93/VII/8 (b).
58. Press cuttings in JRF JRCT93/VII/8 (d), (f).
59. *The Friend*, 29 August 1930, 790; *Yorkshire Observer* report in JRF JRCT93/VII/8 (d).
60. *The Friend*, 31 August 1928, 784.
61. As before, the figures given here on the amount and duration of funding are taken from the JRCT financial records. Lorna Gold has compiled a complete database of peace and international relations funding, showing both size and longevity of JRCT financial support for a variety of organisations and individuals throughout its entire existence. I am grateful to her for her permission to report figures from this database.
62. On the declared objectives of the peace ballot, see Adelaide Livingstone, *The peace ballot: the official history*, 1935, 6-7; for a historical assessment, Martin Ceadel, 'The first British referendum: the peace ballot 1934-1935', *English Historical Review* xcv (1980), 810-39; on some of the controversies to which

it gave rise, Michael Pugh, 'Pacifism and politics in Britain 1931-1935', *Historical Journal* xxiii (1980), 652ff; J. A. Thompson, 'The "Peace Ballot" and the "Rainbow" controversy', *Journal of British Studies* xx (1981), 150-70; Donald S. Birn, 'The League of Nations Union and collective security', *Journal of Contemporary History* ix/3 (1974), 131-59.

63. Livingstone, *Peace ballot*, 9-10; Thompson, 'Peace Ballot', 154-7.

64. Livingstone, *Peace ballot*, 11. According to Ceadel, the Christian pacifist option was included as a result of pressure from members of the Society of Friends, who 'felt unable to answer "no" to sanctions because they wished to disagree with the question's implication that a nation could "insist" on attacking another' (Ceadel, 'First British referendum', 831 n. 4).

65. In the general election the National government won 429 seats (388 Conservatives, 33 National Liberal, 8 National Labour), and the opposition parties 184, including 21 Liberals. The figure of 11,640,066, and the table of results in the following note, are from Ceadel, 'First British referendum', 828, 833, modifying Livingstone, *Peace ballot*, 34 and supplementary sheet.

66. The full results were as follows:

Question	Yes	No	Doubtful	No answer
1	11,166,818	357,930	10,528	104,790
2	10,542,738	868,431	12,138	216,759
3	9,600,274	1,699,989	17,063	322,740
4	10,489,145	780,350	15,157	355,414
5a	10,096,626	636,195	27,369	862,707
5b	6,833,803	2,366,184	41,058	2,381,485

By the time the official account of the ballot was published, 13,395 had taken the Christian pacifist position on question 5a, and 16,702 on question 5b (see note 64 above). These figures do not come from the same date as Ceadel's, and it is not clear whether the Christian pacifist answers are included in the 'doubtfuls' or the 'no answers' in Ceadel's table. In any case, the number of Christian pacifist answers was negligible in the context of the ballot as a whole. Indeed, Ceadel remarks that this option was frequently ignored by local volunteers ('First British referendum', 831).

67. Lord Cecil, 'Conclusion', in Livingstone, *Peace ballot*, 63.

68. Ceadel, 'First British referendum', 810.

69. J. A. Thompson, 'Lord Cecil and the pacifists in the League of Nations Union', *Historical Journal* xx (1977), 954.

70. Ceadel, 'First British referendum', 825.

71. Ceadel, *Pacifism*; see also Z. D. Bliss, 'Pacifism, politics and the Peace Pledge Union', unpublished MA dissertation, University of Glasgow, 1996.

72. Between May 1937 and April 1938 the PPU distributed 2,000 books, over 8,000 posters, 73,000 pamphlets and over 1.7 million items of propagandist literature. By the end of 1938, its weekly publication *Peace News* enjoyed a circulation of about 20,000 (Bliss, 'Pacifism, politics and the PPU', 12).

73. However, the trustees did award small grants of between £750 and £1,500 between 1979 and 1988.

74. Bliss, 'Pacifism, politics and the PPU', 6.

75. At least, it 'seems' that Wilkinson was a sponsor in 1936 (Ceadel, *Pacifism*, 321).

76. Pugh, 'Pacifism and politics', 644-5.

77. Ibid. 643.

78. Thompson, 'League of Nations Union', 143.

79. Ceadel, 'First British referendum', 839.

80. Including the 'chocolate for Spain' initiative of 1937, by which the Trust granted £180 towards the cost of sending a ton of chocolate per month for six months from Rowntree and Company to victims of the Spanish civil war: JRCT minute book, no. 3, minute no. 463 (a).

81. Birn, 'League of Nations Union', 148.

82. Philip John Baker did not formally become Philip John Noel-Baker by adding his wife's name to his own until 1943; however, he was using the name Noel-Baker in the 1930s, and had married in 1915. For an account of his life, see David J. Whittaker, *Fighter for peace: Philip Noel-Baker 1889-1982*, York 1989.

83. Noel-Baker to Rowntree, 6 March 1936, and other letters in JRF JRCT93/VII/2.

84. Ernest E. Taylor, 'The European situation: urgent appeal from Lord Cecil through Noel Baker [*sic*]', 10 March 1936, JRF JRCT93/VII/2.

85. This information is largely taken from the items in JRF JRCT93/VII/2.

86. Birn, 'League of Nations Union', 149-51.

87. Ibid., 159; Ceadel, 'First British referendum', 835 n. 2.

88. JRCT minute book, no. 3, minute nos. 528 (c), 560 (e); and minute no. 528 (b) for a refusal in response to an application by the LNU.

89. See above, pp. 148-9.

90. JRCT minute book, no. 3, minute no. 428 (a).

91. Ibid. minute no. 437.

92. Ibid. Note, however, that the bulk of Pickard's funding came from the JRSST: Rowntree, 'Report on the work and objects of the JRCT', 9.

93. Ibid.

94. JRCT financial records.

95. Ceadel, 'First British referendum', 838 n. 1.

96. Birn, 'League of Nations Union', 148-9.

97. The average for the years 1935-39 (in unadjusted cash figures) was £17,730: JRCT financial records. See appendix.

98. Taylor to Cecil, 7 August 1936, JRF JRCT93/VII/2.

99. Quoted in Briggs, *Seebohm Rowntree*, 220.

100. *The Friend*, 9 August 1918, 492.

101. JRCT Minute book, no. 3, minute no. 492 (5) (a)-(j). The numbering style of the minutes changed, for this meeting only.

102. Ibid. minute no. 529.

103. Ibid. minute no. 550 (meeting on 6 March 1939).

104. Rowntree, 'Report on the work done by the JRCT', 20.

105. Arnold Rowntree and Ernest Taylor, in their response to Seebohm's review and proposals, concentrated on the educational side of the Trust's work and did not deal with the peace question: Rowntree and Taylor, 'Notes on B. S. Rowntree's memorandum', JRF JRCT93/I/11 (e).

106 JRCT, Trust Deed, 3. See p. 147 above.

CHAPTER 7

The second world war and its aftermath

THE YEARS leading up to the war, and the outbreak of the war itself, shook the foundations of the Quaker peace testimony, and, although in the short term the continental upheavals of the 1930s stimulated a revival of the kind of 'fundamentalist' pacifism epitomised by Dick Sheppard and his successors in the Peace Pledge Union, many pacifists came to believe that a war against the tyranny of central Europe might be necessary, inevitable – even 'just'. We have seen how Seebohm Rowntree believed that only 'superior force' could deal with the Hitler threat; another striking example of the intellectual difficulties attendant on the Quaker pacifist position comes from Roger Wilson, who was to join the JRCT in 1941 and who had worked in the Friends' relief schemes in south Wales during the depression. Writing in *The Friend* in 1938, in the aftermath of Munich, Wilson, while maintaining his strict pacifism, candidly expressed his internal difficulties:

> My pacifist convictions have been strengthened rather than weakened by recent events ... But I should welcome guidance on an even more pressing question, because until we have an answer we are evading the chief issue which our countrymen are facing. And that question is: How do you propose to deal with Hitler here and now? ... I believe Hitler was stopped by threat of war and that his vision of 'Germanhood' is by no means fulfilled. I do not believe people in this country want rearmament because they want to fight or even because they are willing to fight. I think all that most of them think they are doing is to call Hitler's bluff. We do not approve of all this, but have we any convincing evidence or faith that Hitler can be treated successfully in any other way? ... We believe that all men can be reached by searching for that of God within them. But we can only help some people with the assistance of a mental home. What happens when the head of a great State is as impervious to ordinary reason as mental patients? I ask this question because it is the one to which so many

non-pacifists want the pacifist answer, and I can only give the long term answer.[1]

In the face of this internal confusion, probably representative of the body of the membership of the Society of Friends as a whole,[2] it may have come as something of a relief for the uncertainty to be brought to an end on 3 September 1939, and the opportunities opened up for the kind of Quaker service that had been undertaken during the first world war. The support of individual conscience and the expression of pacifism was second nature to the Society, and on top of this the outbreak of war saw a revival of many of the forms of service in which Quakers had previously been engaged.

Even before the onset of the war, plans were in hand to revive the Friends Ambulance Unit, which Arnold Rowntree again supported and in which his son Michael came to play a prominent role, along with his brother Richard, and Paul Cadbury.[3] A training camp was rapidly established, at Manor Farm at Northfield near Birmingham, and considerable financial support obtained from the Cadbury family. The JRCT also supported the FAU, which it had not done during the first world war, the minutes referring to 'the large donations given by [Joseph Rowntree personally] to the funds of a similar unit during the last war', and acknowledging that 'it will probably be much more difficult to raise necessary money this time'.[4] The Trust supported the FAU to the extent of about £600 a year throughout the war, and, as during the previous conflict, came to view it as a potential training ground for future service in times of peace. As was the case during the 1914-18 war, the FAU was never an official Society of Friends body. As Elfrida Vipont explained in her biography of Arnold Rowntree, official Yearly Meeting sanctioning of such activity would compromise the Quaker peace testimony:

> The Society of Friends ... neither prepares for war in times of peace nor sets up committees to seek out opportunities for service to be undertaken by its younger members in the event of war. Quaker service has its mainspring in the meeting for worship, and is the Quaker response to a specific need. Organisation is, of course, essential, but the organisation is the expression of the concern, not the begetter of it. Thus there were some misgivings when the question of reviving the [FAU] was raised, and it was only the obvious fact that the Friends responsible for raising it were acting under a deep sense of concern that made the Society of Friends eventually accept the Unit as a valuable form of Quaker service, though necessarily unsponsored by the Society as a whole.[5]

Yearly Meeting did, however, sanction the Friends Relief Service (FRS), the new name for the WVRC, which worked with evacuees and the elderly:[6] evacuees in particular, along with international refugees, became

169

a popular 'target' of Quaker relief. Even the FRS, however, was the subject of some misgivings among members of the Society, the matter coming to a head in 1944 and 1945 when the issue of whether a Quaker working in this service should wear the khaki uniform that was demanded by the military authorities became the subject of fierce debate.[7] Whatever the subtleties of the Quaker position during the war, however, one undeniable result was a slight expansion in membership of the Society: in 1939 there were 262 new members, in 1940 as many as 272, and in the following year 217, whereas in no other year between 1935 and 1964 was the number of new members greater than 185 (in 1938).[8]

Increased membership, however, did not necessarily imply increased vigour, and it was a matter of concern to the JRCT and to other Quaker groups and individuals throughout the war that the opportunity should be grasped to strengthen the vitality of Meetings and the intensity of Quaker social concern. Francis Sturge felt that 'the war has drawn groups of Friends closer together',[9] but the clearest example of this was to be found in international service rather than in the life of domestic Quaker Meetings. One exception to this can be found in the work of the domestic Quaker peace bodies, the Friends Peace Committee and the Northern Friends Peace Board, both of which received JRCT support throughout the war. Many of the other grants in the peace field were quietly abandoned, although Walter Ayles received personal support for the duration of the war, while minor backing was given to groups such as the Friendly Alien Protection Society (1940), the Spiceland centre in Devon for training relief workers (1940),[10] the FRS (1943-7), the German Refugee Group on Educational Reconstruction (1944) and the National Commission for Rescue from Nazi Terror (1944). A longer-term funding relationship with the United Nations Association was developed from 1946.[11] Perhaps the most significant relationship that developed in this field during the war, however, was with the International Voluntary Service for Peace (IVSP), established in 1931 to provide civilian service for conscientious objectors, which the Trust had begun to fund in 1936. The IVSP was the British branch of Service Civil International, which was established in 1921 by Pierre Ceresole, who was inspired by the activities of the FAU and later joined the Society of Friends. The IVSP was involved in projects at home and abroad, and was chaired by John W. Harvey, one of the newly recruited trustees of the JRCT. The IVSP was not a pacifist body,[12] and had no official association with the Society of Friends, although it carried out work very similar to that undertaken by the WVRC and other Quaker bodies. By 1943 the JRCT recorded that the IVSP was attracting good publicity, and was trying to develop a junior section, possibly with the assistance of the Quaker schools at Bootham and The Mount.[13]

Despite the importance of these international and domestic relief projects, and despite their declared intention to scale down their support for the ESA, education remained the most significant area of expenditure for the JRCT throughout the war. Bootham and The Mount suffered from the war: both were temporarily evacuated, Bootham to the Roman Catholic school at Ampleforth and The Mount to the guest house at Cober Hill, while The Mount ran into serious financial difficulties and received additional JRCT support in 1940.[14] Trust servants and the secretary, Roland Whiting, visited the schools regularly as part of their continuing service to the Society of Friends. It was considered that Constance Nightingale, The Mount's headmistress, should be invited to attend trustees' meetings (although not be asked to serve as a trustee),[15] while prize essay schemes continued during the war.[16] At the same time, the needs of young Quakers were recognised through the award of £50 a year for two years to George Gorman, travelling secretary of the Young Friends Committee, to support his visitation work and his studies at Woodbrooke.[17] In the wider work of educating members of the Society of Friends, the trustees found that the *Friends Quarterly Examiner* would need extra support, and would need to be guided in the post-war years if it was to continue to achieve the influence on British Quakerism that they wished for it; while the distribution of volumes of the Quaker histories had to stop because of the lowness of stocks, the impossibility of reprinting due to wartime restrictions, and an air raid on London which destroyed many copies.[18]

The outbreak of war represented something of a stay of execution for the educational settlements as far as JRCT funding was concerned. The implementation of W. E. Williams's recommendations and the cuts in support to the ESA were delayed, and modified, by the national emergency. The settlements responded to the war in a variety of ways, and on the whole their staffs tended to find that the outbreak of hostilities did not curtail their activities to the extent that might have been expected. In a report prepared for the JRCT early in 1940, it was noted that only the Balham settlement had closed down,[19] although the Bristol Folk House and the John Woolman Settlement in London were both bombed out in 1941.[20] Indeed, it was emphasised that '[e]vents since the 3rd September last [1939] have shown that the services and educational opportunities provided by Educational Settlements and Residential Colleges, which have been built up in times of peace, are more than ever needed in the present time of war.'[21] Most settlements found that their student numbers had fallen, partly because of enlistment and partly because the blackout made travelling more difficult: at Leeds, for example, the average student travelled over two miles to reach the settlement; and at York this problem was partially overcome by holding small-group discussions in private homes across the city.[22] Most settlements operated a revised programme of educational activities, and these were supplemented by responses to the wartime emergency such as the establishment of Citizens' Advice Bureaux, work with evacuees at those settlements housed in reception areas (including settlements as diverse in location and origin as Letchworth and Maryport), and the provision of assistance for refugees (a particular concern of the Beacon Guild at Wilmslow, where a refugee club was established, which hoped to 'arrange a First Aid Class taught by a German').[23] At Maes-yr-Haf, various work was provided for disabled men who were unable to serve in the armed forces.[24] The work of the residential colleges was harder to maintain than the work of the non-residential settlements, and those especially established to cater for the unemployed were quickly killed off by the war.[25] Ruskin College, Oxford, became a hospital, although even this was seen by the JRCT as an opportunity, as the warden, Alfred Barratt Brown, was thereby freed to carry out Quaker work and to involve himself in the renewed fundraising efforts of the ESA.[26] Similarly, Avoncroft College was closed down for the duration of the war, and the JRCT responded by giving the warden, James Dudley, a grant to work with Quakers in Cambridge, and later in Lancashire.[27] In general, however, as A. J. Allaway explained in his history of the ESA, 'long-term residential adult education suffered a great set back' as a result of the war.[28]

Woodbrooke, in some respects the most vulnerable of the residential colleges, but also the institution most treasured (for all its admitted faults) by Friends, suffered from many of the same problems as the other colleges.[29] Although the premises were not seriously damaged by enemy action, several incendiary bombs fell in the grounds, and much of the college's work took place in the cellars for the first three years of the war. The size and location of Woodbrooke made it an attractive potential resource for the war effort, and government departments seriously considered requisitioning the buildings. Therefore, as the wartime warden's wife later recalled, 'Woodbrooke's first pre-occupation during the early part of the War was to keep its own identity', and '[i]t seemed, to those responsible for Woodbrooke, that it was worth a great effort to keep in being this little oasis where international values and Quaker ideals would still take first place.'[30] Woodbrooke was, at least, able to stay open, a circumstance gladly reported to the JRCT by Frank Sturge in October 1939;[31] and although it was deprived of almost all its international students, and of men and women of military age, it remained 'full to capacity' throughout most of the war.[32] Some medical students and trainee teachers stayed at the college, and they were joined at various times by victims of the air raids on Birmingham, some conscientious objectors, and members of the FAU who were in training at nearby Manor Farm.

Few students were enrolled on Bible or Quaker courses, but Sturge reported to the JRCT that '[t]he wardens see that the Friend [*sic*] influence is maintained.'[33] Although the peace testimony discouraged most residents from actively supporting the war effort in any way, the flower beds were turned into vegetable patches in the spirit of self-sufficiency. What would appear to many outside observers as the contrariness of the institution was confirmed by the appointment of a German, Konrad Braun, as 'International Lecturer': he and his wife had left Germany in 1937, become naturalised British subjects, and joined the Society of Friends.[34]

The other favourite Quaker provider of adult education, the adult school movement, continued to suffer the depredations of competition from other bodies, and its problems were intensified by the war. Total membership stood at over 30,000 in 1937-8 – low by historic standards, but still a significant body of men and women – but fell to just 13,000 by 1946-7, and it appeared that in a time of conflict little could be done to reverse the receding tide of membership. In 1941 the council of the National Adult School Union met only once, and the schools were further hampered by the impracticability of holding summer schools or conferences in wartime.[35] Some attempts were made to broaden the schools' appeal, or at least to retain what they could of the existing membership: the lesson handbook continued to appear annually, albeit in smaller runs given wartime printing restrictions, and the hymnbook continued to sell. The man for whom the hymnbook had been a central feature of a lifetime's work, Frederick Gillman, had in 1939 called for a more 'missionary' outlook among adult school workers, and this need became paramount by the end of the war, by which time the Education and Social Service Committee of the NASU was considering the possibility of establishing a residential college to serve the movement and of reverting to home-centred discussion groups in an attempt to overcome the apathy encountered in the schools' institutional work.[36] At length, it was also agreed that adult schools needed to develop an all-week programme of activities to release themselves from the straitjacket of limited Sunday morning educational provision, which was becoming less appropriate and less enticing as the opportunities for alternative leisure pursuits expanded. There was also some discussion of schemes aimed at spreading adult school work to the new housing estates.[37] Few of these new endeavours, however, even where they were actually put into practice, did much to stop the long-term decline in the membership and influence of the schools, which were becoming little more than a footnote in the substantial volume of adult education that would be available when the war ended. It should also be added that the movement suffered from the death or retirement of many of its most active pioneers during this period – including Joseph

Rowntree Gillett (died in 1940), George Peverett (retired as general secretary in 1942), Ernest Dodgshun (died in 1944) and Frederick Gillman (died in 1949) – which deprived it of the dynamic leadership it had enjoyed in more pioneering times.

Having said this, some adult school activists were still campaigning hard to reinvigorate the movement. Writing in 1941, Ernest Champness of Surrey, who was later to become president of the NASU and who had been active in the 1930s in the promotion of adult education in India,[38] recognised that

> There has been an alteration in the attitude of men and women to religion, which has not tended to aid Adult School work ... the modern tendency to broaden our religious ideas has been associated with a decrease of conviction, while the reaction from this attitude has been in the direction of a Fundamentalism, which it is difficult to harmonize with Adult School ideas of free inquiry.[39]

Nevertheless, he insisted that the religious dimension of the adult schools must be preserved, if necessary by starting a new movement with a new set of pioneers, and expressed hope that the post-war world might bring new opportunities to reintroduce the Bible to lives that had long been deprived of it.[40] The JRCT felt that this task must now fall to younger Quakers, although the trustees were willing to provide financial support: at one meeting, '[m]ention was made of the vigorous missionary work carried on by men like [Edwin] Gilbert [the first organising secretary of the National Council of Adult School Unions] in the early days of the movement and more money might well be given for the support of leaders of his calibre if they could be found.'[41] One such leader was Gwen Porteous, employed by the JRCT in the interwar period, and based in Sheffield, who took over the secretaryship of the NASU in 1945 and held it for a further twenty-four years; another was Redford Crosfield Harris, treasurer from 1939 to 1977, who also joined the JRCT in 1948.[42] Nevertheless, despite the able leadership of such individuals, the Society of Friends was ultimately unable to save the adult schools from a dwindling membership in a secularising world.

The subject most regularly discussed by the trustees during the war years was the religious life of the Society of Friends, and ways in which it might be stimulated through the active service of individuals. Arguably the two most effective Trust employees, Neave Brayshaw and John Hughes, both died during the war, in 1940 and 1942 respectively, and it was a matter of concern to the trustees that there appeared to be few successors who would be able and willing to carry on their work. This kind of service was the fundamental expression of Quaker concern; thus, following Brayshaw's death, the trustees recorded the need 'to find the right Friend to undertake that rare and difficult, yet most necessary form of service of influencing young people helpfully through personal friendship. Such a service requires natural gifts and a strong sense of concern. Preparation for it should begin early in life.'[43] It was important to find young Quakers eager to spend their lives in spiritual service; and the trustees were conscious that their own advancing ages made their active involvement in such a project inappropriate except in an advisory capacity: 'Whilst older people may guide, the decisions must be those of the young.'[44] In this context it was hoped that Roger Wilson and other comparatively young Friends would be able to find and inspire the right young people and draw the trustees' attention to them. Their own war work with the FAU and FRS brought them into contact with a variety of young Quakers – and many non-Quakers who were drawn to the Quaker peace testimony and other aspects of the Society's religious and social thought – and it was hoped that these bodies might serve as useful recruiting grounds for future Trust employees. Wilson later recalled that '[w]hat kept us vigorously engaged during the war years was the nurture and future of religious conviction in the lives of a younger generation, conceived of very largely in terms of pacifism and service.'[45]

To an extent this concern reflected a minor revival of the idea of Quaker social service, a revival which owed a great deal to men like Wilson who had received their training during the interwar period and were now acknowledged as future leaders in the field. Their work with the FAU, WVRC and other relief bodies during the war gave them the opportunity to work in close fellowship with other Friends and non-Friends, and through this they came to adopt a wider view of the concepts of fellowship and service. In 1942 Wilson expressed his regret that non-Friends who worked in the FAU and WRVC showed little inclination to join the Society;[46] but by 1945 he was arguing that the whole idea of membership – or at least Quakers' concentration on (and arguably fetishisation of) the idea of membership – was damaging to the prospects of Quakerism.[47] The other trustees were sympathetic to this view, agreeing that '[t]here is a tendency on the part of a number of members to attach too much importance to the fact of membership and to regard the Society as an institution rather than as a seeking and governing fellowship', and that this made collaboration between Friends and non-Friends more difficult.[48] These concerns echoed those expressed in the later 1920s by Rufus Jones, whose idea of the 'Wider Quaker Fellowship' entailed the building of cross-denominational alliances in the interests of developing the kinds of social service of which the Society ultimately approved. Jones had been accused of advocating a two-tier membership of the Society, and on these grounds his scheme had been effectively sidelined by the mainstream of British Quakerism; but Wilson's ideas benefited from lacking this obvious (in Quaker eyes) fault by downgrading the idea of membership and concentrating rather on the opportunities for the individual, inspired by the Inner Light, to experience active service and fellowship without the need for membership or the invidious kind of affiliate membership that Jones was (wrongly) understood to have been proposing.

The continuing influence of the ageing Rufus Jones, still living in America, was seen when the trustees sought his advice on the possibility of supporting one of his countrymen, W. O. Mendenhall, a former president of Whittier College in California, to travel to Britain and carry out an inquiry into the position and prospects of British Quakerism, an idea that was regularly floated at JRCT meetings during the war.[49] Nevertheless, as Arnold Rowntree recognised, such an inquiry (which Seebohm supported, having, after all, spent most of his life making inquiries of one sort or another) would in some respects defeat the object of encouraging a new generation of Friends to take on board the responsibilities that the trustees and their collaborators had borne in previous years.[50] The practical result of these deliberations was a long series of conferences, beginning in 1941 and continuing until at least 1949, at which either the trustees met by themselves to discuss what could be done to reinvigorate the Society or, more usually, the trustees met with groups of interested parties to recommend the directions that future leadership within the Society should take. The basic problem, in Roland Whiting's view, was a result of the expansion and diversification of secular leisure opportunites available to the young, which turned practical Quakerism into a part-time activity:

> The circumstances of our time are very different from those of 50 years ago. Mission Meetings, large Sunday Schools, the round of activities we associate with a vigorous Non-conformist church are rarely to be found. Instead the characteristics is [*sic*] that the group of a higher [than] average intellectual attainment, people who rarely meet each other except on the Sunday and who devote themselves in their spare time to a variety of outside interests, including public and social work, and cultural and recreational pursuits.[51]

Nevertheless, it was recognised that some of the problems echoed those of the 1890s, when a limited vocal ministry was compounded by a membership (or body of attenders) full of evangelical fervour but without the necessary 'understanding of Quaker principles', and hence able to 'contribute very little to the building up of the congregation'.[52] If the war had attracted many individuals to Quakerism, most had little understanding of it and appeared sufficiently cynical, irreligious or cautious to rule out actually joining the Society. This was certainly the case among members of the FAU and other relief bodies. Thus a conference was held on 1 January 1942, in 'an endeavour to find out whether in the ranks of the F.A.U. and [WVRC] there is a yearning after a deeper spiritual life'. This conference agreed that

There did not seem much indication of the thoughts of the members of these services turning in that direction. The emphasis is naturally at the present time on action and there is a sense of futility arising from a certain amount of enforced inactivity ... [therefore t]he present seems to be a time for preparing the ground rather than for rapid growth.[53]

Some observers may have noted that the time for preparing the ground had lasted rather a long time already – similar phraseology had been employed by John Hughes in the early 1930s[54] – but some grounds were found for hope. The series of conferences stopped for a while in late 1942 and early 1943, apparently because the concern as expressed by the trustees 'had to some extent laid hold of the Society as a whole'.[55] Some constructive suggestions were put forward, all of which ultimately entailed the identification, training and employment of suitable individuals, preferably from among the youth of the Society, to work in and strengthen local Meetings. One such model was drawn from the example of the educational settlement movement: it was suggested that a similar kind of experiment could be initiated in some Meetings, involving the residence of young workers, preferably a married couple, in a Meeting, where they would organise a range of non-worship activities, and keep a hearth and home where members and seekers could be accommodated and receive personal spiritual guidance. This would have the effect of improving the quality of Bible teaching at the level of the Meeting.[56] One manifestation of this idea was the work of the young Friend Hugh Doncaster and his wife in Cardiff, where they acted as 'caretakers' in the local Meeting, and were recommended as useful future workers in the John Hughes tradition.[57] Other suggestions that cropped up were a mixture of the traditional and the innovative, including the training of individuals for the vocal ministry; improved premises for Meeting houses; the encouragement of interpersonal contact between the older and younger members of individual Meetings; more summer schools and lecture courses, especially at Woodbrooke; the establishment of junior Quarterly Meetings as had recently been pioneered in London; and, as ever, more trained leaders in the mould of John Hughes and Neave Brayshaw.[58] Some of these suggestions, however, were always likely to arouse suspicion among the more conservative members of the Society of Friends: thus, following one conference in 1943, Ernest Taylor aggrievedly recorded that '[w]hen it was suggested that we should lay hands on young people like Hugh Doncaster who showed clear signs of a call to Quaker work, one Friend queried whether we were in danger of setting up pastors.'[59]

This was precisely one of the queries that had arisen in the 1890s, when the Home Mission Committee sent paid workers out to Quarterly Meetings to improve the vocal ministry and hence provoked reservations about the creation of a separate ministry.[60] Yet recollections of the 1890s inevitably evoked the spirit of the Manchester conference and the immense missionary efforts that it had initiated among the young generation of Friends under the influence of John Wilhelm Rowntree. The members of the JRCT were well aware that the jubilee of the Manchester conference would fall in 1945, and hoped that a similar gathering held in connection with the anniversary would bring in its train a similar outpouring of social concern.[61] There is no indication that such a jubilee conference actually took place; however, the JRCT did support, to the extent of over £300, a conference at Cober Hill in 1947 to commemorate the jubilee of the first Quaker summer school at Scarborough in 1897. About a hundred Friends attended this conference, and a follow-up event was held at Easter 1948.[62] Under the inspiration of John S. Hoyland – a veteran of the influential Young Friends' conference at Swanwick in 1911 and in the 1930s warden of Holland House at Woodbrooke – there was also a revival of the Quaker tramps that had so motivated men like Neave Brayshaw in the Edwardian period.[63] Others hoped for a revival of other traditional forms of Quaker service, such as the adult school movement, which the new NASU secretary (and later its historian) Arnold Hall hoped would be one of the main beneficiaries of a Quaker revival;[64] while the JRCT itself established a Trust Visitation Group, with the aim of organising visits to Meetings where required, acting in concert with the Yorkshire Friends Service Committee. As this group[65] explained in 1944, '[m]any Friends are so pressed in their duties during the week that they have no time to visit at weekends. Yet the visit [made] under concern is one of the most important means of deepening the spiritual life.'[66]

After the war a fresh challenge to Quakers to use this deepening religious faith as a means of broadening their religious and social outlook was made by John W. Harvey in the Swarthmore lecture for 1947, published under the title *The salt and the leaven*. Linking the two greatest traditional areas of Quaker social concern – peace and education – with the Society's special forms of worship, Harvey urged Friends to worship with a greater sense of purpose, arguing that 'quietude' need not and should not entail introversion, and nor was it simply a case of 'meditation'.[67] Worship, he told his audience, must 'be concerned primarily with the divine Being whom we worship and very much less with ourselves and our states of mind'.[68] The traditional Quaker 'mistrust of formulating religious creeds' could all too easily resolve itself into an attitude of passive negativity in which positive thought and action were implicitly discouraged.[69] On the other hand, like Roger Wilson, Harvey felt that the fetishisation of the concept of membership could develop a sense of 'corporate feeling' so strong that it acted as an 'impediment to effective Christian action'.[70] Harvey compared the period he and his contemporaries were then living through to the period in which Quakerism had been founded almost three centuries previously: England was emerging from a devastating war, resulting in an urgent need both for the preservation of traditional religious values in a climate of rapid and uncertain change, and for the development of new forms of social action.[71] In no period of history was careful and rigorous religious thought needed more, for 'religious faith is not only the essential rehabilitator and preserver of acknowledged values [the salt], but the essential spring of energy in working them out on new fields and in unfamiliar applications [the leaven]'.[72] Harvey's emphasis on religious thought as the mainspring of action was perhaps a timely reminder to many in York Meeting, some of whose members were, according to David Rubinstein, beginning to have reservations about the apparent concentration of the Society on 'good works' to the detriment of the theological dimension of its distinctively Christian character.[73] Harvey, however, urged socially concerned Quakers to link religious thought and social concern, hoping that the inward strength generated by the careful fostering of a deeper spirituality within a revitalised Meeting for Worship would enable the individual to express his or her concern in the form of action. Social action, especially in the areas of peace and education chosen by Harvey, remained the necessary practical expression of concern.

Harvey was one of many Quakers associated with the JRCT who attended the third world conference of Friends, held in Oxford in 1952, to commemorate the Society's tercentenary.[74] This conference enabled English Quakers to contextualise their post-war concerns within a more global perspective: perhaps inevitably, east-west relations formed the core of the discussions on the peace testimony. Although the eclecticism of the Quakerism represented at the conference ensured that most of the discussion took place at a generalised and theoretical level, the call for a revitalisation of Quaker service, strengthened by recent memories of non-combatant wartime activities, was heard with particular resonance, and was expressed within the same context of Quaker worship that Harvey had addressed in 1947. In the uncompromisingly religious language that some in the Society felt was being threatened by the secularisation of social concern, study groups at the third world conference reported that

> Quaker service springs from the roots of our faith. It grows out of the inner experience of that deep compassion and sense of oneness with all mankind which Jesus Christ revealed as the eternal love of God for men. We must seek to live our whole lives in the awareness of this presence of the love of God, giving time gladly to meditation and worship, to the outreach of preaching from the heart, and to the compassionate sharing of the burdens of our neighbours.[75]

The state of the post-war world, the conference was told, necessitated Friends' involvement in 'civic and political action', and an outgoingness that would find opportunities for service outside the confines of the Society. Having said this, these opportunities were likely to arise through the experience of local Meetings, and perhaps Friends' schools, which should encourage wider participation in service; while the conference also endorsed the kind of sabbatical attachment to voluntary service that the JRCT had frequently supported in the past.[76] Quakers were urged to recognise that they were mainly 'citizens of privileged countries', a status which entailed a series of social duties including 'radical changes in our use of property, in our use of time, and in our privileged social position'.[77] These thoughts reflected the ambitions of bodies like the JRCT and the other Rowntree Trusts, which sought through the promotion of social action solutions to the 'underlying causes of weakness or evil'.[78] They were also inherent in the religious and social philosophy of many of the institutions supported by the Trust: thus John S. Hoyland told a conference of the Woodbrooke Extension Committee in 1941 of the pressing need to merge 'ideas' and 'action', emphasising that 'the gap between middle class Quakerism and the masses of the people could only be bridged by action'.[79]

The link between 'social thought' and 'social action' was fully expressed in Seebohm Rowntree's work. As the epigraph to his study of Rowntree, entitled *Social thought and social action*, Asa Briggs chose the words of the educationalist Kurt Hahn: 'The World of Action and the World of Thought are divided today, often even hostile. I pin my hope to those few men who feel "called upon both to think and to act."' Rowntree's activities during the war continued to be dominated by social investigation, and he was involved in a number of schemes, some political and some administrative, connected with national reconstruction, just as he had been during the previous conflict. His second survey of York, *Poverty and progress*, was eventually published in 1941, although the bulk of the research had been carried out in 1936, and by the time it appeared he had already moved on to new areas of work. He spent much of the war working with his long-time collaborator F. D. Stuart on investigations for the Liberal party's Reconstruction Committee, work which the JRCT supported despite the questionability of its charitable status.[80] More importantly, he was involved at various stages in the framing of the Beveridge proposals for the reform of statutory social welfare provision: he corresponded regularly with Beveridge, who, like Rowntree, had worked on the investigation of unemployment in the Edwardian period.[81] Rowntree sat on Beveridge's 'Sub-Committee of Experts', and warmly endorsed most of the proposals in the report on 'Social Insurance and Allied Services' that appeared in 1942, although he recognised that they would not by themselves abolish poverty.[82] He was generally impressed by the post-war reconstruction policies and the schemes that had been established to develop them: he contrasted the second world war with the first, remembering how 'in the last war we were all looking for a wonderful new world afterwards and what a ghastly mess we made of it'.[83] For the new post-war world he was optimistic about the prospect of the trade unions being drawn into governance in a kind of corporate state, believing that this augured well for the reforms he had hoped to stimulate through his books, and which he had already undertaken with some success in his own cocoa and confectionery business.[84] However, although relatively sanguine about the prospects of 'planning', he believed that ill-considered economic reform was undesirable, and the object of the Liberal reconstruction programme to which he contributed was to avoid the extremes of both the free market and the heavily planned economy. We have seen how he feared possible extremism of left and right after the war,[85] and in 1943 he told the JRCT that his reconstruction work aimed 'to present the middle view avoiding on the one hand a completely planned system, and on the other the evils of unrestricted freedom of enterprise'.[86] If the experiences of the war and the memories of the 1930s drove many in Britain into the socialist camp, the same cannot be said of Seebohm Rowntree, who remained committed to a decaying Liberal creed.

Once again, Seebohm's wartime and post-war interests reflected a mixture of old and new approaches to the investigation of social problems. He continued his inquiries into the employment of leisure time, which he had begun for the 1936 survey of York. In particular, he was interested in the recreational opportunities available for youths aged between fourteen and twenty, the crucial period of adolescence when many of the future habits of a lifetime were acquired. In 1941 he told the trustees that there was only one club in York for boys and one for girls, and that '[p]arental responsibility and the hold of the churches has immensely weakened, so that many young people are just drifting … just as serious attempts were required to prevent grave moral deterioration among young people as had been taken to deal with ill-health and malnutrition.'[87] In many respects this echoed the widespread concern about problems of 'boy life' in the Edwardian period, when fears of the moral consequences of 'blind-alley' employment and poor recreational provision prompted a number of surveys of the conditions of juvenile life and labour.[88] Another issue that he had first examined in the Edwardian period, the impact of gambling, was addressed again in the 1940s. In 1941 Rowntree declared that gambling was now 'Public Enemy No. 1',[89] and in subsequent years the JRCT awarded substantial sums to the National League for Education Against Gambling. For the Rowntrees, as always, there was an important spiritual dimension to this concern, Seebohm explaining that 'there is no hope for modern civilization unless it rests on a more spiritual basis'.[90] Broadening his interest from measurable material poverty to the spiritual and moral condition of the nation, after the war Seebohm, working closely with his 'research secretary' G. Russell

Lavers,[91] 'devoted much time to ascertaining the facts relating to the moral fibre of the nation', including leisure pursuits, church attendance, 'standards of honesty', 'sexual immorality' and 'the extent and effects of communism'. This involved interviews with churchmen, a census of church attendance, personal visits to clubs, and so on.[92] The result was the co-written volume *English life and leisure* (1951), in which Rowntree and Lavers called for a spiritual reawakening without which the social renewal that they believed necessary could not take place.[93]

Nowhere was this made more clear than in their chapter on religion, which as well as attempting to enumerate outward expressions of religious observance and to describe social activities ancillary to religious organisations such as adult schools, also drew readers' attention to the importance of spirituality and asked '[t]o what extent do people in Britain believe that Christianity is relevant to life in a scientific age?'[94] (These questions had long been of interest to Quakers.)[95] Rowntree and Lavers acknowledged the apparent irrelevance of the churches, and pointed to the 'great resurgence of brutality' during the second world war, taking as their example the bombing of German cities that they condemned as 'a series of acts of savagery that not only marked a sharp regression in the national character, but has also had a brutalizing effect that it may take years to expunge'.[96] Nevertheless, it was clear to them that despite these discouraging trends there was much scope for an expansion of Christianity through active religious leadership that could draw on the reserves of spirituality existing at the individual level, especially among the young. They dismissed the practices of the (expanding) Roman Catholic church as 'spiritual totalitarianism',[97] suggesting that the greatest need in the post-war world was 'a new presentation of the true values of Christianity, shorn of the embellishments and dogmatic assertions it has picked up from the time of its first revelation onwards'.[98] Behind these pleas for a spiritual awakening lay a continued emphasis on moral questions, and some of this was echoed in the individual case study reports that made up the first section of the book. These reveal various long-standing hostilities, especially towards socialism, Catholicism, divorce, tobacco, alcohol and gambling; and although mostly carried out by Lavers with the help of various assistants, they display a concern for personal and religious morality that echoes the Victorian background of the main author. Even so broadly sympathetic a biographer as Asa Briggs finds *English life and leisure* 'an interesting but a far from satisfactory volume',[99] although he does see it as a 'pioneer study' which helped to draw 'mass culture' closer to the mainstream of sociological inquiry.[100] Investigating the problem of leisure, begun for the 1936 survey of York, was not only an important aspect of Rowntree's social inquiries, but also reflected the social priorities of the Trust which funded much of his work. The implications of this for the JRCT's work in adult education will be explored in the next chapter.

Some of this work on leisure and religion exhibited a moral judgmentalism which was beginning to be viewed as rather outmoded among the growing community of academic sociologists; and some of the descriptions of individual case-studies in *English life and leisure* make for entertaining reading. 'Mr. H.', for example, a 22-year old publican's son, 'smokes heavily and considers himself something of a Don Juan', 'has no discernible interests except gambling, women, and drink' and was all in all a 'nasty bit of work'.[101] One rather pitiable woman, 'Mrs. W.',

> is distrustful of her fellow humans for most of them look down on her and show it. She might be any age between 40 and 55, but says she is 39. She is enormously fat, to an extent that defies description, and ... she is a complete slattern. She goes about with her clothes unfastened, bare feet thrust into muddy carpet slippers, long black hair uncombed, dirty hands and dirty face. Two men live with her, to one of whom she is married, and her children are divided between them. She is now pregnant again and it is astonishing that either of the men – both decent working-class types – could copulate with such a monstrous creature.[102]

'Mr. C', a 53-year old bachelor, 'is mildly homosexual and this had obviously sapped his moral fibre';[103] 'Mrs. Z.', a colonial widow, 'probably does not stop talking long enough to enable a man to make improper advances';[104] while a 54-year old vicar attributed his lack of interest in sex 'primarily to the excessive sweating when he worked in a foundry'.[105] One more irresistible example is 'Mr. P.', whose 'two interests are games and women – cricket in summer, football in winter, and copulation all the year round ... Not a churchgoer.'[106] It is difficult to see the value of the 220 case histories presented in *English life and leisure* in terms of sociological analysis, but Rowntree continued on this theme, beginning (but never completing) work on a study of the 'moral fibre of the nation', which was to concentrate on religion and the influence of communism.[107] It is to be presumed that Lavers carried out most of the work for these studies – and almost certain that he wrote up the case histories quoted above – but these inquiries did little for Rowntree's reputation. Indeed, although Rowntree, by now a widower, was dependent on Lavers for many of his personal as well as professional needs, concerns were being expressed by trustees and by the wider sociological community that Rowntree's postwar work was damaging his reputation as a social investigator.[108]

Rowntree and Lavers also collaborated on a third social survey of York, also published in 1951 and showing that the problem of measurable poverty had further declined in extent since 1936; and it may have been the general optimism of the early years of the welfare state that encouraged Rowntree to examine a different set of social problems in his final years. The old category of 'secondary poverty' was expunged from the survey, and a small margin was again allowed in the poverty line calculations for expenditure on non-essentials such as beer and tobacco. Using this standard, only a very small proportion of the population of York remained in poverty in 1950 (the year during which it was actually carried out). One of the most notable 'facts' to emerge from the survey was that in the case of over two-thirds of all households living in poverty the cause of that poverty could be attributed to the old age of the chief wage earner, which had in previous surveys been only a minor cause.[109] This reflects a shifting emphasis in poverty research in the post-war years, and a steady realisation that old age was a pressing problem in terms of social welfare. As early as 1943 Arnold Rowntree raised at a JRCT meeting the problems of old people, especially in times of war when it was difficult for them to obtain the level of domestic assistance that was available to them in peacetime.[110] During the war Seebohm was appointed chairman of a Nuffield Foundation committee to investigate problems of old age in a number of towns; and the Village Trust also commissioned a survey of the elderly in York.[111] This research presaged the increasing attention the subject would receive from academic sociologists after the war, most notably Peter Townsend, whose first major work at the outset of a career in poverty research was a study of *The family life of old people*, an inquiry carried out in East London and first published in 1957.

Although secondary poverty was not considered a valid category for the 1951 survey, which announced itself as a study 'dealing only with economic questions', Rowntree did not lose interest in it, recognising that his survey 'necessarily assumes the competent management of income – a condition which is far from fully achieved',[112] and began a secondary poverty survey, which was to be based on evidence gathered from intensive house-to-house surveys in Hull, Fulham and elsewhere. Such a study would clearly necessitate the use of case-work – a method Rowntree was employing more frequently towards the end of his life – rather than a statistical survey, and he was able to secure the cooperation of a number of religious authorities in the carrying out the survey, as well as the Labour MP for Camberwell Peckham, Freda Corbett.[113] It was probably good for Rowntree's reputation that this survey was never published, as some of the information recorded on the household schedules that have survived tells us much more about the moral preoccupations of the investigators than the people who are described on them.[114] Nevertheless, lest this brief examination of Seebohm Rowntree's last years should seem excessively critical, we should bear in mind that in memoranda and at Trust meetings in this period he suggested many avenues for future work that did presage later social research agendas, especially work on the problems of adolescence (a concern which Rowntree and Lavers voiced in *English life and leisure*),[115] race relations, old age, B.B.C. listener research and, more traditionally but no less important in the context of a resurgence of interest in the subject among Church leaders in the post-war years, the problem of gambling.[116]

These surveys represented Seebohm's swansong in the work of social inquiry, and his cousin Arnold was also enjoying his last few years pursuing the work of adult education and trying to shape its future. Between them these two men dominated the JRCT in the late 1940s, although it was realised that this domination could not last much longer. Roger Wilson, who succeeded Arnold as Trust chairman in 1950, has left a valuable record of trustees' meetings in the 1940s, bringing out some of the tensions between members of the Rowntree family that characterised many of their deliberations. This is worth quoting at some length, as it reveals much about the interaction between trustees that the minute books do not record:

> When I began to attend Trust meetings in 1941 ... the effective weight of Trust business lay on the shoulders of Arnold Rowntree, Chairman, and Seebohm Rowntree. Essentially, Trust meetings were somewhat spikey dialogues between ASR [Arnold Rowntree] and BSR [Seebohm Rowntree], with occasional abrasive contributions from Arthur Gillett (who always maintained that J[oseph] R[owntree] had appointed him a Trustee with instructions to keep an eye on ASR's 'sanctified ingenuity' – the phrase was Henry Cadbury's in respect of Quaker relief work – in guiding Trust charity). The other senior Trustees, all close relatives of ASR and BSR, were of the same generation and were largely silent, yet weighty. At the other end of the age range were [Christopher Rowntree], his sister Tessa and I, all in our early mid-thirties. We met on Mondays in a great first-floor reception room at the Station Hotel, looking out on the Minster – I loved it.

Arnold and Seebohm disputed their points in front of an awed, and at times perhaps somewhat embarrassed, audience:

> The dialogues between ASR and BSR were often emotionally painful, but they weren't negligible ... It was unmistakably clear that here were two very remarkable men who had used charitable funds, each in his own way ... ASR's vision had given a new dimension to adult education that has endured and developed. BSR had been a key contributor to the whole changing pattern of socio-economic thought in the country. It was humbling just to sit round the table with them, treated as an equal, even though they were now getting old, used to perceiving what needed to be done and doing it in their own way, without much question but with full explanation ... The styles of ASR and

BSR were totally different. ASR would, as it were, stretch out his arms to embrace the whole body of Trustees and bring them to enjoyment of his proposition and point of view by the yearning warmth of his affection. BSR's response tended to be to escape the embrace by suggesting that the true issue was different, so that they talked past each other. When BSR was taking the initiative, his method tended to be rational, point by point, without much emphasis on faith or personal vision or settings, so that it was difficult to raise large issues of principle with him. ASR had vast tolerance and the humour of warmth. BSR was not very tolerant, but had a twinkling wit that could ease difficult situations.[117]

It was clear to Wilson even at this early stage that significant changes were soon to occur in the composition of the body of trustees. The JRSST had already begun to diversify the profile of its trustees with the addition of new members in the late 1930s. With the exception of John Bowes Morrell, who was appointed a trustee in 1906 (and was to serve until 1963), until 1938 all members of the JRSST were also trustees of the JRCT (Richard Cross and William Braithwaite served on both Trusts, and Ernest Taylor joined the JRSST in 1925, having joined the JRCT ten years earlier). However, in 1938 William Bowes Morrell, son of John Bowes Morrell, and Seebohm Rowntree's son Philip were added to the JRSST, and Seebohm Rowntree's long-time collaborator F. D. Stuart served from 1941 until his death in 1946. (Christopher Rowntree and John W. Harvey did not join the JRSST.) A number of new appointments were made after the war. Similarly, the JRVT, which had appointed Thomas H. Appleton (who served from 1906 to 1933) and Richard Cross (1913-16) before the first world war, was joined by Peter Rowntree, another son of Seebohm, and William Wallace (a solicitor, civil servant and industrialist closely associated with Rowntree and Company, and another of Seebohm's collaborators) in 1933. F. D. Stuart also joined the JRVT in 1941, and was followed by John Wilhelm's daughter Jean Rowntree in 1943; again, there were a number of new appointments after the war.[118]

The senior trustees were keen to see that their younger colleagues appreciated what Joseph Rowntree had had in mind when establishing his Trusts. Thus Arnold Rowntree, writing in 1946, remembered his own conversations with 'JR' in the early 1900s, and remarked that '[w]hilst he felt sure that the Trustees he was hoping to appoint knew his mind and outlook regarding these problems – looking into the indefinite future he felt that however carefully new trustees were chosen – they could not understand his wishes in the same way as those whom he was then appointing and who he hoped for years would have the opportunity of associating with him and sitting with him in the administration of the Trust.'[119] Nevertheless, as the Trust had been reconstituted after the expiration of

186

its initial thirty-five-year lifespan in 1939, there was by this stage little choice but to appoint new trustees to carry its work forward. With the single exception of Christopher Rowntree, the trustees of the JRCT at the outbreak of war were all born in the nineteenth century (even John Harvey was aged 50 in 1939) and were becoming unable to undertake personally the kind of practical work which they were keen to support. It was therefore clear that some more representation from among the younger generation would be helpful to the work of the Trust; this was symptomatic of a more general problem, as we have seen, of an ageing body of trustees who were beginning to find their work something of a strain, while the Trust secretary J. Roland Whiting was approaching retirement. The trustees were conscious of the fact that they were no longer in such close touch with the individuals and organisations they supported as they had been in earlier times. It was therefore agreed in 1939 that 'additional younger trustees should soon be appointed';[120] and once again Roger Wilson's name was mentioned as a possible candidate.[121] He and Arnold Rowntree's daughter Tessa (who married John H. (Jack) Cadbury in 1942) began attending meetings in 1941. However, it was not until after the war that any formal appointments were made.

The new appointments to the JRCT reflected a mixture of conservatism and forward-thinking. The first of these was Michael Rowntree, son of Arnold, educated at Bootham and Oxford, and a prominent member of the FAU during the war. Appointed in 1947, Michael was beginning a career in newspapers, and would spend some 30 years in Oxford before returning to York. He was followed by Roger Wilson in 1948, and in the same year by William Braithwaite's son Alfred and by Redford Crosfield Harris, a London Quaker accountant, treasurer of the Friends Home Service Committee and the NASU, and assistant clerk to Yearly Meeting. Braithwaite and Harris had been suggested as possible candidates for trusteeships in 1945,[122] and all four of the new intake had considerable experience of working directly in some or all of the fields that the JRCT remained concerned to support. Braithwaite, for example, was treasurer of Woodbrooke, and, as a trained solicitor working in insurance, also brought valuable legal and financial expertise to the Trust. The familial links with the older (and previous) trustees reflect Arnold Rowntree's conservative leanings in the matter of new appointments, while the early acceptance of Wilson and the comparative youth of the new intake suggest that the older trustees recognised the importance of drawing in the younger elements of the Society of Friends. Arthur Gillett's son Nicholas joined the Trust in 1951: he was married to Ruth Cadbury and a lecturer at the Dudley Training College for Teachers, as well as chairman of the Fircroft executive committee.[123] (In 1946 the trustees also approached, among others, Duncan Fairn, now running the prison officers' training school at Wakefield, but he was unable to take on the additional commitment.)[124] In 1947, Eric Cleaver, an engineer in his early forties working at the British Thomson-Houston works in Rugby, became a Trust employee, with the intention that he would replace J. Roland Whiting as Trust secretary when the latter retired in 1949: Cleaver was involved with the FRS and wanted to work with conscientious objectors.[125] Roger Wilson, whose experience of the Trust went back to the early years of the war, thoroughly welcomed the changes in Trust practice and policy that these new appointments engendered:

> there was now a strong body of Trustees who were used to exploring the minds of other people with whom they met without a common family background, and most of whom had a fairly wide experience of the Society in other relationships than that of their own meetings. Trust discussions, therefore, steadily became far more wide-ranging, far more participant, and much less centred on the personal active responsibility of individual Trustees, a guideline indicated by J.R. in the 1904 memorandum.[126]

Nevertheless, the trustees, no doubt in the light of Arnold's reservations about leaving the future direction of the Trust in the hands of those who had not known the Founder personally, 'instituted the practice of reading extracts from the 1904 memorandum',[127] to keep themselves reminded of the objects that Joseph Rowntree had in view. Whether this was at the rather pompous insistence of Arnold or Seebohm, or initiated by the younger trustees as the result of a genuine desire to understand the wishes of the Founder, is unclear. What is clear, however, is that all the trustees were conscious that they were embarking on a period of transition; and this transition, as the next chapter will show, entailed not only wholesale changes to the personnel of the JRCT, but also a significant and arguably fundamental change in the focus of its grant-making.

NOTES

1. *The Friend*, 4 November 1938, quoted in Brown, *Making of a modern Quaker*, 62-3.
2. On the impact the second world war on York Quakers, see David Rubinstein, *Faithful to ourselves and the outside world: York Quakers during the twentieth century*, York 2001, 73-99; Allott, *Friends in York*, 109-13.
3. See Greenwood, *Friends and relief*, York 1995, ch. 16, esp. 277, and for the FAU ch. 17; for the official history of the FAU during the second world war see A. Tegla Davies, *Friends Ambulance Unit: the story of the FAU in the second world war 1939-1946*, 1947.
4. JRCT minute book, no. 4, minute no. 567 (g).
5. Vipont, *Arnold Rowntree*, 104-5.
6. Heron, *Quakers in Britain*, 45-7; Greenwood, *Friends and relief*, 275-6.

7. Brown, *Making of a modern Quaker*, 112-14; Heron, *Quakers in Britain*, 46-7. As Heron points out, it was argued that the wearing of a khaki uniform would identify FRS workers as allies of the British cause, and eventually a grey uniform was agreed upon; however, '[i]t does not seem to have occurred to anyone ... that the uniform of the German army was also grey.'
8. Heron, *Quakers in Britain*, 45.
9. JRCT minute book, no. 4, minute no. 44 (b).
10. See Stanley Smith, *Spiceland Quaker training centre*, York 1990.
11. Information on the initiation and duration of funding relationships are taken, with permission, from the database of JRCT peace grantees created by Lorna Gold.
12. See Basil Eastland, Derek Edwards and David Sainty (eds), *Volunteers for peace: field reports on relief work in Europe 1944-1949 by International Voluntary Service for Peace*, Kelso 1998, 13. Most of the general information on the IVSP is taken from this volume.
13. JRCT minute book, no. 4, minute no 202 (c).
14. Ibid. minute no. 68.
15. Ibid. minute no. 28.
16. JRCT, 'Review of operations for the year 1942', 6, JRF JRCT93/I/11 (b).
17. JRCT, 'Review of operations for the year 1944', 4, JRF JRCT93/I/11 (b).
18. JRCT, 'Review of operations for the period 14 December 1939 to 31 December 1941', 5, JRF JRCT93/I/11 (b).
19. 'Summary of reports of educational settlements and residential colleges concerning the work they were able to undertake after the outbreak of war', 1, JRF JRCT93/IV/1 (d).
20. Allaway, *Educational centres movement*, 38-9.
21. 'Summary of reports of educational settlements and residential colleges', 1.
22. Ibid. 3-4, 10.
23. Ibid. 9.
24. Naylor, *Quakers in the Rhondda*, 65ff.
25. Allaway, *Educational centres movement*, 37.
26. JRCT minute book, no. 4, minute nos. 9, 44 (c).
27. Ibid. minute nos. 54 (a), 63. The Cadburys also supported Dudley's work.
28. Allaway, *Educational centres movement*, 38.
29. Much of the following account is taken from Edith R. Richards, 'The second world war', in Davis, *Woodbrooke*, 73-8.
30. Ibid. 73.
31. JRCT minute book, no. 4, minute no. 564 (c).
32. Ibid. minute nos. 196 (a), 263 (a).
33. Ibid. minute no. 196 (a).
34. Richards, 'Second world war', 77.
35. Hall, *Adult school movement*, 153.
36. Ibid. 147-8, 160-1.
37. JRCT minute book, no. 3, minute no. 468 (c).
38. Hall, *Adult school movement*, 146.
39. Champness, *Adult schools*, 68-9.
40. Ibid. 71-2, 78.
41. JRCT minute book, no. 4, minute no. 18.

42. See Hall, *Adult school movement*, 168.
43. JRCT minute book, no. 4, minute no. 13.
44. Ibid. minute no. 128.
45. Roger C. Wilson, 'Some reflections on being a member of the Joseph Rowntree Charitable Trust 1941-1977', 1977, 2, JRF Library, HA3/ROW (oversize).
46. JRCT minute book, no. 4, minute no. 147.
47. Ibid. minute no. 328.
48. Ibid. minute no. 354.
49. Ibid. minute no. 260.
50. Ibid. minute no. 128. See also [Ernest Taylor?], memorandum, 'Quaker enquiry', 17 February 1942, JRF JRCT93/VI/4; and for Seebohm Rowntree's enthusiasm for such an inquiry, 'Report on the work done by the JRCT', 19.
51. J. Roland Whiting, draft memorandum, 5 June 1941, JRF JRCT93/VI/4.
52. Ibid.
53. Memorandum for JRCT meeting held on 2 March 1942, reporting four conferences including one held on 1 January 1942, JRF JRCT93/VI/4.
54. Hughes, referring to his role of 'husbandry in the Society [of Friends]', told Ernest Taylor that it was a 'preparative time', with no obvious signs of a great spiritual awakening (Hughes to Taylor, n.d. [1931], JRF JRCT93/VI/2 (a)). See above, p. 117.
55. Memorandum, 'The religious life of the Society of Friends', 30 March 1943, JRF JRCT93/VI/5, reproducing JRCT minute book, no. 4, minute no. 197 (h).
56. JRCT minute book, no. 4, minute nos. 214, 248; report on Friends Home Service Committee conference, 20 May 1941, JRF JRCT93/VI/4.
57. JRCT minute book, no 4, minute no. 156; reports in JRF JRCT93/VI/5.
58. See for example JRCT minute book, no. 4, minute no. 290; report on 'Conference on the Society of Friends and its new need held at the Penn Club', 1 July 1943, JRF JRCT93/VI/5.
59. Report on London conference, 6 July 1943, JRF JRCT93/VI/5.
60. Whiting, draft memorandum, 5 June 1941.
61. JRCT minute book, no. 4, minute no. 290; JRCT, 'Review of operations for the year 1944', 3-4.
62. JRCT, 'Review of operations for the year 1947', 4, JRF JRCT93/I/11 (b).
63. JRCT minute book, no. 4, minute no. 264 (g).
64. Ibid. minute no. 214.
65. Comprising in 1944 Ernest Taylor, Herbert Waller, Wilfred Allott, J. Roland Whiting and John Hunter, secretary of the Yorkshire Friends Service Committee.
66. Memorandum of Trust Visitation Group, meeting at Leeds, 10 February 1944, JRF JRCT93/VI/5.
67. John W. Harvey, *The salt and the leaven*, 1947, 72-3. For the significance of this lecture, see Heron, *Quakers in Britain*, 51.
68. Harvey, *Salt and leaven*, 79.
69. Ibid.
70. Ibid. 20ff.

71. Ibid. 7-8.
72. Ibid. 16.
73. Rubinstein, *Faithful to ourselves*, 124-5, 127-8.
74. Delegates included Wilfrid Allott, Gerald Bailey, Eric Cleaver, John S. Hoyland, Richard K. Ullmann, Roger Wilson and Herbert Wood. A list can be found in Friends World Committee for Consultation (FWCC), *Friends face their fourth century: the third world conference of Friends*, 1952, 93-110. Redford Crosfield Harris also attended (p. 83), but is not included in the list of delegates.
75. FWCC, *Friends face their fourth century*, 43.
76. Ibid. 44-6.
77. Ibid. 44.
78. Founder's memorandum, 4.
79. Report of Woodbrooke Extension Committee conference, 13-14 September 1941, JRF JRCT93/VI/4.
80. See Briggs, *Seebohm Rowntree*, 310ff.
81. W. H. Beveridge, *Unemployment: a problem of industry*, 1909; Rowntree and Lasker, *Unemployment*.
82. Briggs, *Seebohm Rowntree*, 306-10.
83. Ibid. 306 n. 8.
84. Ibid. 304-5.
85. See above, pp. 140-1.
86. JRCT minute book, no. 4, minute no. 201.
87. Ibid. minute no. 81 (a).
88. On Edwardian attitudes to adolescence see for example Harry Hendrick, *Images of youth: age, class and the male youth problem 1880-1920*, Oxford 1990.
89. Rowntree, *Poverty and progress*, 399.
90. JRCT minute book, no. 4, minute no. 18.
91. Briggs, *Seebohm Rowntree*, 319. Lavers was appointed following the death of F. D. Stuart in 1946.
92. JRCT, 'Review of operations for the year 1947', 6.
93. See in particular their chapter on religion: Rowntree and Lavers, *English life and leisure*, 339-74.
94. Ibid. 366.
95. See for example Arthur Stanley Eddington's Swarthmore lecture, *Science and the unseen world*, 1929.
96. Rowntree and Lavers, *English life and leisure*, 369-70.
97. Ibid. 374.
98. Ibid. 373.
99. Briggs, *Seebohm Rowntree*, 323.
100. Ibid. 327.
101. Rowntree and Lavers, *English life and leisure*, 102.
102. Ibid. 5.
103. Ibid. 19.
104. Ibid. 36.
105. Ibid. 60.
106. Ibid. 2-3.
107. JRCT minute book, no. 4, minute no. 508.

108. Wilson to Eric Cleaver, 1 April 1953, JRCT basement archive, box 22.
109. B. Seebohm Rowntree and G. R. Lavers, *Poverty and the welfare state: a third social survey of York, dealing only with economic questions*, 1951, 34-6.
110. JRCT minute book, no. 4, minute no. 220.
111. Ibid. minute no. 298 (d); JRCT, 'Review of operations for the year 1944', 7; Research Services Ltd, 'A survey of aged people in York', 1949, JRF BSR93/XI/6.
112. JRCT minute book, no. 4, minute no. 823 (c).
113. Ibid. minute nos. 837 (c), 854 (c).
114. The original schedules are in JRF BSR93/XI/5 (a)-(c).
115. Rowntree and Lavers, *English life and leisure*, 109-21: case histories of young people under the age of twenty.
116. Ibid. 122-58; Briggs, *Seebohm Rowntree*, 322-3, 342; JRCT minute book, no. 4, minute no. 508 for a list of future concerns including listener research, minute no. 889 (d) for 'racial intolerance'; see also JRCT, 'Review of operations for the year 1947', 7.
117. Wilson, 'Some reflections', 1-2. It was not strictly the case that the other senior trustees were 'all close relatives' of Arnold and Seebohm Rowntree, as Ernest Taylor was not related to the Rowntree family in any way. The remainder – Gillett, Sturge and Harvey – were all related to Arnold Rowntree by marriage.
118. For a list of JRSST/JRRT and JRVT/JRMT/JRF trustees to 1994, see *The Joseph Rowntree inheritance*, 33, 40.
119. Arnold Rowntree, memorandum, 30 January 1946, JRF JR93/VIII/5.
120. JRCT minute book, no. 3, minute no. 568.
121. JRCT Minute book, no. 4, minute no. 28.
122. Ibid. minute no. 349.
123. Ibid. minute no. 870.
124. Ibid. minute nos. 437, 456, 481.
125. Ibid. minute nos. 517, 535. Cleaver was appointed in 1947, but his employment did not begin until January 1948.
126. Wilson, 'Some reflections', 3.
127. Ibid. 3-4.

CHAPTER 8

Adult education and beyond

IN 1945 EDUCATION was as important a cornerstone of the national
reconstruction programme as it had been after the first world war, and
adult education was expected to undergo a substantial reorganisation in
the light of wartime and pre-war experiences. Mass mobilisation into the
armed forces had allowed scope for adult educationalists to develop
schemes of teaching that were likely to attract a high demand, partly
because the audience was to an extent captive, and partly because of the
absence of alternative recreational opportunities. Even before the war
started a Central Council for Adult Education in HM Forces was established, with representatives from various adult education bodies, providing lectures for servicemen. Basil Yeaxlee, former secretary of the ESA
and an important figure in the NCSS's New Estates Community
Committee, was general secretary of this Council, before moving onto a
readership in religious education at the University of Oxford. There was
also an Army Bureau of Current Affairs (ABCA), directed by W. E.
Williams, who had prepared the scathing report on the state of the educational settlement movement for the JRCT in 1938. The ABCA was
influenced by the methods pioneered by the BBC, itself another important stimulant to the diffusion of adult education: the ABCA focused its
activities on the discussion group method favoured by broadcasters. To
some extent the educational settlement model permeated the wartime
efforts: Williams described army study centres as 'Educational
Settlements on active service'.[1] Apart from Yeaxlee and Williams, others
who had been involved in the ESA and its constituent bodies moved
through Forces' education during the war: Frank Milligan, for example,
Horace Fleming's successor as warden of Beechcroft, joined the Army
Education Corps, and then became secretary of the NCSS's Community
Centres and Associations Committee.[2] The ESA reported that involvement in the Forces and in non-combatant service developed in many individuals an ability and willingness to lead in post-war education, and shared
the JRCT's hopes that FAU and FRS veterans might be drawn into the
movement.[3] Essentially, wartime developments helped to hone the skills

and broaden the outlook of many adult educationalists and, just as importantly, to bring many men into adult education who might otherwise never have passed through the doors of an educational settlement, an adult school or any other institution.

In the light of the wartime experience of adult education, the authors of the Education Act of 1944 intended to expand local education authority provision after the war. LEAs, as J. F. C. Harrison has emphasised, were numerically the largest providers before the war, with 70,000 students taking their courses in 1937-8 in Yorkshire alone;[4] but as N. A. Jepson pointed out in 1959, their pre-war role had been 'largely confined to trying to remedy at an adult level the deficiencies of primary education, and to the provision of vocational and technical training'.[5] The 1944 Act envisaged a much larger role, embracing commercial education, the arts and cultural and recreational activities, incorporating much of the work that had previously been carried out by voluntary bodies, and was being pioneered in community associations. For the first time, local authority involvement in adult education became a statutory duty, LEAs coming under obligation 'to secure the provision for its area of adequate facilities for further education', which included 'leisure-time occupation, in such organized cultural training as are suited to their requirements, for any persons over compulsory school age who are able and willing to profit by the facilities for that purpose'.[6] Under the Act, each authority was required to carry out a large survey of its own area, and this in turn resulted in the preparation of a national plan, whereby a further education college would serve each large centre of population, surrounded by a network of smaller institutions such as community centres and youth clubs.[7] Such a plan, if universally adopted, might have modified the haphazard nature of adult education provision in Britain, but the economic climate of the post-war period prevented its full realisation. Nevertheless, some authorities, notably Kent County Council, developed a series of centres, supporting courses organised by the LEA and voluntary bodies, each enjoying a measure of autonomy. There were seven such centres in the county by 1954.[8] Earlier, the Cambridgeshire Education Committee had initiated a scheme of village colleges, beginning at Sawston in 1930; the best known was Impington, established in 1939, at which 'technical' courses organised by the WEA and other bodies, and 'cultural' or 'recreational' courses in needlework, cookery, art and so on, were provided. By 1943 there were about 400 regular users of the library, about 200 regular users of the other facilities including the canteen, and many other 'occasional users' who attended lectures, concerts and other events.[9] Other notable local authority adult education provision was to be found in Manchester and London. These developments reflected a steady encroachment of official provision into the field of adult education: with the widening demand, encouraged by the experience of war, for adult education of all kinds, it was becoming clear that 'private resources [such as those employed by the ESA] were clearly insufficient to meet the national need'.[10]

Nevertheless, voluntarily provided adult education remained important, both for the voluntarists themselves – the ESA viewed LEA centres as 'merely a second best' to the educational settlements – and for the Ministry of Education and the local authorities. The Education Act also required LEAs to consult with other bodies involved in adult education: as one Ministry of Education circular urged, 'the first need is co-operative action by authorities, universities, and voluntary organisations of every kind'.[11] Many of these bodies had collaborated in an investigation instituted in 1942 under the auspices of the British Institute of Adult Education (BIAE), published as *Adult education after the war* in 1945. The inquiry committee was chaired by the Institute's president, Viscount Sankey, and included representatives from the NCSS, local authorities and the Army Education Corps; and although the ESA was not directly represented, W. E. Williams and Basil Yeaxlee were both members, as was James Dudley, former warden of Avoncroft residential college, who drafted the report. The committee's recommendations centred on the financing of adult education: it called for a variety of provision, with better premises, more dispersal to include rural areas, more use of films and broadcasting as educational tools, efforts to recruit staff from the armed forces and other sources and the improvement and standardisation of conditions of employment in the sector, all to be funded either centrally by the Board of Education (the Ministry of Education after the war) or through the devolved local education authorities. Recognising the importance of the institutional provision of adult education, as pioneered by the ESA, the report declared bluntly that '[t]he initial cost and upkeep of the building and the expense of the salary of a full-time warden will continue to limit the development of adult education in institutional forms by voluntary organizations unless they receive financial aid from public funds.'[12] Institutions like London's City Literary Institute and the Cambridgeshire village colleges were cited as examples of what could be achieved given this kind of support; the limited expansion of the ESA was used as an example of what happened when such support was denied.[13]

The diverse spectrum of voluntarily provided or inspired adult education examined by this report was described by J. F. C. Harrison as a 'jungle of adult learning'. The jungle was not necessarily impenetrable: indeed, although it was initially indicative of a 'regrettable administrative confusion', Harrison argued that it soon 'began to appear rather as a normal part of a mature system of adult education in a mass democracy'.[14] Undoubtedly a wide range of different kinds of institutional and non-institutional provision was appropriate to the more complex forms of social organisation that characterised the mid-twentieth century. Two corners of the jungle that expanded significantly in the 1940s were the WEA and university extension. The number of grant-aided classes provided by the WEA expanded from 793 in the 1937-8 academic year to 3580 in 1948-9, while grant-aided extension classes grew in number from 1374 to 3441.[15] The university extension sector was positively flourishing in the 1950s,[16] buoyed by the establishment of adult education departments such as the Department of Extra-Mural Studies at the University of Leeds in 1946, and imaginative appointments such as that of Roger Wilson to a chair in education at the University of Bristol.[17] (Wilson was lured to Bristol by the vice-chancellor, Sir Philip Morris, who had run the Kent Education Committee before acting as Director-General of Army Education at the end of the war.) Indeed, ultimately this expansion threatened the WEA, which by the 1950s was experiencing a 'relative slowing-down' in growth and facing possible obsolescence: 'The W.E.A. belonged to a great tradition, and there were signs that this tradition had passed its prime, that parts of it indeed had been eroded away.'[18] In essence, it was felt by many, rightly or wrongly, that the development of university extension – assisted by comparatively generous state support – represented a professionalisation of adult education and an effacement of the ideals and practice of voluntarism that had underpinned the WEA and other providers including the ESA. Thus Eric Ashby (vice-chancellor of Queen's University, Belfast, and later Master of Clare College, Cambridge, knighted in 1956) argued in 1955 that universities embodied a particular examination-based, and hence compartmentalising, attitude to knowledge, against which the voluntary spirit offered an important counterweight. It was therefore a matter for concern that 'the voluntary spirit as exemplified by the W.E.A. has in some ways lost its momentum and its sense of dedication'.[19] Whether professionalisation as a result of the spread of university extension should have been a matter for concern – and J. F. C. Harrison, for one, argued that Ashby's concern was misplaced[20] – it did seem to many contemporaries that the benefits of voluntarism were being lost, as universities embraced a duty of moral leadership under the executive leadership of the LEAs as provided for in the 1944 Act.[21] To emphasise this, the educational settlement movement's first historian A. J. Allaway, in his inaugural lecture as professor of adult education at University College Leicester in 1951, was able to declare that adult education was 'no longer a charity graciously bestowed ... but a public service which everyone ... is able to enjoy as of right'.[22]

Eric Ashby was only one of a range of defenders of the voluntary principle in adult education in the post-war period. The BIAE, in *Adult education after the war*, observed that, although the development of British welfare services in the nineteenth and twentieth centuries had generally followed a pattern whereby voluntarily provided services were gradually taken over by the state, this process was 'not inevitable or stereotyped, or even always desirable or necessary'.[23] The committee recognised that the withdrawal of voluntary bodies in the wake of the provision of Board of Education or local authority grants was tempting, 'in these days of "planning" and in the light of what is happening in other forms of social service', but asserted that 'in spite of the advantages from an administrative point of view, of a unified service under central control, this would be contrary to the true interests of adult education'.[24] Indeed, while Allaway pointed to the need for 'education for politico-economic responsibility' within the planned or 'purposive' economy,[25] the JRCT saw voluntarily provided adult education as offering a counterweight to the potential excesses of 'planning':

> In the present progressively socialised world it would appear to be the part of voluntary enterprise to pioneer experiments which require a more audacious vision than statutory authorities dare to command. It is imperative that this service should be rendered, and the influence of such pioneer endeavours is often vastly in excess of their size.[26]

At the ESA's[27] annual general meeting in 1948, in the wake of serious concerns about its future policy (and, indeed, its whole future),[28] it was agreed that there was a 'need for an Association to keep alive the voluntary spirit at a time when administration threatened to slow down the whole movement of Adult Education'.[29] Indeed, when government and local authority spending cuts in the later 1940s and early 1950s threatened many of the advances made in adult education since the end of the war, the JRCT heard that it was the duty of voluntary bodies to maintain 'vigilance' in the wake of such retrenchment.[30]

The ESA was struggling to maintain its own clearing in the 'jungle of adult learning' within which it could prosper, and was concerned that, as the long-term poor relation of the WEA and university extension, it could be marginalised even further by the expansion of local authority provision and the widespread adoption of the 'centre idea' by LEAs. The ESA retained its status as a 'Responsible Body', eligible to receive grants-in-aid from the Ministry for its recognised courses: indeed, in the 1946-7 academic year it submitted more courses for recognition than in any previous year.[31] The executive saw this as one of the Association's main functions in a period of increasing uncertainty as to its role. Much of the language employed by the Association and its spokesmen appealed to the same considerations as the early pioneers had done at York, Leeds and Birkenhead. Thus the ESA claimed credit for the widespread acceptance of the model of non-residential institutional adult education that its settlements had pioneered, and applauded the recognition of this importance in the white paper on educational reconstruction on which the 1944

Act was based;[32] particular pride was taken in the white paper's emphasis on the value of centres which 'will not only provide the educational courses which the adult population may need, but will add to them the values associated with the life of a corporate institution'.[33] William Hazelton, still the ESA's secretary, addressing a JRCT meeting in December 1944, 'emphasised the significant fact of the recognition by the Ministry and by some L.E.A.s that Adult Education should take place in a "hearth and home" atmosphere rather than that of a school; a principle which E.S.A. Settlements were the first to put into practice'.[34] Addressing the JRCT in 1948, Hazelton (by now treasurer of the ESA and vice-chairman of its executive committee) maintained that the primary aim of this form of adult education was the provision of 'the right kind of atmosphere and spirit';[35] while in 1949 the same Trust congratulated itself on its success in 'maintaining and extending the type of education with a spiritual context in an atmosphere of "hearth and home" for which [it] has always stood'.[36]

Nevertheless, it was clear that the ESA needed to adapt itself and its associated institutions to the needs of the post-war environment. Change was already happening at the level of the individual settlements: at St. Mary's in York, for example, A. J. Peacock notes that 'more and more craft courses, do-it-yourself courses that were a response to appeals for help with the war effort' had been instituted in the early 1940s, and '[b]y the time the war ended the programme [of courses] had altered so drastically that it bore practically no resemblance to that of [Duncan] Fairn's time.'[37] The curriculum was packed with woodwork and dressmaking, along with language classes and flourishing ballet and dramatic activities: the settlement had become 'something very similar to a modern evening centre', 'a very different place from the one Arnold Rowntree had envisaged'.[38] Changes like these entailed a reinterpretation of the ESA's continuing insistence that the 'primary function' of an educational settlement was 'the progressive development of the individual through mental training, self-effort and the exercise of personal responsibility'.[39] At a central level, it was realised that the patrician image (and, to an extent, practices) of the settlements left them open to the criticism that the form of education they provided was unsuited to the more democratic age that the war appeared to have instituted. It was admitted that 'the word "Settlement" is not as acceptable to-day as it was in times past',[40] and the ESA finally abandoned its titular associations with Canon Barnett in 1946 when it changed its name to the Educational Centres Association (ECA). This was accompanied by more substantive change: in 1947 a new constitution was agreed which gave its members more say in its governance to counterbalance the disproportionate influence previously wielded by Arnold Rowntree and the other members of the ESA's executive committee.[41] However, even this did not prevent the warden of the Pontypool settlement asking '[w]hen would the E.C.A. cease to be a rich man's plaything?'[42] The climate within the ECA, together with his own failing health, precipitated Rowntree's resignation in 1948, and William Hazelton left the offices of treasurer and chairman of the executive committee at around the same time. Like the JRCT, the ECA was experiencing a significant set of changes of personnel. In 1946 Harold Marks, an Oxford graduate and former university extension tutor, was appointed the ECA's education officer, and Wells Houghton, who had been involved in military education during the war, became its information officer.

It was becoming clear to most in the ESA/ECA that the future of the model of institutional adult education that they sought to promote lay, at least as far as the voluntary sector was concerned, in the hands of community associations. Arnold Rowntree told the ESA executive in 1945 that, following discussion with community association leaders, it had become clear to him that 'the future of that movement was very closely related to the future of our own movement', and argued that the ESA and the National Federation of Community Associations (NFCA) should share offices and have a joint staff.[43] The NFCA was the post-war successor to the NCSS's Community Centres and Associations Committee: both Marks and Houghton worked for the NFCA, and it was not long before Houghton was entirely occupied with community association work.[44] William Hazelton and Ernest Taylor both agreed with Arnold Rowntree that 'the future of Adult Education is closely bound up with the development of Community Centres',[45] which offered a whole new arena for the promotion of what the ESA before the war had called 'community education'.[46] Although little educational work was carried on in the new institutions as yet, the ESA discerned substantial scope for the permeation of community centres with their ideals and expertise, claiming in 1945 that '[t]he aim of the founders of the Educational Settlement movement has now an ampler setting, and doors to its fulfilment seem about to open.'[47] The JRCT shared the ESA's optimism for the ideals of community education, and remained hopeful that other funding bodies would assume the lion's share of the financial support for both educational settlements and community centres in the post-war years. The extent of the trustees' ambition is indicated by a proposal at a Trust meeting in December 1945 to establish a new 'Community Education Trust', to which the JRCT and the JRVT between them would contribute £100,000, and which it was envisaged would be able to raise a total of a million pounds or more for expenditure on educational work, mainly in community centres.[48] Indeed, although Arthur Gillett dissented from the JRCT's resolution in 1946 to donate £50,000 over five years to the proposed new Trust, the remainder of the trustees clearly felt that the continuance of large-scale JRCT support for adult education was worthwhile only if directed along the new vectors of community social organisation provided by community associations and centres.[49]

In the event the establishment of a new Trust proved more difficult than anticipated. Although Arnold Rowntree believed that the Founder had intended the JRVT 'to advance the cause of good community living',[50] the latter was advised that donations to the proposed Trust would not fall within the terms of its Trust Deed. The solution adopted was the establishment of two separate Trusts, both essentially fulfilling the same functions. Like Joseph Rowntree in 1904, the new educational pioneers of the 1940s found that legal barriers compromised the unified scheme of philanthropy they hoped to promote. The result was a Community Education Trust (CEdT), funded by the JRCT, which was established 'for the purpose of providing leisure time educational facilities for persons over compulsory school age', and a Community Equipment Trust (CEqT), 'for the purpose of improving and ameliorating and promoting the improvement and amelioration of the living conditions of the working classes', a more ambiguous wording that reflected the JRVT's origins as a housing Trust.[51] The CEdT's Trust Deed explicitly included in its remit the establishment and support of educational settlements or centres, the training of staff and the possible establishment of a training college, the provision of bursaries to support training of wardens of staff, the allocation of grants to the ECA, NFCA and NASU, and expenditure on publicity to support these objectives.[52] The CEqT could support the establishment and maintenance of community centres and award grants to the NFCA, and was also allowed to support staff training and publicity.[53] In practice, all decisions were made by the two trusts acting in collaboration: as with the three Joseph Rowntree Trusts at their inception, the same individuals were the trustees of both the CEdT and CEqT, namely Arnold Rowntree, Ernest Taylor and Lewis Waddilove, who had become the JRVT's executive officer in 1946 and was to remain associated with it in its various incarnations until his death in August 2000.[54]

Much of the work of the CEdT and CEqT was motivated by the belief – first widely propounded in the interwar years – that one of the dangers facing post-war society lay in the expansion of leisure and the limited spread of educational opportunities: in 1939, as a CEdT memorandum of 1946 pointed out, less than one in a hundred of the adult population was attending classes at any adult education institution, while

> At the same time it is clear that a great and ever increasing number of people are spending a considerable part of their leisure time in attending cinemas, 'dog tracks', football matches and other places of amusement. It is probable that many of those who patronise these forms of entertainment do so, not out of any intrinsic interest in the

particular activity concerned, but because they are in need of some distraction.[55]

This depressing and somewhat patronising diagnosis of the social life of the nation was more than borne out by Seebohm Rowntree's study of *English life and leisure*, which presented the multiplication of commercialised entertainment as a potentially corrupting and undoubtedly counter-educational tendency. Addressing his personal concern in his later years for the 'moral fibre of the British people' – a subject on which other members of the JRCT were very willing to advise him at some length[56] – Rowntree struck a note of rather unquakerly evangelism in his call for a national spiritual reawakening, a project in which he believed that adult education would play a vital role. Although his own direct connection with adult education had by now largely eroded, he nevertheless saw a solution to the problem of leisure in the provision of wisely directed educational opportunities. He would, therefore, have been glad to hear William Hazelton tell the JRCT in 1948 that community centres were beginning to realise the importance of 'more culture' and 'an inspired service', even if Hazelton's optimism was probably somewhat misplaced.[57] The close links between Seebohm's interest in leisure and this aspect of community education was emphasised by the CEdT and CEqT's joint report for 1947, in which the trustees recognised the essentially experimental nature of the projects they supported: 'until B. S. Rowntree's comprehensive investigation into the ways in which people spend their leisure time was completed and available, the Trustees did not consider that they were in possession of the fullest factual information upon which plans for large and judicious spending could be formed'.[58]

However, the spirit that animated many of the efforts of the CEdT and CEqT in this period bore many similarities to that which had driven the pioneers of the educational settlement movement, similarities which can be discerned in the ambivalence with which the Rowntrees and their associates continued to approach the question of democratic governance in the settlements. During and after the war the clamour for education in the interests of democracy was heard from all quarters, echoing the language employed by Arnold Rowntree and Horace Fleming some decades earlier. The universities were engaged in 'education for citizenship',[59] while Harold Shearman (later chairman of the Inner London Education Authority and the Greater London Council), the WEA's education officer, called for 'education for constructive democracy' in the context of competing theories of economic organisation.[60] Arnold Rowntree agreed, telling the ESA in 1945 that settlements sought 'to raise the level of civic life by the energizing power of example and by the influx of [their] members into the fields of active citizenship'.[61] The BIAE put the point even more forcefully in 1945:

In this country we have accepted the principle of democratic government, not only in the control of the affairs of the nation, but in nearly
all our smaller groupings and associations, but we have hardly, as yet,
begun to realize how much this requires of us as individuals ... [W]e
have done almost nothing to ensure that we shall be equipped to make
effective use of our privileges. Indeed, we are so ill-equipped as a
people at present, that it is a question whether any form of democratic machinery can hold its own effectively against the growing tendency to mass regimentation in one direction or another, unless we
have an immediate and widespread development of adult education.[62]

The CEdT and CEqT shared the Institute's concerns, and, at the level
of the governance of the educational institution itself, insisted that centres must grow democratically from local grass-roots activity, as opposed
to the patrician practice of 'settling', or 'planting the most perfect Model,
as if it had dropped down from Mars'.[63] The constitution of the ESA,
agreed in 1935, had declared unambiguously that '[m]embers of the settlement ... shall share responsibility for its government'.[64] Yet they were
only to *share* in the government: limitations to the practicabilities of the
democratic control of educational centres were set after the war. The
CEdT's secretary, in a co-authored memorandum written in 1946,
asserted: 'In our view a balance has to be struck which allows a full democratic control but at the same time preserves by the right kind of guidance a higher standard of taste and of recreational and educational
interests than might be achieved by the untutored voice of the majority.'[65]
The concerns of Ernest Taylor nearly three decades earlier about the
spread of democracy in the York settlement were echoed by those who
sought in the post-war years to maintain themselves as guardians of the
public taste; such an attitude left itself open to caricature. Thus in 1944
Harold Shearman denounced the fundamentally (though arguably necessarily) anti-democratic nature of many wartime experiments in adult
education, in terms that might equally be applied to the settlements:

Some ... of the projects for post-war Adult Education bear a strong
family resemblance to the elaborate and expensive provision for
'workers' leisure' which Fascist Italy developed under the title of
Dopolavoro[66] ... Some of the current talk about post-war Adult
Education is in terms of education for other people. It has the stamp
of philanthropy or benevolent paternalism which is, of course, nothing new in English life. It sometimes provokes an impatient reaction
towards emphasising the right of adult men and women to live their
own lives without being 'done good to' ... It cannot too often be
repeated that Adult Education must have a genuinely democratic
foundation; and there was never a time when this more needed saying
than towards the end of a period when, in highly artificial conditions,
it has been organised on a large scale from above and not from below.[67]

The settlements always embodied a contradiction arguably inherent in any such educational establishment: the genuine desire to concede democratic governance could conflict with the aim of imposing what was viewed as a suitable curriculum and ethos onto the institution. If the community centres movement represented an abandonment of the 'philanthropy or benevolent paternalism' that had characterised many educational experiments, it also, through its concentration on recreational as opposed to educational projects, appeared to entail an abandonment of education; and this clearly begged the question as to what role a philanthropic and educational Trust could or should play in its development.

The most distinctive role that the CEdT, CEqT and their parent Trusts could find for themselves was in the expression of the voluntary spirit in adult education through the maintenance of the spiritual dimension of educational service. The ESA/ECA had always viewed this as a defining feature of its own contribution, suggesting in 1945 that

> Man's knowledge of himself and of the world in which he has to live was never more urgently necessary than it is to-day, and the acquisition of such knowledge never more clearly a duty which he must undertake in the years of his maturity. But factual knowledge of the world is not enough; there must also be a deepening sense of the spiritual life, without which there can be no democratic society – without which there can be no greater good for all. 'Democracy is not primarily a matter of political organisation. It is a quality of personal life'...[68]

As early as 1940, John Hughes, reporting on his work among the troops stationed at Strensall near York, referred to 'the complete disillusionment of so many of the troops he had come across, their dull apathy, and ignorance of religion, a disastrous result of the secularisation of education'.[69] Hughes did not live to contribute to the battle against this secularisation after the war, but if he had done, he would probably have been one of a group of socially concerned Quakers who sought to bring religious influences to the new secular community institutions. A notable example was John W. Harvey, who, in his Swarthmore lecture for 1947, argued that, through the new community centres and associations, individual Friends, labouring under the same concern that had animated the founders of the ESA, may find the opportunity to promote the kind of community education that the older institutions had pioneered. This social and spiritual dimension transcended the institutional provision that the JRCT had hitherto supported:

> we cannot for a moment do without institutions. But we often need new ones to meet new, or newly-recognized, needs, and in no sphere so clearly as in education is it possible for the old to become the obsolete, so that the old bottle impairs the new wine. An institution begins

by being the arsenal of a new idea, militant and on the march: then it becomes a fortress to defend it: then (too often) a prison to immure it: and lastly, perhaps, a museum to exhibit it as a mere lifeless effigy.[70]

Community associations were generally suspicious of both 'education' and 'religion', but, Harvey told his audience, at least 'the movement is alive', and might even be modified if Quakers were more imaginative, for example in using Meeting Houses for community centre-type work.[71] This echoed William Hazelton's call in 1944 for each Meeting House to be made 'a centre of vital adult education', open every day and staffed by a 'capable' and 'concerned' Friend, and, if in a pleasant area, to be used for weekend and summer residential schools.[72] Such a channeling of adult education through the Meeting might effect a re-connection of practical Quakerism to adult education. This was one way in which the secularised atmosphere of post-war adult education might be challenged; and one area in which the ESA and other Quaker bodies could maintain their influence on the ethos of adult education in Britain.

For the JRCT, the preservation and reinvigoration of the adult school movement, from which the educational settlements had originally sprung, was a priority in this context: Gwen Porteous, addressing the trustees in 1952, emphasised 'the need for keeping alive, among the many bodies concerned with Adult Education, the one which retains both its concern for integrating Education and Religion and its fully voluntary status'.[73] By contrast, Lewis Waddilove, describing the importance of religious faith to the work and atmosphere of the educational settlements, asked rhetorically '[b]y what faith is the wider movement of community associations and centres inspired? At present the answer is in doubt...'[74] There was no doubt as to the moving faith of the adult schools, but rather more doubt as to whether they would survive for much longer. Unlike the educational settlements, the adult schools enjoyed no official support at all – the NASU did not even apply for any Ministry of Education funding until 1955, when the first of three unsuccessful applications was initiated[75] – and despite the efforts of active Friends such as Gwen Porteous, the movement was largely unsuccessful in evangelising itself. To promote the adult school movement, from the late 1940s the JRCT supported a scheme whereby paid paid tutor-organisers would attempt to establish a base for the movement in some of England's larger cities. Richard Ullmann – a German-born schoolteacher of Jewish ancestry, a Buchenwald survivor and a veteran of the FAU[76] – was sent to Birmingham, and Percy Pitman, formerly of the WEA, went to Manchester, supported by the Trust to the extent of £1,000 a year for three years.[77] Although Ullmann 'wasn't an extension worker', and soon shifted to direct JRCT employment working in the peace field,[78] schemes like this represented a continuation of Trust support for declining bodies like the NASU that the trustees still felt to be playing an important role. The NASU was represented on the JRCT from 1948 by its treasurer, Redford Crosfield Harris, who was able to report back regularly on the continuing decline of the schools, which the tutor-organiser scheme and other initiatives could do little to arrest. Ironically, just as the BIAE was recommending more widespread use of the kind of short-term intensive course such as the weekend school, often held at the adult school guest houses such as Cober Hill,[79] many of these guest houses were having to close down through lack of use.[80] At the same time, a number of new short-term residential colleges were being established by other providers – 25 in the period 1944-50[81] – mostly without the religious influence that lay behind the adult school institutions.

The role of charitable trusts such as the JRCT in maintaining this religious influence in adult education was becoming, it was thought, more important, as the numbers of individuals able to give their time voluntarily to such educational ventures was diminishing even further in the post-war period, and as alternative opportunities for useful service at home and internationally were expanding. The Quaker, and more generally the Christian, element in adult education needed to halt the demise that it was experiencing as a result of the decline of the adult schools and the effacement of the educational settlements by the community centres movement. Richard Rowntree, Arnold's son, who was not at this time a trustee of any of Joseph Rowntree's foundations but who had joined the CEdT and CEqT soon after their establishment, argued that these developments necessitated a fundamental change of strategy on the part of charitable trusts. In a memorandum of 1949 he predicted that

> in the near future the unique contribution to society that was formerly made by concerned members of the 'leisured classes' will be almost entirely lost, and this will throw an immense responsibility on those Trusts with capital resources; for they, almost alone, will have the necessary means to help fill the gap thus created. It is a very serious gap, for it is in the spiritual approach to life and its many social problems that such people have made their greatest contribution, and it is just this approach that is in so much danger of being weakened in the modern 'welfare state'.[82]

What was needed, he argued throughout the late 1940s, was an 'Income Trust', which would augment its capital resources through the solicitation of donations, and would also use its influence and expertise to assist the sort of bodies that the JRCT supported to obtain their own financial security through independent fund-raising.[83] Rowntree's vision was something of a triumph of hope over experience, as this had been precisely the aim of the CEdT and the CEqT, which aimed to raise a million pounds but which in fact received almost no support apart from that provided by the JRCT and JRVT. Nevertheless, Lewis Waddilove agreed that fund-raising in the future needed to be carried out with a broader base of support, and that the age of the wealthy individual like Joseph Rowntree, able and willing to pour large sums of money into new movements like the ESA, was practically over.[84]

Joseph Rowntree's conception of the kind of philanthropy in which he wanted his Trusts to engage, however, was still followed in these post-war educational ventures; in particular, the CEdT and CEqT largely followed his advice and did not spend money on buildings or educational premises. This advice had featured in his memorandum on the establishment of the Trusts in 1904 and his subsequent memorandum of 1919,[85] and had by and large been followed by the JRCT in the intervening years. (Some exceptions were made in the 1940s: the freehold of the Lemington-on-Tyne settlement was still held, and the JRCT owned some property used by the York settlement, while the damages of war necessitated some rebuilding work, notably at the Folk House in Bristol, which was funded by the CEqT. Joseph Rowntree's remarks on buildings were clearly less applicable to the JRVT, one of the initial purposes of which had been the construction of houses.) Those involved in the community centres and educational settlements after the war were generally agreed that it was in the provision of well-trained and suitable individuals that voluntary service could make its greatest contribution. William Hazelton uncompromisingly told the JRCT that 'the choice of a good Warden is fundamental';[86] while the CEdT secretary Roger Pulbrook argued that wardens needed to enjoy professional status and respect, along with higher salaries.[87] Although this conception of staffing retained some elements of the Victorian 'settlement' ideal – Pulbrook hoped to attract 'those who have had a public school education'[88] – the quality of leadership was the essential criterion by which the CEdT and CEqT would judge an institution. As we have seen, both Trust Deeds incorporated the provision of training as one of the permitted items of expenditure, and Harold Marks organised summer schools for wardens and community centre leaders under the joint auspices of the ECA and NFCA.[89] The CEdT and CEqT's proposals to establish a joint training scheme to serve settlements and community centres was frustrated by confusion as to the purpose of such training and by the limited enthusiasm for the idea on the part of Ministry of Education;[90] but bursaries were provided for the training and education of future wardens and staff, at the Primrose Hill teacher training college and elsewhere.

Despite these initiatives and the enthusiasm with which they were approached in the 1940s and early 1950s, the long-term involvement of the JRCT in adult education did not survive the mid-1950s. A combination of the increased statutory support for adult education, the growth of the community centres movement and the failures of the CEdT and CEqT to attract support and to grasp new opportunities in the sphere of community education provoked a reassessment of Trust priorities.[91] The trustees could claim that they had achieved many of the aims of the Founder in pioneering and establishing a movement which was by this time, if not flourishing, then at least able to support itself through local fundraising and through the accessibility of publicly provided financial support. It was recognised at quite an early stage that the ambitions of the new Trusts had been set too high: community centres had not proved to be as open to educational endeavour as had been hoped. In 1951 Seebohm Rowntree and Russell Lavers reported at best a mixed success in bringing education to the community centres: 'at their best they are making an immensely useful but intangible contribution to what might be described as "education for living," at their worst they are mere places of amusement of no educational significance'.[92] In any case, it was realised that centralised effort at a national level was probably not the way to go about promoting community education.[93] The CEdT and CEqT admitted in 1948 that 'the permeation of the community centre and association movement with the ideals of educational centres cannot be achieved through central bodies',[94] while Lewis Waddilove noted in the same year that the 'tendency towards centralisation' among post-war voluntary institutions, paralleling the continuing growth of the state, had been counterproductive.[95] Thus the offices of the CEdT in London were closed down at the end of 1949, and the work transferred to the JRCT offices in York, while the ECA abandoned its Bloomsbury premises and attached its central work to the Walthamstow settlement, under the wardenship of Ray Lamb, who was appointed honorary secretary of the Association at that year's annual general meeting.[96] The crisis among the settlements was highlighted by the ECA's chairman A. J. Allaway,[97] present by invitation at a JRCT meeting in December 1953, who echoed W. E. Williams fifteen years earlier in bluntly telling the trustees that settlement premises were poor, the quality of staff variable and the wardens poorly remunerated (despite the efforts of the CEdT and CEqT), administration frequently inadequate, the work lacking cohesion, and membership numerically satisfactory but lacking the 'intimate and corporate sense of "belonging"' that such institutions were intended to foster.[98] This bleak diagnosis was unlikely to encourage the JRCT to throw any more money at what appeared to be decaying educational institutions.

Having said this, the trustees recognised that the ECA would continue to have a role, not only as a Responsible Body for the provision of courses, but also as an advisory and propagandist organisation. Although the ECA feared that it might become 'merely a Conference calling body',[99] the JRCT still saw it as an important feature of the educational environment, awarding (through the CEdT) over £1,200 in the year to June

1948.[100] Essentially, the ECA came to serve as 'a centre for consultation and advice for wardens', but ceased to be the channel through which funding to individual settlements was provided.[101] It is clear, however, that there was considerable confusion about the role of the JRCT and its allied trusts and associations in adult education in this period, and the dominant attitude seems to have been one of 'wait and see'. In 1950 the responsibility of the CEdT was defined as 'largely that of holding a watching brief in the field of Adult Education generally, maintaining contacts in that field, and above all, watching for new growing points and fresh opportunities'.[102] It is hardly surprising that, in this climate of vagueness, it did not seem worthwhile to continue with the CEdT and CEqT, which were duly wound up in 1953 and 1954 respectively.[103] They were replaced by a short-lived Adult Education Sub-Committee, reporting to the JRCT and still involving Lewis Waddilove and Richard Rowntree, but this sub-committee found itself unable or unwilling in 1952 to spend its limited budget of £1,000 and was itself discontinued in December of the following year.[104] By this time Arnold Rowntree, the guiding spirit of the JRCT's adult education funding across the previous five decades, was dead, and grant-making in this area was haphazard and ill-directed. The Trust's new chairman, Roger Wilson, wondered in 1952 exactly 'who comes within the scope of what kind of education and what is its scope?',[105] reflecting the confusion and, perhaps, the lack of interest among the younger trustees. It was agreed in 1954 that the JRCT might continue to give limited assistance to individual educational centres, and possibly some support to the ECA, and would probably continue its support for individuals in the form of bursaries[106] – indeed grants were given under the general heading of 'adult education and settlements' until 1969 – but the era of large-scale support in this area was clearly now over.[107]

A new generation of trustees held different visions of the future of adult education, and interpreted their grant-making responsibilities in different terms from those who had served the Trust for half a century. Following the deaths of Arnold and Stephen Rowntree in 1951, and the retirement of Ernest Taylor and Arthur Gillett from their trusteeships, also in 1951,[108] the board of trustees now consisted, with the exception of Seebohm Rowntree, entirely of people appointed during the previous fifteen years, with John W. Harvey by some way the oldest. Seebohm's advancing age, failing health and geographical remoteness from York – he was now living in Benjamin Disraeli's old home at Hughenden Manor in Buckinghamshire – and his attachment in his last years to the social studies carried out in association with Russell Lavers, took him away from the affairs of the JRCT; and the real power lay with Roger Wilson, appointed chairman in 1950 with Christopher Rowntree as his vice-chairman, and the other younger trustees. These people had their own favoured

208

projects, and although they tried hard to apply the principles outlined by Joseph Rowntree in his 1904 memorandum, it was clear that in practice their grant-making would differ from his and that of his family. This was evident in the attitude of the new trustees to the Society of Friends. Whereas men like Joseph and Arnold Rowntree had been essentially 'a family group of deeply concerned Yorkshire Friends ... whose attitude to the Society could perhaps be fairly described as paternal rather than participant', the younger trustees tended to be more closely connected with the 'central life of the Society', Quakerism 'as expressed through its institutions'.[109] There had long been a tension within the Society between those institutions that were formally sanctioned by Yearly Meeting or Meeting for Sufferings on the one hand and those that were the product of independent activity by concerned Friends on the other. The original trustees and their immediate successors had been more provincial in outlook, and less concerned to view and to enhance Quakerism at a national level. Their localist outlook was reflected in their grants to local projects such as the Yorkshire 1905 Committee, itinerant Yorkshire-based Quaker lecturers, the Leeds and York settlements and the York Quaker boarding schools. Their successors, living in different cities, located their grant-making at a more national level and interpreted the likely impact of their financial support in somewhat larger terms. The new trustees had never been fully and directly exposed to the Victorian conception of philanthropy that lay behind the practices and principles of the JRCT in the early years of its existence, and had more faith in the support of existing bodies and in collectivist schemes of social reform. No less significantly, the original trustees had been Liberals in politics, whereas men like Roger Wilson broadly identified themselves as socialists, at a time when the Labour party was in government and taking the country in directions about which men like Seebohm Rowntree found themselves uneasy.[110]

The newer trustees also challenged the Rowntree family dominance of JRCT meetings from the late 1940s. We have seen how Arnold and Seebohm Rowntree dominated Trust proceedings in the 1940s, and Roger Wilson clearly had a difficult relationship with both of them. Notable evidence of this comes from 'a very frank discussion' at a trustees' meeting in 1949 on the Trust's policy of assisting family members: some (unnamed) trustees had reservations about this, but discussion was apparently curtailed when Arnold Rowntree, still the Trust chairman, decreed that Joseph Rowntree would have approved of such expenditure.[111] Some months later, the Trust awarded financial support to Seebohm Rowntree's daughter and granddaughter,[112] while in 1951 Seebohm's assistant Russell Lavers wrote asking for money for the upkeep of Hughenden Manor.[113] By 1951 Wilson and Redford Crosfield Harris were doubtful about the value of continuing the large grants to Seebohm,[114] who was not thought to be producing work of much quality or usefulness. Seebohm himself had 'always been querulous' about grants given to Horace Fleming's widow Cecilie (Fleming had died in 1941), a reflection no doubt of ancient personal rivalries, and Wilson found Seebohm's 'smallmindedness on some of these issues very tiresome'.[115] The impact of the generation gap was being felt on an interpersonal level as well as in terms of grant-making.

It was evident that new post-war concerns would need to be addressed by the Trust. One entirely new experience for Britain in the 1940s was peacetime conscription under the National Service Act, which continued until 1960. Eric Cleaver, Trust secretary from 1949, was particularly concerned to work with conscientious objectors to national service, while Roger Wilson expressed the hope that a proposed merger of the FAU into a larger civilian service for COs would prepare these reluctant conscripts for 'educational and social service careers', thus assisting the other projects supported by the Trust.[116] The coming of the cold war necessitated another reappraisal of funding in the area of peace, and so although some traditional favourites such as the Northern Friends Peace Board were still given small grants, the focus of awards in this area was moving, as predicted by Seebohm Rowntree in 1939 and 1941, towards larger-scale ventures and towards peace research. There was support for a Quaker body, the East/West Relations Committee of British Friends, from which arose the Quaker Mission to Moscow in 1951; for the Quaker United Nations Programme in New York; and for a Conference on Christian Approaches to Defence and Disarmament.[117] The United Nations Association, successor to the League of Nations Union, has also been a long-term beneficiary of JRCT support. Perhaps the most important new work in the field of peace was the support of Gerald Bailey, a brilliant researcher and peace campaigner but also something of a loose cannon who was unable to find himself a job with an official Quaker peace body: this support was indicative of a broadening of Trust concern and a willingness to embrace new approaches to peace research (although Seebohm Rowntree was hostile to the support of Bailey's work when it was first discussed by the trustees at length in 1950).[118] Bailey's subsequent involvement with the East/West Relations Committee was later recalled by Roger Wilson as one of the most significant achievements of the Trust during that period; and Wilson also remarked on the usefulness of Richard Ullmann's contribution in this field, to which Ullmann was clearly more suited than to adult school work.[119]

It was notable in the post-war period how many of the trustees began to look abroad for the fulfilment of some of their philanthropic ambitions, and especially to the 'third world'. To an extent this turning outwards was prompted by the involvement of trustees in international projects during the war, especially Harvey's work with the IVSP, Roger Wilson's experiences in the FRS and Michael Rowntree's service in the FAU. When Rowntree was first discussed as a possible future trustee in 1946 (he was formally appointed in the following year), '[i]t was felt that it would be an advantage to have the help of a youngish Friend with the freshness of outlook derived from a varied experience abroad.'[120] Perhaps the clearest expression of an increasingly outgoing collective disposition was to be found in the links with Africa that were developed in this period. As Grigor McClelland has explained, the Trust had given its first grant (also in the field of education) to an African project as early as 1910, 'but serious interest of the trustees in Africa dates from 1954, when the focus was on the development of those former British colonies which were gaining their independence'.[121] In fact, it was through the educational activities of William Hazelton that the trustees were first alerted to the opportunities for development work of this kind: the joint committee of the NFCA and ESA held conferences with western Africans in 1946 to discuss the promotion of adult education,[122] and Hazelton followed up these initiatives with further consultations in 1947.[123] Eric Cleaver and Richard Rowntree visited Kenya in 1954, at the invitation of the Friends Service Council, and these visits instituted a funding relationship with southern Africa that lasted throughout the second half of the twentieth century, focusing on development, especially in the context of the apartheid system in South Africa.[124] Even Seebohm Rowntree turned some of his attention overseas, in 1953 accepting the presidency of War on Want, a propagandist and fund-raising organisation which aimed to place public awareness of poverty within a global context. As Asa Briggs has explained,

> Its objective was a logical international extension of the cause which had always meant so much to him – 'forming a public opinion that will demand that the poverty problem shall be effectively dealt with throughout the world'. However old-fashioned 'traditional' poverty surveys might seem to be in post-war Britain, they were still relevant in most other parts of the world.[125]

It was partly the optimism generated by the post-war establishment of the welfare state in Britain, partly the increased funds available as a result of the abandonment of the large-scale support of educational settlements, and partly the personal interests of trustees and Trust employees, that made African projects a major priority for the JRCT in the second half of the twentieth century.

Having said all this, some of the traditional areas of concern were followed up by the newer trustees. Research into the history of Quakerism appeared to be at a low ebb (although Ernest Taylor published his account of *The valiant sixty* in 1947, and it was reprinted in 1951), at least compared with the days of William Braithwaite and Rufus Jones, and in 1952 the Trust aimed to encourage further work by establishing a short-lived sub-committee, which decided to attempt to reissue some of the old Quaker histories, stocks of which were running low.[126] Henry Cadbury undertook the task of revising and updating Braithwaite's *Beginnings of Quakerism* and *Second period of Quakerism*, which were published by Cambridge University Press in 1955 and 1961 respectively. Similarly, the Founder's interest in the Quaker schools was not forgotten: these institutions found themselves in some financial difficulty after the war, and in 1949 the trustees contributed £5,000 to an appeal at Bootham that sought to raise £100,000, and £1,000 to a similar venture at Ackworth aiming at £75,000; they also donated £2,500 to The Mount in 1951.[127] Following Arnold Rowntree's death in 1951, a small grant of £50 was given towards the memorials to him at each of the York schools: a new entrance drive at The Mount, and a cricket scorebox at Bootham, reflecting Arnold's interest in the sport.[128] A continued interest in children's education – though not specifically Quaker education in this case – was confirmed by the appointment in 1950 of Joyce Aspden, headmistress of the Queen Anne Grammar School in York, as a trustee in 1950.[129] Aspden, a Friend, began attending Trust meetings in 1949; and was a member of the Adult Education Sub-Committee. Woodbrooke also continued to receive support. Although Frank Sturge died in 1948, links with the college were maintained through the appointment of Alfred Braithwaite to the JRCT in the same year; and, as Braithwaite began attending meetings soon after the end of the war, he was able to report that the 1945-6 academic year was already showing signs of a return to normal, with a welcome increase in the numbers of students taking the religious courses.[130] Woodbrooke remained a source of some concern: in 1950, it was reported that Birmingham University had abandoned the collaborative arrangement for teaching the now somewhat outdated diploma in social study, and that the college was still struggling to attract an acceptable intake of British Quakers.[131] Nevertheless, Woodbrooke continues to enjoy a funding relationship with the JRCT today, almost a century after the first grants were given: the peculiarly Quaker nature of the institution, and the continued hopes for it as a resource for Meetings across Britain, as well as the sentimental links with the Founder and with John Wilhelm Rowntree, have preserved the association. At the same time, the JRCT continued to receive applications from an array of groups and individuals: to take random examples as illustrations, grants were made in 1946 to the Liverpool Friends Service Committee, the *Friends Quarterly Examiner* and the Maurice L. Rowntree Memorial Fund,[132] while refusals of support in the following year included the Sheffield University Development Campaign, the World Conference of Christian Youth and the British Council of Churches.[133]

Although much of the day-to-day work of the Trust went on as normal, the younger trustees needed to familiarise themselves with some of the projects that had been funded by their predecessors for many years, and in this period a series of semi-formal reassessments were carried out, in the form of trustees' meetings to which grant-holders were invited. This had for a long time been the procedure followed for the assessment of the work of men like Edward Grubb, John Hughes and Herbert Waller, but it became more systematised in the post-war period as a series of conferences of this kind considered the affairs of the adult school movement, Woodbrooke, the educational settlements and JRCT-funded social research. This last meeting, in December 1953,[134] coming as it did only a few months before the death of Seebohm Rowntree, was especially significant, and from it can be dated the new kinds of social work that the Trust would involve itself with during the next two decades. The trustees discussed a memorandum (which does not appear to have survived) entitled 'Social Research and Action under the Aegis of the JRCT', which reflected Seebohm's optimism about economic poverty and reorientation towards problems of community life and social morality:

> Whilst the misery of primary poverty in the country had very nearly been removed, there remains a great deal of social disease in the life of the community due to the weaknesses of personal and social relationships. These two fields of investigation are closely related and as far as this Trust is concerned represent spheres of action which were evidently much in the mind of the Founder.[135]

The poverty survey, as pioneered by Seebohm Rowntree, seemed an obsolete mechanism for social improvement in post-war Britain, and the trustees pointed approvingly to projects such as the Case Work Centre, later the Consultation Centre, in Hull, which worked with 'social casualties' and with which Roger Wilson had been associated through his work at the University of Hull.[136] Among many other things, this project offered marriage guidance services; and the Marriage Guidance Council, established in 1938 and expanding rapidly in the post-war years, was another recipient of JRCT support.[137] Another venture praised at this time was the 'Bristol Resettlement project', similar to the Hull scheme, and involving Wilson and Lulie Shaw, who was herself to be appointed to the JRCT in 1956.[138]

Notwithstanding the misplaced optimism among this generation of trustees as the removal of 'primary poverty', these new projects undoubtedly reflected a more generally optimistic outlook as a result of the establishment of the welfare state in the post-war years. It appeared that voluntarists could now concentrate their attention on other areas, in which the careful and considered personal involvement of individuals could be seen to make a difference. The third world conference of Friends at Oxford

213

in 1952 recognised the 'tremendous needs and opportunities for constructive action in dealing with such problems as racial discrimination, mental health, the right use of leisure, and the whole fabric of community and family life':[139] all problems which were foregrounded by the voluntary sector in the 1950s. The JRCT began funding work in the area of race relations in 1969,[140] and in the 1950s and 1960s supported various schemes aimed at the strengthening of family life: as well as the funding of marriage guidance, the trustees supported projects such as play centres and family organisations (in the 1980s they even funded the Family Welfare Association, the new incarnation of the Charity Organisation Society). However, adolescence was perhaps the most significant area of JRCT involvement in these early post-war years. This was appropriate in the context of the Trust's history: Seebohm Rowntree and many other social investigators in the Edwardian period had examined the economic and moral consequences of 'blind alley' work among juvenile labourers,[141] and although the raising of the school leaving age had ameliorated the worst effects of this kind of employment, the longer-term results of the post-war 'baby boom' were to be seen in cultural disaffection among the newly rediscovered 'teenagers' in the years to come. Although not all the trustees were happy about the amount of money channelled into projects dealing with adolescents, educationalists like Roger Wilson saw this kind of work as the natural extension of the adult education projects supported during the first five decades of the Trust's existence. Wilson recognised this, and in applying for support for another experimental scheme to work with adolescents in Bristol in 1960, he explained his vision of the future importance of this kind of work:

> I should like to ask the Trust to think of this not as an isolated effort but as part of a policy based on the assumption that over the next 20 years the question of the relationships between adolescents and the grown-up world will be a major one, parallel in importance to the work which the Trust did in pioneering adult education during the first half of this century.[142]

If the Trust had moved beyond its focus on education, the ideals of education, in its broadest and most informal sense, continued to motivate many of the trustees, and were applied to a new series of concerns in the second half of the twentieth century.

The Victorian conception of philanthropy promoted by Joseph Rowntree and his early collaborators in the work of his Trusts, although it survived well into the interwar period, appeared obsolete by the time of what was effectively a complete reconstitution of the board of trustees of the JRCT in the 1940s and early 1950s. The period through which these new trustees were living, the new social concerns that arose in the wake of the establishment of the welfare state, and the new threats to world peace and security as a consequence of the development of weapons of mass destruction all contributed to a reassessment of where the money available to the Trust should be directed. Above all, however, these new trustees were essentially men and women of the twentieth century, raised in a different environment from that experienced by Arnold, Seebohm and Stephen Rowntree, who were, like the Founder, essentially Victorian people expounding what we may loosely term Victorian values. It is therefore appropriate to end this history with the death of the last of these eminent Victorians, Seebohm Rowntree, in 1954; although it should also be noted that the longest-serving of the Friends 'liberated' for service by the JRCT, Herbert Waller, died two years later, representing the end of a funding relationship that stretched back to 1906. With the death of Seebohm, the last direct link with the Founder of the Trust was ended, and the JRCT (and its sister Trusts) entered a new era of grant-making in the fields that its newer members thought appropriate to the social problems, and the concerns of the Society of Friends, of the second half of the twentieth century. Nevertheless, it was by Seebohm, together with Arnold Rowntree and the other senior trustees, that the new group of trustees were schooled in the implications of what Joseph Rowntree had told his family in 1904. Thus, in minuting Seebohm's death fifty years later, the JRCT recorded that he 'was able again and again to show by his example how the vision and profound concern of his father a generation ago could be interpreted in a living way to meet the changing needs and problems of the contemporary world'.[143] Joseph Rowntree's trustees were to attempt to follow this example in the decades that followed.

NOTES
1. ESA, 'The Educational Settlements Association' [typescript, 1945], 6, JRF JRCT93/IV/8 (a).
2. Ibid. 14.
3. Ibid. 18-19.
4. Harrison, *Learning and living*, 314.
5. N. A. Jepson, 'Local authorities and adult education', in S. G. Raybould (ed.), *Trends in English adult education*, 1959, 83, quoted in Roger Fieldhouse, 'The Labour government's further education policy 1945-1951', *History of Education* xxiii (1994), 290.
6. Quoted in Harrison, *Learning and living*, 314.
7. Fieldhouse, 'Labour government's further education policy', 290-6.
8. Allaway, *Educational centres movement*, 53-5.
9. Ibid. 51-3; figures from H. C. Wiltshire, 'Impington and adult education', *Adult Education* xvii (1944), 125-34.
10. Allaway, *Educational centres movement*, 55.
11. Quoted in Fieldhouse, 'Labour government's further education policy', 297.
12. BIAE, *Adult education after the war*, Oxford 1945, 22.

215

13. Ibid.
14. Harrison, *Learning and living*, 327.
15. S. G. Raybould, *The English universities and adult education*, 1951, 118. The figures for university extension courses are obtained by adding together Raybould's categories of advanced and three-year tutorial classes and other university classes.
16. J. W. Saunders, 'University extension renascent', in Raybould, *Trends in English adult education*, 52-82; Harrison, *Learning and living*, 345ff.
17. Harrison, *Learning and living*, 341; Brown, *Making of a modern Quaker*, 145-6, 147ff.
18. Harrison, *Learning and living*, 348-9.
19. Eric Ashby, *The pathology of adult education*, Belfast 1955, 8-15 (quote at 9).
20. Harrison, *Learning and living*, 351ff.
21. A. J. Allaway, *Adult education in a changing society: an inaugural lecture delivered at University College Leicester, 1 May 1951*, Leicester 1951, 28.
22. BIAE, *Adult education after the war*, 25.
23. Ibid. 34.
24. Ibid. 35-6.
25. Allaway, *Adult education in a changing society*, 22.
26. [Roger Pulbrook and Kenneth Bowden,] memorandum to CEdT, December 1946, part C, section 2, JRF JRCT93/V/1 (a).
27. By this time the ESA had changed its name to the ECA (see below).
28. Allaway, *Educational centres movement*, 45-8.
29. ECA, annual general meeting minutes, 19 September 1948, JRF JRCT93/V/1 (c).
30. JRCT minute book, no. 4, minute no. 864 (8 December 1951).
31. CEdT, report 1946, JRF JRCT93/V/1 (d).
32. ESA, 'Educational Settlements Association', 5-6.
33. Ibid. 5.
34. JRCT Minute book, no. 4, minute no. 308.
35. Ibid. minute no. 597.
36. Ibid. minute no. 675.
37. Peacock, 'Adult education in York', 300.
38. Ibid. 300-1.
39. ESA, memorandum on educational settlements in post-war years, January 1943. I am grateful to Konrad Elsdon for supplying me with a copy of this memorandum.
40. CEdT report, 1946.
41. Allaway, *Educational centres movement*, 44-5.
42. Ibid. 45.
43. Ibid. 41.
44. Ibid. 43; CEdT report 1946.
45. JRCT minute book, no. 4, minute no. 394.
46. ESA, *Community education*.
47. ESA, 'Educational Settlements Association', 22.
48. JRCT minute book, no. 4, minute no. 394.
49. Ibid. minute no. 396.
50. Arnold Rowntree, memorandum, 30 January 1946, JRF JR93/VIII/5.

51. CEdT and CEqT, report 1947, JRF JRCT93/V/1 (d).
52. CEdT Trust Deed, 18 July 1947, JRF JRCT93/V/1 (a).
53. CEqT Trust Deed, 18 July 1947, JRF JRCT93/V/1 (a).
54. *The Joseph Rowntree inheritance*, 35.
55. Pulbrook and Bowden, memorandum to CEdT. No part or section given. Part C, section 2 is attached (see note 26 above).
56. JRCT minute book, no. 4, minute no. 508, reports a long discussion of Rowntree's proposed book on the subject and a long series of points raised by trustees reflecting many of the social and spiritual concerns of the period.
57. JRCT minute book, no. 4, minute no. 597.
58. CEdT and CEqT, report 1947.
59. Raybould, *English universities*, p. 14.
60. Harold C. Shearman, *Adult education for democracy*, 1944, p. 26-7 and passim.
61. ESA council minutes, 15-16 September 1945, JRF JRCT93/IV/6.
62. BIAE, *Adult education after the war*, 6.
63. Pulbrook and Bowden, memorandum to CEdT, part C, section 2.
64. ESA constitution, JRF JRCT93/IV/8 (b).
65. Pulbrook and Bowden, memorandum to CEdT, part C, section 2.
66. The National Institute for the Organisation of Workers' Leisure, the name Dopolavoro being derived from the Italian abbreviation.
67. Shearman, *Adult education for democracy*, 55.
68. ESA, 'Educational Settlements Association', 22.
69. JRCT minute book, no. 4, minute no. 33.
70. Harvey, *Salt and leaven*, 61; partly quoted in Heron, *Quakers in Britain*, 51.
71. Harvey, *Salt and leaven*, 63-4.
72. William Hazelton, 'Adult education and national reconstruction', *Friends Quarterly Examiner* lxxviii (1944), 118.
73. JRCT minute book, no. 4, minute no. 887.
74. Lewis E. Waddilove, memorandum on the future of the CEdT and CEqT, n.d. [1949], JRF JRCT93/V/1 (c).
75. Hall, *Adult school movement*, 164-5.
76. For a brief account of Ullmann's life see 'Testimony to the grace of god in the life of Richard K. Ullmann', typescript, Woodbrooke Quaker Study Centre library: biography pamphlet ULL/WAR.
77. JRCT minute book, no. 4, minute nos. 634, 905.
78. Wilson, 'Some reflections', 7-8.
79. BIAE, *Adult education after the war*, 26, 58; Walter Drews and Roger Fieldhouse, 'Residential colleges and non-residential settlements and centres', in Fieldhouse and associates, *History of modern British adult education*, 257.
80. Hall, *Adult school movement*, 172.
81. Drews and Fieldhouse, 'Residential colleges and non-residential settlements', 255-6; see also Guy Hunter, 'Residential colleges for adult education', in Raybould, *Trends in English adult education*, 120-36.
82. Richard S. Rowntree, memorandum, 2 May 1949, JRF JRCT93/V/1 (c).
83. Ibid.; Richard S. Rowntree, memorandum 18 July 1948, JRF JRCT93/V/1 (c).

84. Waddilove, memorandum on the future of the CEdT and CEqT.
85. Founder's memorandum, 2; Joseph Rowntree, memorandum of 16 April 1919; quoted in CEdT and CEqT, report to the JRCT and JRVT for 1949, JRF JRCT93/V/1 (d).
86. JRCT minute book, no. 4, minute no. 597.
87. Pulbrook and Bowden, memorandum to CEdT.
88. Ibid.
89. CEdT, report 1946.
90. CEdT and CEqT, report 1948, JRF JRCT93/V/1 (d).
91. Davies and Freeman, 'Education for citizenship'.
92. Rowntree and Lavers, *English life and leisure*, 331.
93. JRCT minute book, no. 4, minute no. 675 (12-13 June 1949).
94. CEdT and CEqT, report 1948.
95. Waddilove, memorandum on the future of the CEdT and CEqT.
96. CEdT and CEqT, report 1949, JRF JRCT93/V/1 (d); Allaway, *Educational centres movement*, 46-8.
97. He was also at this time Head of the Department of Adult Education, Vaughan College, Leicester, and was in the process of touring settlements and centres, a venture which was later drawn on in his *Educational centres movement*.
98. JRCT minute book, no. 4, minute no. 988.
99. ECA, annual general meeting minutes, 19 September 1948.
100. CEdT and CEqT, income and expenditure account, JRF JRCT93/V/1 (c).
101. CEdT and CEqT, report 1949.
102. JRCT minute book, no. 4, minute no. 791.
103. The decision to wind up the Trusts was taken in 1952.
104. Only £844 was spent: JRCT minute book, no. 4, minute nos. 977, 998; JRCT Adult Education Sub-Committee, summary report of activities, year ending 31 December 1952, JRCT basement archive, box 62.
105. JRCT Adult Education Sub-Committee, minute book, 6 May 1952, JRCT basement archive, box 62.
106. JRCT minute book, no. 4, minute no. 1015.
107. Some adult education initiatives in Africa have since been supported by the JRCT.
108. *The Joseph Rowntree inheritance*, p. 45, and JRCT, *Triennial report 1988-90*, 6, JRCT library, both record Gillett's trusteeship as ending in 1954, the year of his death. His resignation in 1951 and replacement by his son Nicholas is recorded in JRCT, minute book, no. 4, minute nos. 849, 869.
109. Wilson, 'Some reflections', 3.
110. See Brown, *Making of a modern Quaker*, passim, esp. 147; JRCT minute book, no. 4, minute no. 201, for Rowntree's uneasiness about planning.
111. JRCT minute book, no. 4, minute no. 694.
112. Wilson, 'Some reflections', 11.
113. Lavers to Wilson, 29 January 1951, JRCT basement archive, box 22; see also JRCT minute book, no. 4, minute no. 1010.
114. Harris to Wilson, 9 February 1951, JRCT basement archive, box 22.
115. Wilson, 'Some reflections', 4.
116. JRCT minute book, no. 4, minute nos. 535, 544.

117. Wilson, *Money and power*, 4.
118. Wilson, 'Some reflections', 6.
119. Ibid. 7-8.
120. JRCT minute book, no. 4, minute no. 456.
121. *The Joseph Rowntree inheritance*, 43.
122. CEdT, report 1946.
123. JRCT minute book, no. 4, minute no. 491 (c).
124. See the reports on Cleaver's visits to Africa in JRF JRCT93/VII/11-12.
125. Briggs, *Seebohm Rowntree*, 332; see also Greenwood, *Friends and relief*, 333.
126. JRCT minute book, no. 4, minute nos. 908, 919.
127. Ibid. minute nos. 650, 878.
128. Ibid. minute no. 790 (h); Vipont, *Arnold Rowntree*, 83-4.
129. JRCT minute book, no. 4, minute nos. 695, 718, 794, 824.
130. JRCT minute book, no. 4, minute no. 401 (a).
131. Ibid. minute no. 799.
132. Ibid. minute no. 440.
133. Ibid. minute no. 530.
134. Ibid. minute no. 990.
135. Ibid.
136. Ibid. minute nos. 732, 922 (f), 1052.
137. Ibid. minute no. 1031 (h).
138. Brown, *Making of a modern Quaker*, 158-60.
139. FWCC, *Friends face their fourth century*, 45.
140. *The Joseph Rowntree inheritance*, 42.
141. Rowntree and and Lasker, *Unemployment*, esp. ch. 1; Hendrick, *Images of youth*. See above, pp. 43-4.
142. Roger Wilson, draft memorandum, 'Adolescents', May 1960, JRCT basement archive, box 24.
143. JRCT minute book, no. 4, minute no. 1051.

Epilogue and conclusion

THIS ACCOUNT of the first fifty years of the JRCT has concentrated on the educational settlement movement and the Trust's role in it; a less central role has been given to the trustees' activities in the promotion of peace and the financing and execution of social inquiry. Needless to say, the different areas of grant-making were closely associated in the minds of the trustees, who tended to view their organisation as a single grant-making body addressing the needs of British Quakerism and the society it served. This has been the history of an organisation, and of the individuals who created it, shaped it and changed it; but it is also a chapter in the history of adult education, and in the history of the Society of Friends. It has not purported to be a full history of the Educational Settlements Association or of the educational settlement movement as a whole: with the exception of A. J. Allaway's brief institutional history of the ESA, and the various short accounts of individual settlements or groups of settlements, there remains no history of the institutions to which so much of the JRCT's money was directed in its first fifty years of existence. However, the foregoing account represents a striking, and important, example of the effacement of voluntarily provided adult educational institutions in a period when the state and local authorities were gradually assuming more responsibilities in the field, especially in the wake of the Education Acts of 1918 and 1944. The relationship between the voluntary providers and official bodies was often uneasy, and always existed in the context of insufficient funds to support the needs and desires of adult education institutions. The JRCT, as a small grant-making body with limited resources at its disposal and many other commitments, was able to occupy only a small corner of the field, a corner which few other trusts or groups seemed willing to share with them. Perhaps inevitably, then, this has been the story of the failure of the educational settlement movement, a movement bypassed by other developments, marginalised in a field which also contained university extension classes, the WEA, community centres and local authority centres. Although the educational settlements retained some distinctiveness in the field of adult education, they lacked the resources or the appeal to maintain the Quaker dimension that was, in most cases, their *raison d'être*, and in the end the ESA recognised that their future could be secured only in harness with other bodies that concentrated less on purely educational activities and relied less on voluntarism.

Nevertheless, the educational settlement model of adult education provision was being adopted by other movements in this period, and the educational settlement movement can take some credit, at least indirectly, for many of the developments in post-war adult education. The ESA was claiming a somewhat Pyrrhic victory for its conception of the educational centre as early as 1945: as its own institutions struggled to survive, other bodies, especially LEAs, were seizing on the centre model and establishing non-residential institutions of adult education underpinned by many of the same philosophies that characterised the educational settlement movement. In addition, the residential centres in membership of the ESA remained important institutions, albeit attracting a very atypical kind of adult student. By extension, the JRCT's foresightedness in its support of the early educational settlements, and its substantial support for the ESA in the interwar period, can be viewed as having enabled the model to prosper and to succeed for long enough to prove to other, wealthier bodies, that it was worth appropriating and developing. Joseph Rowntree was right that the JRCT would have to 'start the movement first' and then withdraw so that other bodies could take it forward.[1] The problem with this was that the movement itself, as established by the JRCT and its collaborators, had two substantial flaws: first, its association with the adult schools, and, second, its links (arguably more apparent than real) with the social settlement model as pioneered by Canon Barnett at Toynbee Hall. Established by a generation of eminent Victorians, most notably Arnold Rowntree, and initiated and driven by Quakers, it was essential to the survival of the movement that others took it on and remodelled it: the Quaker model of adult education, as epitomised by the adult schools which were becoming increasingly marginalised, seemed incapable of making the necessary changes which would fit the educational settlements for the circumstances of the interwar and post-second world war periods. If the educational settlements were originally established as outgrowths of the adult school movement, they were very quickly taken further, given institutional form (albeit somewhat precarious, given the state of their finances), and developed along more 'mainstream' adult educational lines. Only the 'atmosphere' at some settlements appeared to retain a Quaker influence, and this was viewed, even by sympathetic observers such as W. E. Williams, as an unattractive feature.

At the same time, British Quakerism itself was evolving, as the implications of the 'Quaker Renaissance' and the 'new Quakerism' led by John Wilhelm Rowntree and his successors became clearer in the aftermath of the first world war. Thomas C. Kennedy has shown how the experience of the war cemented the leadership in the Society of Friends of the absolutist war-resisters (actually a small minority of Quakers), and at the same

221

time radicalised the Society, or at least sections of it, and brought a new degree of political conscience to its members. The practical results of this, seen in the Quaker response to the general strike and the distress in the coalfields, especially in south Wales, rather overtook the JRCT, which was not equipped to deal either with intense political controversy or with the scale of interwar social distress. Trustees were often concerned about political activity in the educational settlements, and the difficulties of these institutions were felt even more keenly in the Special Areas settlements, where the activities of Quakers could be viewed as palliatives to 'keep the jobless occupied' and divert their attentions from political activity.[2] Clearly the severest test of Quaker beliefs in the interwar period, however, was the rise of totalitarianism on mainland Europe, and the framing of a response to the imminent threat of war. As we have seen, even lifelong pacifists in the Society of Friends were won over to the belief that the Hitler threat could be met only by superior military force. The failure of the liberal internationalism that had been enthusiastically promoted by the League of Nations Union and other bodies may have confirmed some Friends in their adherence to an absolutist interpretation of their peace testimony, but many more were drawn to bear arms against the Nazi menace. The JRCT's peace activities in this period reflected the confusion among British Quakers, being directed towards a range of pacifist and internationalist bodies and individuals, and the balance of interests meant that grant-making in this area could not easily be rationalised. The development of a more internationalist outlook among Quakers was largely continued after the second world war – the JRCT supported the United Nations Association, for example – and this has persisted, perhaps most significantly inspiring many Friends' associations with environmental campaigns, although this is an area in which the JRCT has not yet made its presence felt.

From its early existence as a small family concern, supporting marginal, provincial initiatives, the JRCT transformed itself during the twentieth century into a large grant-making Trust, supporting significant research and innovation across a range of areas at a national and international level. Although the JRCT today retains some specific Yorkshire connections, and has maintained unbroken a funding relationship with Woodbrooke, it is now able and willing to support national quasi-political campaigns (in recent years, for example, for freedom of information and democratic accountability at a central government level), and at the same time is probably more closely integrated into 'mainstream' British Quakerism, insofar as such a thing exists, than it was during the lifetime of the Founder. The JRCT is willing to move further afield, away from the 'traditional' areas of Quaker social concern and social action, and into a range of social and political activity. Educational settlements, and indeed adult education in general, are no longer of much interest to the Trust, and the story of the educational settlement movement is no longer of any direct relevance to the JRCT. It is questionable whether there are any direct implications of the account presented in this book for the JRCT or for other grant-making bodies, Quaker or otherwise, today. What the story of the JRCT's first fifty years does show is that the funding priorities changed with altered political, economic and social circumstances, and above all with the involvement of successive generations of British Quakers in the distribution and administration of grants. Even the great twenti-eth-century Quaker constant, the peace testimony, was reinterpreted over the course of the most turbulent of centuries, and today the grants made in this area (which represented the largest area of JRCT expenditure at the start of the twenty-first century) are usually aimed at very different ventures from the grants of the early 1920s. Politically, whereas the early trustees generally identified themselves with the Liberal party, the next generation was more sympathetic to socialism and generally supported the Labour party, especially during the years after the second world war. Today the trustees subscribe, if not to the 'third way', then certainly to a broadly social democratic political agenda, epitomised by their sympathy for constitutional reform.

During the first fifty years of the JRCT, although trustees frequently disagreed and were forced to compromise with each other and with the recipients of their limited benevolence, grant-making was invested with a vague but important 'joined-up' philosophy: the different areas they sup-ported often involved the same individuals, motivated by the same Quaker ideals, and were linked, like the activities of the Friends Social Union under the leadership of Seebohm Rowntree in the Edwardian period, by 'modern principles of integrated social service'.[3] This integration is much less easily discernible in the JRCT's grant-making in the early twenty-first century. Today the trustees have much more money at their disposal, in real terms – over £4 million a year – and there are many more trustees: fifteen in 1999 compared with just six in 1904 (and five after the untimely death of John Wilhelm Rowntree). Moreover, the trustees, although all Quakers, are drawn from a wider range of backgrounds, a trend that was already observable by the 1940s. Like the world it which it operates, the JRCT has been become more complicated and more diverse. It has devel-oped particular interests in the politics of southern Africa, in the Irish conflict, and in political accountability and corporate responsibility. Its sister Trusts – now the Joseph Rowntree Reform Trust and the Joseph Rowntree Foundation – have also found new fields for concern, and oper-ate on a similarly expanded scale, especially since the controversial take-over of Rowntree Mackintosh by Nestlé in the late 1980s, which substantially increased the resources at the disposal of all three Trusts. It is much more difficult to operate 'joined-up' grant-making in the early twenty-first century. The JRCT today attempts, with varying degrees of plausibility, to justify its grant-making priorities and practices with reference to Joseph Rowntree, the Founder, and especially his 'splendidly far-sighted' memorandum of 1904. Arguably this document, which applied to all three Trusts, has become a sort of moral constitution by which trustees feel they can and should abide. 'Re-discovered' by the new generation of trustees in the 1940s, this document contains passages that remain clearly resonant for today's generation of Quaker philanthropists, although it might also be noted that Rowntree expected both the JRCT and JRSST to last, initially at least, for a period of only thirty-five years, and that his own words expressed some scepticism as to the longer-term value of reliance on such documents: he admitted the truth of James Lowell's remark, '[n]ew occasions teach new duties: time makes ancient good uncouth'.[4] Nevertheless, through this memorandum and the quotations from it which continue to litter the publications of all three Trusts, Rowntree's conception of philanthropy has at least acquired a memorial, and to an extent remains an influence on British Quaker philanthropic practice at the start of the twenty-first century.

Nevertheless, what this book has shown, mainly through the example of the educational settlement movement, with which the JRCT was so closely associated in the first half of the twentieth century, is that adherence to a single unifying conception of philanthropy, and the substantial financial support given to the institutions whose practices appeared most closely to embody that conception, had, to borrow one Friend's words, 'both its dangers and its advantages'. The disadvantages with which the settlements found themselves encumbered were sometimes susceptible of solution by talented members of staff or the tireless efforts of educational voluntarists; but the failure of the movement to retain the distinctive place in the spectrum of adult education which its pioneers wished for it is indicative of the limited demand for religious adult education and of the frequently noted stuffiness of the settlements. The JRCT, as a body, can take credit for eventually abandoning its support for the educational centres, and for turning its attention to other areas of concern, in particular the problems of family life and the challenges posed by adolescents, in the 1950s and 1960s. Arguably, only the replacement of one generation of trustees by another enabled this abandonment finally to take place; however, the JRCT was always intended to be a pioneering Trust and not one that existed to bail out 'lame duck' ventures like the post-war educational settlements. Trustees identified a new opportunity for the educational settlements to associate themselves more closely with the community associations movement, itself plagued with difficulties but undoubtedly reflecting more closely the needs and concerns of the period from which it emerged than did the settlements, which can be (and were) characterised as hangovers from the late Victorian period. The vaguer educational ideals embodied in the community centres, together with a somewhat updated version of Joseph Rowntree's Victorian insistence of the value of the element of interpersonal connection in the philanthropic relationship, were carried through into the new work of the second half of the twentieth century. As a significant group of Quaker philanthropists responding to changing perceptions of social need in the community in which it has operated during the past century, the Joseph Rowntree Charitable Trust is an important example of the evolution of twentieth-century Quaker social concern.

NOTES

1. JRCT minute book, no. 1, p. 109.
2. Tait, 'Keeping the jobless occupied'.
3. Kennedy, *British Quakerism*, 281 n. 41.
4. Founder's memorandum, 6.

Appendix

ANNUAL EXPENDITURE OF THE JOSEPH ROWNTREE CHARITABLE TRUST, 1913-1954, BY CATEGORY
Source: JRCT financial records, The Garden House, York

Note: the figures for 1923 are for estimated expenditure only. The actual expenditure for that year is unavailable. Financial records for the period 1904-13 are not available. In 1941 the grant for 'Friends and other literature' was included within 'Religious teaching among Friends', and in the above table is included in 'Quaker and other religious concerns'. For 1946 'Miscellaneous grants' is inflated by a one-off donation of £10,000 to Gordonstoun School.

Explanation of categories: These categories of expenditure are derived from the JRCT financial records. As their names and functions changed considerably over time, the categories employed here are usually amalgamations of various original categories. 'Religious teaching and Quaker service' was 'Religious teaching among Friends' until 1944. For 1926 to 1930 inclusive the Trust's short-lived separate category of expenditure 'Friends' research work' is included in 'Religious teaching and Quaker service' in the table. 'Educational grants' is an amalgamation of the categories 'Woodbrooke' and 'Friends' settlements and schools'; for 1913 and 1914 this embraces the separate category 'Friends' schools'. 'Social investigation and welfare' was originally 'Social and economic investigation and education' (and in 1947 was cumbersomely re-labelled 'Investigation into social questions and grants to certain agencies concerned with social reform'). 'Friends' and other literature' remained a separate category throughout this period. 'Adult education and settlements' originated in 1919 as 'Settlement extension grants'. 'Peace and international relations' was variously referred to as 'Peace', 'Peace and international education' and 'Peace and reconstruction'.

As the boundaries of the different categories were ny no means consistent and frequently unclear, the figures should be used only as rough guides to the distribution of JRCT expenditure in this period. The figures are all given to the nearest full pound; they are unadjusted for inflation.

These figures are taken from a larger analysis of JRCT expenditure in the period 1913-99 by Lorna Gold and Mark Freeman, and are used here with the permission of Lorna Gold.

	Religious teaching and Quaker service	Educational grants	Social investigation and welfare	Friends' and other literature	Adult education and settlements	Peace and international relations	Miscellaneous	Sundries and administration	TOTAL EXPENDITURE
1913	£?,850	£1,984	£702	£322				£106	£4,964
1914	£?,055	£3,328	£389	£974				£119	£5,865
1915	£851	£1,821	£766	£457				£90	£3,985
1916	£?,195	£808	£2,448	£0				£158	£4,610
1917	£?,297	£2,460	£275	£61		£657		£60	£4,810
1918	£?,721	£1,884	£100	£339				£98	£4,142
1919	£2,453	£2,407	£150	£462	£4,932			£328	£10,733
1920	£2,212	£7,274	£594	£1,152	£4,402			£511	£16,144
1921	£?,810	£2,287	£842	£1,952	£11,263			£654	£18,809
1922	£?,248	£3,488	£1,127	£679	£11,753	£75		£358	£18,728
1923	£?,424	£4,051	£2,672	£1,750	£10,332	£75		£493	£20,797
1924	£?,329	£3,604	£837	£346	£8,518	£150		£993	£15,778
1925	£?,195	£1,408	£1,127	£439	£7,401	£300		£1,174	£13,045
1926	£?,555	£1,174	£1,091	£280	£7,285	£231		£1,326	£12,942
1927	£?,732	£1,492	£1,292	£365	£7,738	£678		£1,527	£14,825
1928	£?,709	£1,962	£1,739	£203	£7,634	£743		£846	£14,837
1929	£?,521	£2,132	£1,221	£637	£7,620	£1,031		£1,245	£15,407
1930	£2,068	£2,000	£903	£75	£7,662	£935		£1,339	£14,982
1931	Data unavailable for 1931								

	Religious teaching and Quaker service	Educational grants	Social investigation and welfare	Friends' and other literature	Adult education and settlements	Peace and international relations	Miscellaneous	Sundries and administration	TOTAL EXPENDITURE
1932	£1,829	£1,707	£1,070	£22	£7,300	£441		£1,418	£13,787
1933	£1,768	£1,530	£910	£68	£7,696	£507		£482	£12,962
1934	£1,711	£1,563	£1,058	£83	£7,506	£355		£3,566	£15,843
1935	£1,669	£1,721	£2,539	£216	£7,504	£917		£1,516	£16,082
1936	£2,245	£1,606	£3,294	£217	£6,806	£824		£2,113	£17,104
1937	£2,397	£1,843	£2,562	£404	£6,851	£826		£2,107	£16,989
1938	£6,674	£1,889	£2,323	£155	£6,709	£625		£1,782	£20,156
1939	£2,173	£1,988	£2,673	£149	£6,210	£540		£4,585	£18,318
1940	£2,035	£2,599	£2,551	£130	£5,750	£1,085		£2,666	£16,816
1941	£3,580	£2,245	£2,691		£4,550	£920	£1,618	£1,972	£17,577
1942	£2,551	£1,886	£2,007	£483	£3,328	£995	£2,458	£3,452	£17,160
1943	£2,468	£1,677	£1,780	£227	£4,114	£1,732	£1,197	£2,407	£15,603
1944	£2,881	£2,046	£1,975	£254	£4,005	£2,114	£655	£2,279	£16,209
1945	£2,748	£1,598	£2,029	£283	£4,302	£1,482	£2,452	£1,668	£16,560
1946	£3,387	£3,121	£2,397	£224	£11,266	£1,440	£12,025	£2,045	£35,904
1947	£4,863	£1,939	£4,177	£169	£11,316	£4,998	£1,987	£2,739	£32,187
1948	£4,566	£3,136	£5,759	£367	£10,887	£1,783	£3,558	£2,318	£32,373
1949	£6,060	£3,897	£6,381	£279	£268	£2,980	£3,499	£2,428	£25,792
1950	£5,426	£5,186	£7,245	£351	£4,375	£1,392	£2,854	£2,832	£29,661
1951	£4,459	£3,607	£6,247	£323	£2,319	£1,265	£829	£2,656	£21,705
1952	£4,731	£4,022	£3,380	£367	£2,120	£1,269	£791	£2,910	£19,590
1953	£5,197	£3,294	£4,415	£112	£732	£1,686	£655	£2,707	£18,798
1954	£4,897	£2,993	£4,138	£237	£959	£1,854	£930	£5,493	£21,501

Bibliography

Unpublished primary sources

Birmingham, Woodbrooke Quaker Study Centre library
miscellaneous items

London, Friends House library
miscellaneous items

York, Joseph Rowntree Charitable Trust (JRCT)
JRCT financial records
JRCT basement archive
JRCT minute books:
      no. 1: 1904-1921
      no. 2: 1921-1928
      no. 3: 1929-1939
      no. 4: 1939-1954

York, Joseph Rowntree Foundation (JRF)
papers relating to Rowntree family and Trusts (owned jointly by the JRF, JRCT and JRRT)

York, Borthwick Institute of Historical Research
B. Seebohm Rowntree papers

The following unpublished items have been referred to frequently in the text:

ESA, 'The Educational Settlements Association' [typescript, 1945], JRF JRCT93/IV/8 (a)

Fleming, Horace, 'Interim report on the Society of Friends, etc.', 1928, JRF JRCT93/VI/1 (e)

Rowntree, B. Seebohm, 'Report on the work and objects of the JRCT', 1939, JRF, *Basic documents*, JRF library

Rowntree, B. Seebohm, 'Report on the work done by the JRCT 1905-1939 and suggestions ... regarding future policy', 1941, JRF JRCT93/I/11 (d)

Rowntree, Joseph, memorandum of 29 December 1904, 1, JRCT, *Basic documents*, JRCT library (Founder's memorandum)

Rowntree, Joseph, memorandum of 16 April 1919, inset in JRCT minute book, no. 1, pp. 241-2

Williams, W. E., 'The educational settlements: a report prepared for the Joseph Rowntree Charitable Trust', October 1938, JRF JRCT93/IV/2

Wilson, Roger C., 'Some reflections on being a member of the Joseph Rowntree Charitable Trust 1941-1977', 1977, JRF Library, HA3/ROW (oversize)

[Luther Worstenholme], 'Joseph Rowntree (1836-1925): a typescript memoir, and related papers', JRCT library

Periodicals and newspapers

Common Room
The Friend
Friends Quarterly Examiner

Published articles, books and pamphlets

The place of publication is London unless otherwise stated.

Adams, Tony, *A far-seeing vision: the Socialist Quaker Society 1898-1924*, Bedford n. d.

Allaway, A. J., *Adult education in a changing society: an inaugural lecture delivered at University College Leicester, 1 May 1951*, Leicester 1951

Allaway, A. J., *The educational centres movement: a comprehensive survey*, 1961

Allott, Stephen, *Friends in York: the Quaker story in the life of a Meeting*, York 1978

Allott, Stephen, *John Wilhelm Rowntree 1868-1905 and the beginnings of modern Quakerism*, York 1994

Angell, Norman, *The great illusion: a study of the relation of military power in nations to their economic and social advantage*, 1909

Angell, Norman, *After all: the autobiography of Norman Angell*, 1951

Arnove, Robert F. (ed.), *Philanthropy and cultural imperialism: the foundations at home and abroad*, Boston, Mass., 1980

Ashby, Eric, *The pathology of adult education*, Belfast 1955

Astor, J. J. (ed.), *Is unemployment inevitable? An analysis and a forecast*, 1924

Beveridge, W. H., *Unemployment: a problem of industry*, 1909

BIAE, *Adult education after the war*, Oxford 1945

Birn, Donald S., 'The League of Nations Union and collective security', *Journal of Contemporary History* ix/3 (1974), 131-59

Booth, Charles (ed.), *Life and labour of the people in London* (1st edn 2 vols 1889; 2nd edn 10 vols 1892-7), 17 vols 1902-3

Bosanquet, Helen, *Social work in London 1896-1912: a history of the Charity Organisation Society*, 1914

Bowley, A. L. and A. R. Burnett-Hurst, *Livelihood and poverty: a study in the economic conditions of working-class households in Northampton, Warrington, Stanley and Reading*, 1915

Bowley, A. L. and M. H. Hogg, *Has poverty diminished? A sequel to Livelihood and poverty*, 1925

Bowpitt, Graham, 'Poverty and its early critics: the search for a value-free definition of the problem', in Jonathan Bradshaw and Roy Sainsbury (eds), *Getting the measure of poverty: the early legacy of Seebohm Rowntree*, Aldershot 2000, 23-38

Boyd-Orr, John, *Food, health and income: report on a survey of adequacy of diet in relation to income*, 1936

J. Bevan Braithwaite: a Friend of the nineteenth century, by his children, 1909

Braithwaite, William C., *Spiritual guidance in the experience of the Society of Friends*, 1909

Braithwaite, William C., *The beginnings of Quakerism*, 1912

Braithwaite, William C., *The second period of Quakerism*, 1919

Brayshaw, A. Neave, *The Quakers: their story and message*, 1921

Brayshaw, Shipley N., *Unemployment and plenty*, 1933

Briggs, Asa, *Social thought and social action: a study of the work of Seebohm Rowntree*, 1961

Briggs, Asa, 'The welfare state in historical perspective', in *The collected essays of Asa Briggs*, 3 vols Brighton 1985, ii. 177-211

Briggs, Asa, *The story of the Leverhulme Trust: for purposes of research and education*, 1991

Briggs, Asa, and Anne Macartney, *Toynbee Hall: the first hundred years*, 1984

Brock, Peter, *The Quaker peace testimony 1660 to 1914*, York 1990

Brown, Fred, *The making of a modern Quaker: Roger Cowan Wilson 1906-1991*, 1996

Browne, Joan D., 'The Toynbee Travellers' Club', *History of Education* xv (1986), 11-17

Brown, John, 'Charles Booth and labour colonies 1889-1905', *Economic History Review* 2nd ser. xxi (1968), 349-60

Cadbury, George Junior and Tom Bryan, *The land and the landless*, 1908

[Castle, E. B.,] *Quaker education and the Society of Friends*, 1929

Ceadel, Martin, *Pacifism in Britain 1914-1945: the defining of a faith*, Oxford 1980

Ceadel, Martin, 'The first British referendum: the peace ballot 1934-1935', *English Historical Review* xcv (1980), 810-39

Ceadel, Martin, 'Christian pacifism in the era of two world wars', in W. J. Sheils (ed.), *The church and war: papers read at the twenty-first summer meeting and the twenty-second winter meeting of the Ecclesiastical History Society*, Oxford 1983, 391-408

Champness, Ernest F., *Adult schools: a study in pioneering*, Wallington 1941

Checkland, Olive, *Philanthropy in Victorian Scotland: social welfare and the voluntary principle*, Edinburgh 1980

Clark, Ronald William, *A biography of the Nuffield Foundation*, 1972

H. C. [i.e. Henry Clay], *Notes on the countries at war*, n.d.

Cober Hill, Cloughton 1920-1986, York 1986

Davies, George M. L. (ed.), *Joseph Rowntree Gillett: a memoir*, 1942

Davies, A. Tegla, *Friends Ambulance Unit: the story of the FAU in the second world war 1939-1946*, 1947

Davies, J. Elfed, 'Educational settlements in south Wales, with special reference to the Merthyr Tudful settlement', *Transactions of the Honourable Society of Cymmrodorion*, session 1970, part 2, 177-98

Davies, Jonathan S. and Mark Freeman, 'Education for citizenship: the Joseph Rowntree Charitable Trust and the educational settlement movement', *History of Education* xxxii (2003), 303-18

Davies, Jonathan S. and Mark Freeman, 'A case of political philanthropy: the Rowntree family and the campaign for democratic reform', *Quaker Studies* (forthcoming)

Davis, Robert (ed.), *Woodbrooke 1903-1953: a brief history of a Quaker experiment in religious education*, 1953

Letters and other writings of the late Edward Denison, ed. Baldwyn Leighton, 1872

Dickinson, Goldsworthy Lowes, *War: its nature, cause and cure*, 1923

Digby, Anne, 'The relief of poverty in Victorian York: attitudes and policies', in Charles Feinstein (ed.), *York 1831-1981: 150 years of scientific endeavour*, York 1981, 160-87

Dudley, James, *The life of Edward Grubb 1854-1939: a spiritual pilgrimage*, 1946

Eastland, Basil, Derek Edwards and David Sainty (eds), *Volunteers for peace: field reports on relief work in Europe 1944-1949 by International Voluntary Service for Peace*, Kelso 1998

Eddington, Arthur Stanley, *Science and the unseen world*, 1929

Elsdon, K. T., *Centres for adult education*, 1962

Englander, David and Rosemary O'Day (eds), *Retrieved riches: social investigation in Britain 1840-1914*, Aldershot 1995

ESA, *Settlements and their work, from the point of view of the Educational Settlements Association*, ESA papers, no. 2, n.d.

ESA, *Community education, being a description of the work of residential and non-residential colleges for adult education*, 1938

Evans, R. A., 'The university and the city: the educational work of Toynbee Hall', *History of Education* xi (1982), 113-25

Fieldhouse, Roger, 'The Labour government's further education policy 1945-1951', *History of Education* xxiii (1994), 287-99

Fieldhouse, Roger, and associates (eds), *A history of modern British adult education*, Leicester 1996

Finlayson, Geoffrey, *Citizen, state and social welfare in Britain 1830-1990*, Oxford 1994

Finnegan, Frances, *Poverty and prejudice: a study of Irish immigrants in York 1840-1875*, Cork 1982

Fitzgerald, Robert, *Rowntree and the marketing revolution 1862-1969*, Cambridge 1995

Fleming, Horace, *Education through settlements, being an address delivered at the tenth annual conference of educational associations, University College London, on January 6th 1922*, ESA papers, no. 4, 1922

Fleming, Horace, *The lighted mind: the challenge of adult education to Quakerism*, 1929

Fleming, Horace, 'The Educational Settlements Association: retrospect', *Friends Quarterly Examiner* lxv (1931), 62-75

Fleming, Horace, *Beechcroft: the story of the Birkenhead settlement 1914-1924: an experiment in adult education*, 1938

Freeman, Mark, 'The provincial social survey in Edwardian Britain', *Historical Research* lxxv (2002), 73-89

Freeman, Mark, '"No finer school than a settlement": the development of the educational settlement movement', *History of Education* xxxi (2002), 245-62

Freeman, Mark, *Social investigation and rural England 1870-1914*, Woodbridge 2003

Fry, John Pease, 'The function of the Society of Friends with regard to social and industrial questions', *Friends Quarterly Examiner* lxi (1927), 273-9

Fuller, Edward, *She championed children: the story of Eglantyne Jebb* (1st edn 1953), 1956

FWCC, *Friends face their fourth century: the third world conference of Friends*, 1952

Gardiner, A. G., *The life of George Cadbury*, 1923

Gilbert, Bentley B., *The evolution of national insurance in Great Britain: the origins of the welfare state*, 1966

Arthur B. Gillett 1875-1954: memories from some of his friends, Gloucester [1955]

Gillman, Frederick John, *The story of the York adult schools from the commencement to the year 1907*, York 1907

Glasby, Jon (ed.), *'Back to the future': the history of the settlement movement and its relevance for organisations today*, Birmingham 2000

Goldman, Lawrence, 'Intellectuals and the English working class 1870-1945: the case of adult education', *History of Education* xxix (2000), 281-300

Graveson, Caroline C., *Religion and culture*, 1937

Greenwood, John Ormerod, *Quaker encounters, volume I: Friends and relief*, York 1975

Greenwood, John Ormerod, *Quaker encounters, volume III: whispers of truth*, York 1978

Gregg, Pauline, *A social and economic history of Britain 1760-1970* (1st edn 1950), 1971

Grubb, Edward, *The historic and the inward Christ*, 1914

Grubb, Edward, *What is Quakerism? An exposition of the leading principles and practices of the Society of Friends, as based on the experiences of 'the Inward Light'*, 1917

Hake, Barry J., 'The Dutch Woodbrookers movement and the development of residential adult education in the Netherlands 1903-1941', *History of Education* xxv (1996), 335-51

Hall, W. Arnold, *The adult school movement in the twentieth century*, Nottingham 1985

Hannington, Wal, *The problem of the distressed areas*, 1937

Harris, Jose, 'The Webbs, the Charity Organisation Society and the Ratan Tata Foundation: social policy from the perspective of 1912', in Martin Bulmer, Jane Lewis and David Piachaud (eds), *The goals of social policy*, 1989, 27-63

Harris, Jose, *Private lives, public spirit: Britain 1870-1914* (1st edn 1993), Harmondsworth 1994

Harrison, Brian, 'Philanthropy and the Victorians', *Victorian Studies* ix (1966), 353-74

Harrison, J. F. C., *Workers' education in Leeds: a history of the Leeds branch of the Workers' Educational Association 1907-1957*, Leeds 1957

Harrison, J. F. C., *Learning and living 1790-1960: a study in the history of the English adult education movement*, 1961

Harvey, John W., *The salt and the leaven*, 1947

Hatton, Helen E., *The largest amount of good: Quaker relief in Ireland 1654-1921*, Montreal 1993

Hawkins, Lucy M., *Maes-yr-Haf*, n.d.,

Hazelton, William, 'Adult education and national reconstruction', *Friends Quarterly Examiner* lxxviii (1944), 113-19

Hazelton, William, *Maes-yr-Haf 1927-1952: an account of 25 years of work and friendship in the Rhondda valley*, Rhondda [1952]

Hendrick, Harry, *Images of youth: age, class and the male youth problem 1880-1920*, Oxford 1990

Hennock, E. P., *British social reform and German precedents: the case of social insurance 1880-1914*, Oxford 1987

Heron, Alastair, *Quakers in Britain: a century of change 1895-1995*, Kelso 1995

Hewison, Hope Hay, *Hedge of wild almonds: South Africa, the 'Pro-Boers' and the Quaker conscience 1890-1910*, 1989

Hills, R. I., *The inevitable march of Labour? Electoral politics in York 1900-1914*, York 1996

Hinshaw, David, *Rufus Jones: master Quaker*, New York 1951

Hirst, Margaret E., *The Quakers in peace and war: an account of their peace principles and practice, etc.*, 1923

Hobhouse, L. T., *Liberalism*, 1911

Hobhouse, Margaret, *I appeal unto Caesar: the case of the conscientious objector*, 1917

Howard, Ebenezer, *Garden cities of tomorrow* (1st edn 1898), 1902

Howarth, Edward G. and Mona Wilson, *West Ham: a study in social and industrial problems*, 1907

Hoyland, John S., 'The present need of the Society of Friends', *Friends Quarterly Examiner* lxiv (1930), 43-8

Hoyland, John S., 'Woodbrooke and the Selly Oak Colleges', in Davis, *Woodbrooke*, 169-84

Humphreys, Robert, *Sin, organized charity and the poor law in Victorian England*, Basingstoke 1995

Hunter, Guy, 'Residential colleges for adult education', in Raybould, *Trends in English adult education*, 120-36

Isichei, Elizabeth, *Victorian Quakers*, Oxford 1970

Jennings, Hilda, *Brynmawr: a study of a distressed area*, 1934

Jepson, N. A., 'Local authorities and adult education', in Raybould, *Trends in English adult education*, 83-119

Jones, D. Caradog (ed.), *The social survey of Merseyside*, 3 vols Liverpool 1934

Jones, Gareth Stedman, *Outcast London: a study in the relationship between classes in Victorian society* (1st edn 1971), Harmondsworth 1984

Jones, Rufus M., *Quakerism: a religion of life*, 1908

Jones, Rufus M., *The later periods of Quakerism*, 2 vols 1921

Jones, Rufus M., 'That wider fellowship', *The Friend*, 8 November 1929, 993-4

Jordan, W. K., *English philanthropy 1480-1660: a study of the changing pattern of English social aspirations*, 1959

Kelly, Thomas, *A history of adult education in Great Britain*, Liverpool 1962

Kennedy, Thomas C., *The hound of conscience: the story of the No-Conscription Fellowship 1914-1919*, Fayetteville, Arkansas, 1981

Kennedy, Thomas C., *British Quakerism 1860-1920: the transformation of a religious community*, Oxford 2001

Kent, Raymond A., *A history of British empirical sociology*, Aldershot 1981

Kidd, Alan, *State, society and the poor in nineteenth-century England*, 1999

Laybourn, Keith (ed.), *Social conditions, status and community 1860-c.1920*, Stroud 1997

Lewis, Jane, *The voluntary sector, the state and social work in Britain: the Charity Organisation Society/Family Welfare Association since 1869*, Aldershot 1995

Livingstone, Adelaide, *The peace ballot: the official history*, 1935

Lowe, John, *Adult education in England and Wales: a critical survey*, 1970

MacBriar, A. M., *An Edwardian mixed doubles: the Bosanquets versus the Webbs: a study in British social policy 1890-1929*, Oxford 1987

Macnicol, John, *The politics of retirement in Britain 1878-1948*, Cambridge 1998

Official papers by Alfred Marshall, ed. J. M. Keynes, 1926

Manasseh, Pamela, 'Quaker relief work and the Brynmawr experiment', *Woodbrooke Journal* vii (2000), 2-31

Martin, G. Currie, *The adult school movement: its origin and development*, 1924

Meacham, Standish, *Toynbee Hall and social reform 1880-1914: the search for community*, New Haven, Conn., 1987

Mess, Henry A., *Industrial Tyneside: a social survey made for the Bureau of Social Research for Tyneside*, 1928

Ministry of Reconstruction: Adult Education Committee final report, Parliamentary Papers 1919, Cmd. 321

Morland, Lucy Fryer, *The new social outlook*, 1918

Mowat, Charles Loch, *The Charity Organisation Society 1869-1913: its ideas and work*, 1961

Naylor, Barrie, *Quakers in the Rhondda 1926-1986*, Chepstow 1986

O'Day, Rosemary and David Englander, *Mr Charles Booth's inquiry:* Life and labour of the people in London *reconsidered*, 1993

Olechnowicz, Andrzej, *Working-class housing in England between the wars: the Becontree estate*, Oxford 1997

Orwell, George, *The road to Wigan pier* (1st edn 1937), Harmondsworth 1982

Owen, David, *English philanthropy 1660-1960*, Oxford 1965

Peacock, A. J., *York 1900 to 1914*, York 1992

Peacock, A. J., *York in the Great War 1914-1918*, York 1993

Peacock, A. J., 'Adult education in York 1800-1947', in A. J. Peacock (ed.), *Essays in York history*, York 1997, 266-301

Phillips, Alan, *Maes-yr-Haf: the time – the place*, Rhondda [1996]

Picht, Werner, *Toynbee Hall and the English settlement movement*, 1914

Pimlott, J. A. R., *Toynbee Hall: fifty years of social progress*, 1935

Prochaska, F. K., *The voluntary impulse: philanthropy in modern Britain*, 1988

Pugh, Michael, 'Pacifism and politics in Britain 1931-1935', *Historical Journal* xxiii (1980), 641-56

Raybould, S. G., *The English universities and adult education*, 1951

Raybould, S. G., (ed.), *Trends in English adult education*, 1959

Richards, Edith R., 'The second world war', in Davis, *Woodbrooke*, 73-8

Robertson, William, *Welfare in trust: a history of the Carnegie United Kingdom Trust 1913-1963*, Dunfermline 1964

Robson, S. Elizabeth, *Joshua Rowntree*, 1916

Rooff, Madeline, *A hundred years of family welfare: a study of the Family Welfare Association (formerly Charity Organisation Society) 1869-1969*, 1972

Rowntree, Arnold S., *Woodbrooke: its history and aims*, Birmingham 1923

Rowntree, B. Seebohm, *Poverty: a study of town life* (1st edn 1901), 1902

Rowntree, B. Seebohm (ed.), *Betting and gambling: a national evil*, 1905

Rowntree, B. Seebohm, *Land and labour: lessons from Belgium*, 1910

Rowntree, B. Seebohm, *The labourer and the land*, 1914

Rowntree, B. Seebohm, 'Labour unrest', *Contemporary Review* cxii (1917), 368-79

Rowntree, B. Seebohm, *The human needs of labour*, 1918

Rowntree, B. Seebohm, 'Prospects and tasks of social reconstruction', *Contemporary Review* cxv (1919), 1-9

Rowntree, B. Seebohm, 'Labour unrest and the need for a national ideal', *Contemporary Review* cxvi (1919), 496-503

Rowntree, B. Seebohm, *The human factor in business* (1st edn 1921), 1925

Rowntree, B. Seebohm, 'The function of the Society of Friends with regard to social and industrial questions', *Friends Quarterly Examiner* lxi (1927), 265-72

Rowntree, B. Seebohm, *Poverty and progress: a second social survey of York*, 1941

Rowntree, B. Seebohm and Bruno Lasker, *Unemployment: a social study*, 1911

Rowntree, B. Seebohm and May Kendall, *How the labourer lives: a study of the rural labour problem*, 1913

Rowntree, B. Seebohm and Viscount Astor (eds), *Small holdings studies: reports of surveys undertaken by some agricultural economists*, 1939

Rowntree, B. Seebohm and G. R. Lavers, *English life and leisure: a social study*, 1951

Rowntree, B. Seebohm and G. R. Lavers, *Poverty and the welfare state: a third social survey of York, dealing only with economic questions*, 1951

Rowntree, J. S., *The sincere desire: a study in prayer*, 1907

Rowntree, John Wilhelm, *Essays and addresses*, ed. Joshua Rowntree (1st edn 1905), 1906

Rowntree, John Wilhelm and Henry Bryan Binns, *A history of the adult school movement*, 1903

Rowntree, Joseph and Arthur Sherwell, *The temperance problem and social reform*, 1899

The Joseph Rowntree inheritance 1904-1994, York 1994

JRRT, *Trusting in change: a story of reform* (1st edn 1994), York 1998

Rowntree, Joshua, *Social service: its place in the Society of Friends*, 1913

Rubinstein, David, *York Friends and the Great War*, York 1999

Rubinstein, David, *Faithful to ourselves and the outside world: York Quakers during the twentieth century*, York 2001

Russell, Bertrand, *The practice and theory of Bolshevism*, 1920

Saunders, J. W., 'University extension renascent', in Raybould, *Trends in English adult education*, 52-82

Scott, Janet, 'The making of an institution: the Swarthmore lecture 1907-1913', *Journal of Quaker Studies* i (1995): typescript copy in Friends House Library, shelved with *Quaker Studies*

Searle, G. R., *The quest for national efficiency: a study in British politics and political thought 1899-1914* (1st edn 1971),1990

Settlements and their outlook: an account of the first international conference of settlements, Toynbee Hall, London, July 1922, ed. Basil A. Yeaxlee, 1922

Shearman, Harold C., *Adult education for democracy*, 1944

Simon, Brian, *Education and the labour movement 1870-1920*, 1965

Smith, H. Llewellyn (director), *The new survey of London life and labour*, 9 vols 1930-5

Smith, Stanley, *Spiceland Quaker training centre*, York 1990

Stephenson, Flora and Gordon Stephenson, *Community centres: a survey*, 1942

Stevenson, John, *British society 1914-1945*, Harmondsworth 1984

Sturge, Helen M., *Personal religion and the service of humanity*, 1923

Sturge, H. Winifred and Theodora Clark, *The Mount School, York, 1785 to 1814, 1831 to 1931*, 1931

Styler, W. E., *Yorkshire and Yorkshire North: the history of the Yorkshire North district of the Workers' Educational Association 1914-1964*, Leeds 1964

Summers, Anne, 'A home from home – women's philanthropic work in the nineteenth century', in Sandra Burman (ed.), *Fit work for women*, 1979, 33-63

Swanwick, H. M., *Builders of peace, being ten years' history of the Union of Democratic Control*, 1924

Swartz, Marvin, *The Union of Democratic Control in British politics during the first world war*, Oxford 1971

Tait, I., 'Keeping the jobless occupied: voluntary welfare and unemployment in 1930s Britain', in Ian Blanchard (ed.), *New directions in economic and social history: papers presented at the 'new researchers' sessions of the Economic History Society conference held at Edinburgh*, Avonbridge 1995, 57-64

Tatham, Meaburn and James E. Miles (eds), *The Friends' Ambulance Unit 1914-1919: a record*, 1920

Taylor, A. J. P., *The trouble makers: dissent over foreign policy 1792-1939*, 1957

Taylor, Ernest E., *The valiant sixty*, Swindon 1947

Thane, Pat, *The foundations of the welfare state* (1st edn 1982), 1996

Thomas, Anna L. B. and Elizabeth B. Emmott, *William Charles Braithwaite: memoir and papers*, 1931

Thompson, J. A., 'Lord Cecil and the pacifists in the League of Nations Union', *Historical Journal* xx (1977), 949-59

Thompson, J. A., 'The "Peace Ballot" and the "Rainbow" controversy', *Journal of British Studies* xx (1981), 150-70

Tout, Herbert, *The standard of living in Bristol: a preliminary report of the work of the University of Bristol social survey*, Bristol 1938

Townsend, Peter, *The family life of old people*, 1957

Tritton, Frederick J., *Carl Heath: apostle of peace*, n.d.

Twelvetrees, Alan C., *Community associations and centres: a comparative study*, Oxford 1976

Vernon, Anne, *A Quaker business man: the life of Joseph Rowntree 1836-1925*, 1958

Vipont, Elfrida, *Arnold Rowntree: a life*, 1955

Vining, Elizabeth Gray, *Friend of life: the biography of Rufus M. Jones*, Philadelphia and New York 1958

[Waddilove, Lewis E.,] *One man's vision: the story of the Joseph Rowntree Village Trust*, 1954

Waddilove, Lewis E., *Private philanthropy and public welfare: the Joseph Rowntree Memorial Trust 1954-1979*, 1983

Waddilove, Lewis E., *Foundations and trusts – innovators or survivals?*, 1979

Wagner, Gillian, *The chocolate conscience*, 1987

Walvin, James, *The Quakers: money and morals*, 1997

Watkins, Percy E., *A Welshman remembers: an autobiography*, Cardiff 1944

Webb, Beatrice, *My apprenticeship* (1st edn 1926), Harmondsworth 1971

Whitaker, Ben, *The foundations: an anatomy of philanthropy and society*, 1974

Whittaker, David J., *Fighter for peace: Philip Noel-Baker 1889-1982*, York 1989

Whiting, J. Roland, *Ernest E. Taylor: valiant for truth*, 1958

Wilkinson, Ellen, *The town that was murdered: the life-story of Jarrow*, 1939

Wilkinson, Marion (ed.), *E. Richard Cross: a biographical sketch, with literary papers and religious and political addresses*, 1917

Wilson, Roger C., *Money and power: reflections as a trustee*, 1972, (pamphlet reprinted from *Friends' Quarterly*, July 1972)

Wilson, William E., 'Post-war conditions in Woodbrooke', in Davis, *Woodbrooke*, 53-71

Wiltshire, H. C., 'Impington and adult education', *Adult Education* xvii (1944), 125-34

Wood, Herbert G., 'Woodbrooke and the Society of Friends', *Friends Quarterly Examiner* lxiv (1930), 133-45

Wood, Herbert G., 'The first director of studies', in Davis, *Woodbrooke*, 19-30

Wood, Herbert G., 'Wardens and staff', in Davis, *Woodbrooke*, 31-42

Wood, Herbert G., 'The first world war', in Davis, *Woodbrooke*, 43-52

Wood, Herbert G. and Arthur Ball, *Tom Bryan, first warden of Fircroft: a memoir*, 1922

Worsdell, Edward, *The gospel of divine help*, 1886

Wright, Sheila, *Friends in York: the dynamics of Quaker revival 1780-1860*, Keele 1995

Yarrow, C. H. Mike, *Quaker experiences in international conciliation*, New Haven, Conn., 1978

Yeaxlee, Basil A., *Lifelong education: a sketch of the range and significance of the adult education movement*, 1929

Yeo, Eileen Janes, *The contest for social science: relations and representations of gender and class*, 1996

Unpublished dissertations, lectures and papers

Bliss, Z. D., 'Pacifism, politics and the Peace Pledge Union', unpublished MA dissertation, University of Glasgow, 1996

Davies, Jonathan S., 'Grounding the work of the JRCT: the Rowntrees and political and economic democracy'; unpublished paper, University of York, 2001

Freeman, Mark, 'The Outer London Inquiry Committee 1905-1908: a study in Edwardian social investigation', unpublished paper, Economic History Society annual conference, 2000

Freeman, Mark, 'Rowntree and poverty: the perspective of a century', Historical Association/University of York public lecture, 16 October 2001

Kennedy, Thomas C., 'Late Victorian/Edwardian Quakers and early Friends: clean connections or crossed wires?', lecture at Woodbrooke Quaker Study Centre, 1 May 2002

Rose, Michael, '"A microcosm of cultivated society": education, the arts and the social settlements', unpublished paper, University of Manchester, 2001

Index

This book has been indexed as fully as possible consistent with space and user-friendliness. There is not a full entry for the Joseph Rowntree Charitable Trust (JRCT). There is also no full entry for Society of Friends (Quakers). Readers should refer to individuals or groups of Friends who are indexed.

Hughes, John A., 122, 129, 140, 174, 177, 203, 213; warden of St. Mary's, 76, 93; work in the Special Areas, 116-18; in USA, 153

INDEPENDENT Labour Party, 20, 50, 148
International Peace Campaign (IPC), 113, 158-60, 161. *See also* League of Nations Union (LNU)
International Voluntary Service for Peace (IVSP), 138, 170, 211
Inward Light doctrine, 12, 14, 48, 62, 77, 100

JOHN Woolman Settlement, 120, 171
Jones, Henry, 45, 67
Jones, Rufus M., 16, 31, 37, 81, 95-6, 97, 153, 175, 176, 211-12; present at JRCT meeting, 102. *See also* 'Wider Quaker Fellowship'
Joseph Rowntree Charitable Trust (JRCT), Trust Deed, 18-19, 33, 35, 37, 44, 147, 153; expiry in 1939, 139-40; Adult Education Sub-Committee, 208, 212; summary of expenditure, 226-8
Joseph Rowntree Foundation (JRF), 31, 223
Joseph Rowntree Reform Trust (JRRT), 223
Joseph Rowntree Social Service Trust (JRSST), 17, 29, 33, 42, 52, 53, 66, 137, 139, 150, 186, 224
Joseph Rowntree Village Trust (JRVT), 17, 18, 29, 30, 33, 47, 48, 66, 139, 186, 199-200; old age survey, 184. *See also* New Earswick

KINGSMEAD, *see* Selly Oak Colleges

LABOUR exchanges, 8, 44, 47
Labour party, 20, 52, 96, 114 15, 117, 131, 141, 148, 158-9, 223
Lasker, Bruno, 43
Lavers, G. Russell, 181-5, 207, 208, 209

League of Nations Society, 53, 148. *See also* League of Nations Union (LNU)
League of Nations Union (LNU), 50, 76, 147, 148, 153-7, 158, 159-60, 161, 222; York branch, 154; Geneva summer schools, 154-5; peace ballot, 155-7. *See also* International Peace Campaign (IPC)
Left Book Club, 76
Letchworth educational settlement, 68, 78, 172
Liberal party, 8, 30, 31, 34, 42, 130-1, 180, 223; general election victory 1906, 8, 46-7; 'new Liberalism', 8-9, 44-5; Land Enquiry Committee, 34, 42; in the general election of 1945, 140-1. *See also* York Liberal party
Lindsay, A. D., 103, 105, 159
Lindsay, Erica, 105
Liverpool, University of, 45, 90, 134
Lloyd George, David, 31, 34, 35, 51, 54, 131
local education authorities (LEAs),136; role in post-war adult education, 194-5; adoption of the 'centre idea', 197-8, 220-1
Loch, Charles, 9, 20
London County Council, 43, 71, 127
London School of Economics (LSE), 45, 115, 131-2

MACDONALD, J. Ramsay, 52, 80, 114, 131
Maes-yr-Haf, 105-7, 108, 116, 119, 135, 137, 172. *See also* south Wales settlements
Malthouse, *see* Davies, George M. L.
Manchester conference (1895), 14, 30, 34, 37, 63, 94, 97, 178
Mansbridge, Albert, 67, 80. *See also* Workers' Educational Association (WEA)
Marks, Harold, 199, 206
Marriage Guidance Council, 213
Martin, George Currie, 70, 73, 129

appointment to University of
Bristol, 196; JRCT chairman, 208;
socialism, 209
Wood, Herbert, 66, 98, 99, 101
Woodbrooke, 18, 30, 32, 33, 34, 36,
37-9, 45, 54, 65, 66, 75, 77, 78-9,
81, 82, 83, 89, 92, 94, 95, 130,
171, 187, 212, 213, 222;
Woodbrooke Extension
Committee, 36, 37, 39; as a centre
of training for school teachers and
settlement wardens, 38-9, 70, 79,
98, 100, 101, 128-9; and
international students, 39, 79, 99,
150, 151, 172; diploma in social
study, 45, 75, 98, 99, 151, 212;
concerns as to effectiveness of the
work (1920s and 1930s), 98-100,
117, 118; Dutch alumni, 151; as a
centre for missionary training,
152; in second world war, 172-3
Workers' Educational Association
(WEA), 40, 64, 67, 69, 70, 71, 72,
98, 196, 197, 201, 204, 220-1; as
a 'Responsible Body', 68; Leeds
branch, 40, 93; York branch, 49,
92-3; and the Beechcroft
settlement, 91, 100; in County
Durham, 117; in Cambridgeshire,
194
Worsdell, Edward, 14, 30, 33

YEARLY Meeting, 1, 14, 49-50, 116,
137, 209; of 1907, 36; of 1916,
63; of 1918, 62-3, 96; of 1920,
153; of 1924, 94; of 1926, 103
Yeaxlee, Basil, 40, 67, 71, 74, 98,
105, 193, 195
York Liberal Association, *see* York
Liberal party
York Liberal Club, *see* York Liberal
party
York Liberal Party, 1, 32, 52. *See also*
Liberal party
Yorkshire 1905 Committee, 35, 36,
39-40, 47, 53, 73, 80-1, 83, 89,
94, 98, 209. *See also* Yorkshire
Friends Service Committee
Yorkshire Adult School Union, 32,
80. *See also* adult schools
Yorkshire Friends Service
Committee, 80, 118, 119, 130,
138, 140, 178. *See also* Yorkshire
1905 Committee
Yorkshire Quarterly Meeting, 30, 94.
See also Yorkshire 1905
Committee; Yorkshire Friends
Service Committee
Young Men's Christian Association
(YMCA), 52, 126
Youth Hostels Association, 76, 120